4 - 21 - 03

To Courtney
from
Grandpa

Intuition

Its Powers and Perils

David G. Myers

YALE UNIVERSITY PRESS

New Haven & London

pp. 6, 24, 139: Illustrations from David G. Myers, *Psychology*, 6th ed. (New York: Worth, 2001). Used with permission.

p. 7: Illustration courtesy Al Seckel (IllusionWorks.com), from *The Art of Optical Illusions* (London: Carlton, 2000).

p. 53: Illustration courtesy Pawel Lewicki.

pp. 104–108: BB and airplane exercises from Michael McCloskey, "Naive Theories of Motion," in D. Gentner and A. L. Stevens (eds.), *Mental Model* (Hillsdale, N.J.: Erlbaum, 1983). Used with permission. Water-level exercise from H. Hecht and D. R. Proffitt, "The Price of Expertise: Effects of Experience on the Water-Level Task," *Psychological Science* 6 (1995): 90–95. Used with permission.

p. 136: Checkboard illustration courtesy Ruma Falk, Hebrew University, Jerusalem.

p. 221: Table courtesy Chance Team, Dartmouth College, from "Using Lotteries in Teaching a Chance Course," August 1, 1998.

Set in Charter type by Keystone Typesetting, Inc. Printed in the United States of America by R. R. Donnelley & Sons.

Library of Congress Cataloging-in-Publication Data
Myers, David G.
Intuition : its powers and perils / David G. Myers.
    p. cm.
Includes bibliographical references and index.
ISBN 0-300-09531-7 (alk. paper)
1. Intuition. I. Title.
BF315.5 .M94 2003
153.4'4—dc21   2002000881

A catalogue record for this book is available from the British Library.

The paper in this book meets the guidelines for permanence and durability of the Committee on Production Guidelines for Book Longevity of the Council on Library Resources.

10 9 8 7 6 5 4 3 2 1

The heart has its reasons which reason does not know.

    —Pascal, Pensées, *1670*

He that trusteth in his own heart is a fool.

    —Proverbs 28:26

Contents

Acknowledgments

My mission in this book—to plumb what psychological science has to say about intuition, to connect disparate discoveries and to apply them to everyday life—stands on the shoulders of many creative researchers. These include psychologists Daniel Kahneman (Princeton) and the late Amos Tversky (Stanford), whom many of us believe long ago became deserving of a future Nobel Prize for their contributions to behavioral economics. I have also been fascinated and inspired by the clever experiments on human reasoning by

- the Cornell University social psychology group, including Thomas Gilovich and David Dunning,
- John Bargh (New York University) and Tanya Chartrand's (Ohio State) explorations of automatic thinking,
- Nalini Ambady and Robert Rosenthal's demonstrations of our skills at reading thin slices of behavior,
- Timothy Wilson's (Virginia) studies of the unconscious dynamics of attitudes and judgments,
- Robert Zajonc (Stanford) and Anthony Greenwald's (University of Washington) work on unconscious perceptions,
- Pawel Lewicki's studies of nonconscious information processing,
- Robert Sternberg's (Yale) analyses of tacit knowledge,
- John Mayer (New Hampshire) and Peter Salovey's (Yale) concept of emotional intelligence,
- Elizabeth Loftus (University of Washington) and Michael Ross's (Waterloo) revelations of our misremembering our past,
- Daniel Gilbert (Harvard) and George Loewenstein's (Carnegie-Mellon) discoveries of our flawed predictions of our future feelings,
- Neil Weinstein's (Rutgers) demonstrations of our unrealistic optimism,
- Paul Slovic and Baruch Fischhoff's insights into risk intuitions,

- Lee Ross (Stanford) and Richard Nisbett's (Michigan) studies of biases in human inference,
- Seymour Epstein's (Massachusetts) concept of experiential knowing,
- Burton Malkiel's (Princeton) analyses of investment intuitions,
- Richard Thaler (Chicago), Robert Schiller (Yale), and Matthew Rabin's (California, Berkeley) behavioral economics,
- Paul Meehl (Minnesota) and Robyn Dawes' scrutiny of clinical intuition,
- Mark Snyder's (Minnesota) studies of behavioral confirmation,
- and by the pioneering work on intuitive expertise by the late Herbert Simon (Carnegie-Mellon), who did win the Nobel Prize for contributions to economics.

These scholars—and the hundreds of others on whose work I report—built the foundation for this book.

I am additionally grateful to several people who guided and encouraged my writing. Letha Dawson Scanzoni and Judith Rich Harris offered a meticulous and helpful critique of the entire manuscript. Carol Myers, Kathryn Brownson, and Charlotte van Oyen Witvliet also offered dozens of useful suggestions for improving the manuscript. Thomas Gilovich, Robert Emmons, and Robert Sternberg each offered encouragement with specific chapters. Leanne Van Dyk, Steven Chase, Christopher Kaiser, and James Brownson assisted with the pruning and shaping of the final manuscript, which was prepared by Phyllis Vandervelde with her usual diligent attention.

At Yale University Press, my editor Susan Arellano caught and championed the vision for this book. Sarah Lawsky facilitated its progress to a completed product. With great care, Heidi Downey smoothed the rough edges and produced an improved finished work. And Heather D'Auria helped make it available to readers.

With the help of all these people, this book—which was great fun to write—became a better book than I, alone, could have written.

Intuition

Introduction

As a research psychologist and communicator of psychological science, I have spent a career pondering the connections between subjective and objective truth, between feeling and fact, between intuition and reality. I'm predisposed to welcome unbidden hunches, creative ideas, the Spirit's workings. I once took an instant liking to a fellow teenager, to whom I've now been married for nearly forty years. When I meet job applicants, my gut reactions sometimes kick in within seconds, before I can explain my feelings in words. "Not everything that can be counted counts, and not everything that counts can be counted," said a sign in Albert Einstein's office.

But from science and everyday life, I also know that my intuition sometimes errs. My geographical intuition tells me that Reno is east of Los Angeles, that Rome is south of New York, that Atlanta is east of Detroit. But I am wrong, wrong, and wrong. "The first principle," said Einstein's fellow physicist Richard Feynman, "is that you must not fool yourself—and you are the easiest person to fool."

For Webster and for this book, *intuition* is our capacity for direct knowledge, for immediate insight without observation or reason. "Intuitive thinking is perception-like, rapid, effortless," notes Princeton University psychologist Daniel Kahneman. By contrast, "deliberate thinking is reasoning-like, critical, and analytic."

Do we all have untapped intuitive powers? Are we worthy of Shakespeare's acclaim, "in apprehension how like a god!" When hiring, firing, and investing should we plug into our "right brain" premonitions? Should we follow the example of *Star Wars*' Luke Skywalker, by turning off our computers and trusting the Force?

Or are skeptics right to define intuition as our inner knowing that we're right, whether we are or not? Are we like "the hollow men . . . headpiece filled with straw" (T. S. Eliot)? With bright people so often believing demonstrably dumb things, do we instead need more "left brain" rationality? To think and act smarter, should we more energetically check intuition against reality and subject creative hunch to skeptical scrutiny?

THE ACCLAIMED POWERS OF INTUITION

In his BBC Reith Lecture in 2000, Prince Charles lifted up the wisdom of the heart. "Buried deep within each and every one of us there is an instinctive, heart felt awareness that provides—if we allow it to—the most reliable guide as to whether or not our actions are really in the long term interests of our planet and all the life it supports. . . . Wisdom, empathy and compassion have no place in the empirical world yet traditional wisdoms would ask 'without them are we truly human?'" We need, said the future king, "to listen rather more to the common sense emanating from our hearts."

In this postmodernist New Age, Prince Charles has plenty of company. Scholars, popular writers, and workshop gurus are training people to trust their hearts as well as their heads. You have lots of options if you want to develop your intuition—what *Apollo 14* astronaut and Institute of Noetic Sciences founder Edgar Mitchell calls an "experience of inner knowing that [can be] experienced just as concretely as logical thought." You can take a Caribbean Intuition Cruise, where "leading intuitives will offer a comprehensive program for using intuition to enhance every area of your life." To cultivate your "inner, intuitive resources" you can explore the Intuition Network's website. You can listen to "Intuition Training" audiotapes. You can subscribe to *Intuition* magazine to explore the "natural skill anyone can cultivate." In other magazines you can read scores of articles on topics such as how to "let intuition be your guide" (by giving "yourself permission to listen to . . . your intuitive voice" and learning to exercise your "intuitive muscle").

You can go even deeper with one of the dozens of intuition guidebooks that promise to develop your sixth sense, to harness your inner wisdom, to unlock the power of your subconscious mind.

If it's healing you're looking for, *The Intuitive Healer: Accessing Your Inner Physician* suggests how the "personalized medicine chest" in your intuitive mind can help you avert illness. But you can also find "five steps to physical, emotional, and sexual wellness" in *Dr. Judith Orloff's Guide to Intuitive Healing* and learn "how to trust your intuition for guidance and healing" in *The Intuitive Heart*. For cooks and dieters there's even *Intuitive Cooking* and *Intuitive Eating*.

Would you like children to experience "whole-brain" learning? Suggest that their school administrators read *The Intuitive Principal* and their teachers study *Understanding and Teaching the Intuitive Mind*. If your child is academically challenged, you might consider *The Intuitive Approach to Reading and Learning Abilities*. For home use, there is *The Wise Child: A Spiritual Guide to Nurturing Your Child's Intuition*.

Are you a business person, manager, or investor? Perhaps *The Intuitive Manager, The Intuitive Trader,* or *Practical Intuition for Success* would help.

Do you want to expand your spiritual consciousness? There is a buffet of options, including *Intuitive Thinking as a Spiritual Path, Divine Intuition,* and *Intuitive Living: A Sacred Path*.

Or are you simply interested in wisdom and effective living? Then you may want *The Intuitive Edge* or *Practical Intuition*. Perhaps you will want to dig deeper and study *Intuition: The Inside Story*. Where does one begin? If you are an intuitive, *You Already Know What to Do,* asserts my favorite title (by Sharon Franquemont, a delightful intuition trainer whose book declares that "intuition is my passion").

THE POWERS OF INTUITION

Who can disagree with the *Utne Reader*'s observation that "Intuition is hot"? But what shall we make of this new cottage industry? Intuition authors and trainers—"intuitives," as they call themselves—seem largely oblivious to psychology's new explorations of how we process information. Are their intuitions about intuition valid? Is our consciousness sometimes invaded by unbidden truth, which is there for us to behold if only we would listen to the still small voice within? Or are their intuition writings to cognitive science what professional wrestling is to athletics? Do they offer little more than a make-believe world, an illusory reality in substitution for the real thing?

The emerging understanding, as we will see, is double-sided. "There are trivial truths and great truths," declared the physicist Niels Bohr. "The opposite of a trivial truth is plainly false. The opposite of a great truth is also true."* And so it is with human intuition, which has surprising powers and perils. On the one hand, recent cognitive science reveals a fascinating unconscious mind—another mind backstage—that Freud never told us about. More than we realized over a decade ago, thinking occurs not on stage, but off stage, out of sight. As we will see in chapters to come, studies of "automatic processing," "subliminal priming," "implicit memory," "heuristics," "spontaneous trait inference," right-brain processing, instant emotions, nonverbal communication, and creativity unveil our intuitive capacities. Thinking, memory, and attitudes all operate on two levels (conscious and deliberate, and unconscious and automatic)—dual processing, today's researchers call it. We know more than we know we know.

Consider:

Blindsight. Having lost a portion of their brain's visual cortex to surgery or stroke, people may be consciously blind in part of their field of vision. Shown a series of sticks in the blind field, they report seeing nothing. Yet when asked to guess whether the sticks are vertical or horizontal, they may unerringly offer the correct response. When told, "you got them all right," they are astounded. These people clearly know more than they know they know. They may reach to shake an outstretched hand that they cannot see. There are, it seems, little minds—"parallel processing" systems—operating unseen.

Indeed, "sight unseen" is how University of Durham psychologist David Milner describes the brain's two visual systems—"one that gives us our conscious perceptions, and one that guides our actions." The second he calls the "zombie within." Milner describes a brain-damaged woman who can see the hairs on the back of a hand and yet be unable to recognize a hand. Asked to use her thumb and forefinger to estimate an object's size, she can't do it—though when she reaches

*A playful question: If Bohr's statement is a great truth, what is its opposite?

for the object her thumb and forefinger are appropriately placed. She knows more than she is aware of.

Prosopagnosia. Patients with this disorder have suffered damage to a part of the brain involved in face recognition. After losing the pertinent temporal lobe area, patients may have complete sensation but incomplete perception. They can sense visual information—indeed, may accurately report the features of a face yet be unable to recognize it. When shown an unfamiliar face, they do not react. When shown a loved one's face, however, their *body* displays recognition. Their autonomic nervous system responds with measurable perspiration and speeded pulse. What the conscious mind cannot understand, the heart knows.

Everyday perception. Consider your own taken-for-granted capacity to intuitively recognize a face. As you look at a photo, your brain acts like a multitasking computer. It breaks the visual information into subdimensions, such as color, depth, movement, and form, and works on each aspect simultaneously, using different neural networks, before reassembling the components. (Damage the pertinent neural network and you may become unable to perceive a subdimension, such as movement.) Finally, your brain compares the reconstructed image with previously stored images. Voilà! Instantly and effortlessly you recognize, among billions of humans, someone you've not seen in five years.

Neural impulses travel a million times slower than a computer's internal messages, yet our brain humbles any computer with its instant recognition. "You can buy a chess machine that beats a master," notes vision researcher Donald Hoffman, "but can't yet buy a vision machine that beats a toddler's vision." If intuition is immediate knowing, without reasoned analysis, then perceiving is intuition par excellence.

So, is human intelligence more than logic? Is thinking more than ordering words? Is comprehension more than conscious cognition? Absolutely. Cognitive psychologist George Miller embodied this truth by telling of two passengers leaning against the ship's rail, staring at the sea. "'There sure is a lot of water in the ocean,' said one. 'Yes,' answered his friend, 'and we've only seen the top of it.'"

It's true: intuition is not only hot, it is also a big part of human decision making. But the complementary truth is that intuition often errs. Lay aside, for the moment, your rational mind and the analytical tools that serve it. Put down that measuring stick and take a deep breath, relax your body, quiet your "talk-addicted mind," and tune in to that sixth sense. Listen to its soft song as it tells you, immediately and directly . . .

a. How far up this triangle is the dot?

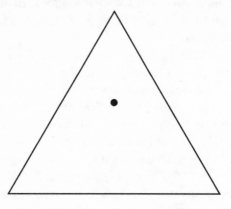

b. Do the dimensions of these two box tops differ?

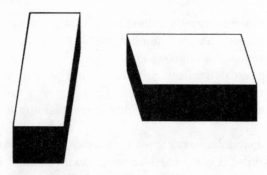

c. Which of these two line segments (AB or BC) is longer?

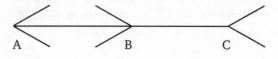

d. Line CD is what percent as long as AB?

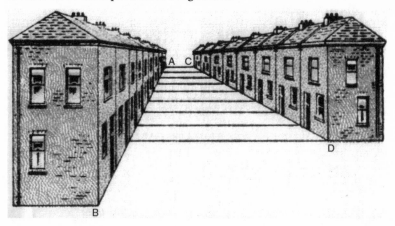

e. Are you familiar with this phrase?

A

BIRD

IN THE

THE HAND

The truths refute our intuition. The dot is exactly halfway up the tri-angle (though our intuition—our direct knowledge—says it's higher). The two box tops, as a measurement or a comparative tracing indi-cates, are identical in size and shape (though our intuition tells us otherwise). Line segment AB is one-third longer (though our intuition tells us the lines are the same). Line segment CD (rowhouses) is 100 percent as long as AB (though our intuition tells us CD is shorter). And you probably are *not* familiar with the phrase "a bird in *the the* hand."

You perhaps have seen some of these perceptual effects, which are among dozens of illustrations of how our brain's rules for perceiving the world—rules that usually enable correct intuition—sometimes lead us astray, as many injured drivers and pilots can testify (and dead ones cannot). Things may appear one way yet really be quite different. Are intuition's errors limited to perceptual tricks? Consider some simple questions. Again, follow the intuitives' advice to silence your linear, logical, left-brain mind, thus opening yourself to the whispers of your inner wisdom.

Imagine (or ask someone to imagine) folding a sheet of paper on itself 100 times. Roughly how thick would it then be?

Given our year with 365 days, a group needs 366 people to ensure that at least two of its members share the same birthday. How big must the group be to have a 50 percent chance of finding a birthday match?

Imagine yourself participating in this study, patterned after a 1930s experiment by psychologist Lloyd Humphreys. On each of 100 trials, you are asked to guess whether a light that goes on 70 percent of the time will go on. You get a dollar each time your guess ("yes" or "no") is correct. Visualize the first ten trials.

Once again, our intuitions usually err. Given a 0.1-millimeter-thick sheet, the thickness after 100 folds, each doubling the preceding thickness, would be 800 trillion times the distance between the earth and the sun. Only twenty-three people are needed to give better than even odds of any two people having the same birthday. (Look out at a soccer match with a referee and the odds are 50–50 that two people on the field have the same birthday.) And though people typically guess "yes" about 70 percent of the time, their intuitions leave them with emptier pockets—about $58—than if they simply guessed "yes" all the time, producing about $70.*

Ah, but shall we say with some postmodernists that intuitive truth is self-validating, and that we must not judge it by the canons of westernized logic? No. With these mind teaser problems, rational analysis defines truth. On the perceptual problems, the ruler rules; it measures an objective reality. On the little gambling game, the rare person who follows logic leaves with enough money to take friends out to a lobster dinner, while the intuitive and friends at the next table can afford only spaghetti.

To be sure, these puzzle games are played on rationality's home court. Logic and measurement, anyone might grant, are ideally suited to such tasks. Consider, then, the tension between intuition and rational analysis in more important realms.

*Guessing "yes" 70 percent of the time would produce about $49 for correct yes's (.7 × 70 = 49) and about $9 for correct no's (.3 × 30 = 9).

The history of science is a story of one challenge to our intuition after another. The heart, our hearts once told us, is the seat of the mind and emotions. Today, the heart remains our symbol for love, but science has long overtaken intuition on this issue. It's your brain, not your heart, that falls in love.

For all human history, our ancestors daily observed the sun cutting across the sky. This had at least two plausible explanations: a) the sun was circling the earth, or b) the earth was spinning while the sun stood still. Intuition preferred the first. Galileo's scientific observations demanded the second.

My own field of psychological science has sometimes confirmed popular intuitions. An enduring, committed marriage *is* conducive to adults' happiness and children's thriving. The media modeling of violent and sexually impulsive behaviors *do* affect viewers' attitudes and actions (though the same studies contradict people's intuitions that it's only *others* who are influenced). Perceived freedom and feelings of control *are* conducive to happiness and achievement. But at the same time, our unaided intuitions may tell us that familiarity breeds contempt, that dreams predict the future, and that high self-esteem is invariably beneficial—ideas that aren't supported by the available evidence. Even the California Task Force to Promote Self-Esteem acknowledged in its report that the "intuitively correct" presumption— that high self-esteem leads to desirable behaviors—has been but weakly confirmed. (It is true that those with high self-esteem are less at risk for depression, but high self-esteem also has a dark side. Much violence results from the puncturing of inflated egos.)

Recent research also relegates other intuitively correct axioms of pop psychology to the dustbin.

- Although genetic predispositions and peer and media influences shape children, direct parental nurture has surprisingly little effect on their developing personalities and tastes. (Adopted siblings do not develop more similar personalities as a result of being reared in the same home. And identical twins are *not* more alike in personality if reared together than if reared in separate homes.)

- People typically do *not* repress acutely painful or upsetting experiences. Holocaust survivors, children who have witnessed a parent's murder, and rape victims remember the horror all too well.

Experiments have similarly deflated people's intuitions that quartz crystals uplift their spirits, that subliminal self-help tapes have reprogrammed their unconscious mind, and that "therapeutic touch" (moving hands near the body) has curative effects. (Those given fake crystals or supposed subliminal tapes, for example, exhibit the same results.)

"Science," said Richard Feynman, "is a long history of learning how not to fool ourselves."

WHY DOES IT MATTER?

Does comprehending the powers and perils of intuition matter? I contend that it matters greatly.

Judges' and jurors' intuitions determine the fate of lives. (Is she telling the truth? Will he do it again if released? Does applying the death penalty deter homicide?)

Investors' intuitions affect fortunes. (Has the market bottomed? Are tech stocks due for another plunge? Is it time to shift into bonds?)

Coaches' intuitions guide their decisions about whom to play. (Does she have the hot hand tonight? Is he in a batting slump?)

Clinicians' intuitions steer their practice. (Is he at risk for suicide? Was she sexually abused?)

Intuitions shape our fears (do we fear the right things?), impressions (are our stereotypes accurate?), and relationships (does she like me?). Intuitions influence presidents in times of crisis, gamblers at the table, and personnel directors when eyeing applicants. As a high-ranking Texas official said of the theory that the death penalty deters murder, "I just feel in my gut it must be true." Our gut-level intuitions have helped us all avert misfortunes, but sometimes they have led us into misfortune. "Nobody can dictate my behavior," said Diana, Princess of Wales, in her last interview before that fateful ride. "I work through instinct, and instinct is my best counselor."

So, yes, it's worth our while to examine the powers and perils of our human intuition. It's worth our while to sift fact from fancy. It's worth our while to seek wisdom. Perhaps, with apologies to Reinhold Niebuhr, we could use a second Serenity Prayer:

God, give us grace
to accept the things that are true,
courage to challenge the things which are untrue,
and the wisdom to distinguish the one from the other.

The Powers of Intuition

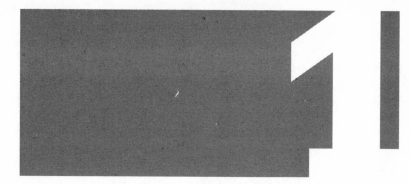

Thinking Without Awareness

How much do we know at any time? Much more, or so I believe, than we know we know!
—*Agatha Christie*, The Moving Finger

Has anyone ever told you that you are amazing? Well, you are. You process vast amounts of information off screen. You effortlessly delegate most of your thinking and decision making to the masses of cognitive workers busily at work in your mind's basement. Only the really important mental tasks reach the executive desk, where your conscious mind works. When you are asked, "What are you thinking?" your mental CEO answers, speaking of worries, hopes, plans, and questions, mindless of all the lower-floor laborers.

This big idea of contemporary psychological science—that most of our everyday thinking, feeling, and acting operate outside conscious awareness—"is a difficult one for people to accept," report John Bargh and Tanya Chartrand, psychologists at New York University. Our consciousness is biased to think that its own intentions and deliberate choices rule our lives (understandably, since tip-of-the-iceberg consciousness is mostly aware of its visible self). But consciousness overrates its own control. Take something as simple as speaking. Strings of words effortlessly spill out of your mouth with near-perfect syntax (amazing, given how many ways there are to mess up). It's as if there were servants downstairs, busily hammering together sentences that get piped up and fluidly shoved out your mouth. You hardly have a clue how you do it. But there it is.

As I typed this last paragraph, the words spilled onto the screen, my fingers galloping across the keyboard under instructions from somewhere—certainly not from my mental CEO's directing each finger one by one. I couldn't, without asking my fingers, tell you where the "w" or the "k" are. If someone enters my office while I'm typing, the smart fingers—actually, the cognitive servants that run them—will finish the sentence while I start up a conversation. More impressive are skilled pianists, who can converse while their fingers play a familiar piece. And then there are the Cornell University students whom psychologists Ulric Neisser, Elizabeth Spelke, and William Hirst trained to copy dictated words with one hand while they read stories with full comprehension. We have, it seems, two minds: one for what we're momentarily aware of, the other for everything else—for doing the computations involved in catching a fly ball, for converting two-dimensional retinal images into three-dimensional perceptions, for taking well-timed breaths, for buttoning a shirt, for coordinating our muscles when signing our names, for knowing to jump at the rustle in the leaves, for intuiting the next master chess move.

Or take driving. When one is learning, driving requires CEO-level attention. We minimize conversation and focus on the road. An American's first week of driving in the United Kingdom or a Brit's first experience driving on the Continent is the new-driver experience over again, requiring concentration as one gradually masters left- or right-sided driving. With time, driving skills are learned, then "overlearned." Like most of life's skills, they become automatic, thus freeing consciousness for executive work. The light turns red and we hit the brake without consciously deciding to do so. While driving home from work we may be engrossed in conversation or worry, so our hands and feet chauffeur us to our destination.

Indeed, sometimes they chauffeur us home when we're supposed to be going elsewhere. "Absent-mindedness is one of the penalties we pay for automatization," notes mental lapse researcher James Reason (who joins animal behavior researchers Robin Fox and Lionel Tiger on my short list of aptly named psychologists). If the boss doesn't direct a different route, the servants—serving our usual interests—do what they're trained to do. But Boss Consciousness can intervene at any time. Unlike Freud's unconscious mind, filled with rebellious, repressed workers in conflict with management, cognitive science's unconscious mental workers are friendlier, more cooperative, and more speedily efficient. Their motto is "we aim to serve."

Be glad for this "automaticity of being." Your capacity for flying through life mostly on autopilot enables your effective functioning. With your mental butlers handling the routine and well-practiced tasks, you can focus on the big stuff. While others take care of the White House lawn, fix meals, and answer the phone the president can ponder international crises and the state of the nation. Much the same is true for you. As the philosopher Alfred North Whitehead observed in 1911, "Civilization advances by extending the number of operations which we can perform without thinking about them."

We have all experienced the automaticity of being. Absentminded professors know the phenomenon well. Sometimes after leaving the bathroom I feel my face to see whether I've shaved. At a late-morning bathroom stop I check the mirror to see whether I've yet combed my hair. After walking down the hall to our department office I'm often without a clue why I'm there (like shaving and hair combing, the automaticity of walking doesn't require our holding our intent in mind).

CHILDREN'S INTUITIVE LEARNING

Some things we know we know, but we don't know *how* we know them. Consider your absorption of language. If you are an average secondary school graduate you know some 80,000 words (likely an underestimate given that you're reading this book). That averages (from age 1 to 18) to nearly 5,000 words learned each year, or 13 each day! How you did it—how the 5,000 words a year you learned could outnumber by so much the roughly 200 words a year that your schoolteachers consciously taught you—is one of the great human wonders. Before you could add 2 + 2 you were creating your own original and grammatically appropriate sentences. Your parents probably would have had trouble stating the rules of syntax. Yet while barely more than a toddler you intuitively comprehended and spoke with a facility that would shame a college student struggling to learn a foreign language or a scientist struggling to simulate natural language on a computer.

Even infants—well before they have begun thinking in words—possess striking intuitive capacities. We are born preferring sights and sounds that facilitate social responsiveness. As newborns, we turned our heads in the direction of human voices. We gazed longer at a drawing of a face-like image than at a bull's-eye pattern, and longer at a bull's-eye pattern (which has contrasts much like those of the human eye) than at a solid disk. We preferred to look at objects eight to twelve inches away, which, wonder of wonders, just happens to be the approximate distance between a nursing infant's eyes and its mother's.

Our perceptual abilities develop continuously during the first months of life. Within days of birth, our brain's neural networks were stamped with the smell of our mother's body. Thus, a week-old nursing baby, placed between a gauze pad from its mother's bra and one from another nursing mother, will usually turn toward its own mother's pad. A three-week-old infant, if given a pacifier that turns on recordings of either its mother's voice or a female stranger's, will suck more vigorously when it hears its now-familiar mother.

Babies also have an intuitive grasp of simple laws of physics. Like adults staring in disbelief at a magic trick, infants look longer at a scene of a ball stopping in midair, a car seeming to pass through a solid object, or an object that seems to disappear. Babies even have a head for numbers. Researcher Karen Wynn showed five-month-old infants one or two objects. Then she hid the objects behind a screen, sometimes removing or adding one through a trap door. When she lifted the screen, the infants often did a double take, staring longer when shown a wrong number of objects. Like animals' native fear of heights, this is intuitive knowledge—unmediated by words or rational analysis.

LEFT BRAIN/RIGHT BRAIN

For more than a century, we've known that the brain's two sides serve differing functions. Accidents, strokes, and tumors in the left hemisphere generally impair activities of the rational, verbal, nonintuitive mind, such as reading, writing, speaking, arithmetic reasoning, and understanding. Similar lesions in the right hemisphere seldom have such dramatic effects.

By 1960 the left hemisphere (or "left brain") was well accepted as the dominant or major hemisphere, and its quieter companion as the subordinate or minor hemisphere. The left hemisphere is rather like the moon's facing side—the one easiest to observe and study. It talks to us. The other side is there, of course, but hidden.

When surgeons first separated the brain's hemispheres as a treatment for severe epilepsy, they effectively created a small population of what have been called the most fascinating people on earth—split-brain people who are literally of two minds. The peculiar nature of our visual wiring enables researchers to send information to either the patient's left or right brain by having the patient stare at a spot and then flashing a stimulus to the right or left of it. (They could do this with you, too, but in your intact brain the telltale hemisphere that received the information would instantly call the news to its partner across the valley. Split-brain surgery severs the phone cables—the corpus callosum—across the valley.) Finally, the researchers quiz each hemisphere separately.

In an early experiment, psychologist Michael Gazzaniga asked split-brain patients to stare at a dot as he flashed HE•ART. Thus HE appeared in their left visual field (which transmits to the right brain) and ART in the right field (which transmits to the left brain). When he then asked them what they had seen, the patients *said* they saw ART and so were startled when their left hands (controlled by the right brain) *pointed* to HE. Given an opportunity to express itself, each hemisphere reported only what it had seen. The left hand intuitively knew what it could not verbally report.

Similarly, when a picture of a spoon was flashed to their right brain, the patients could not say what they saw. But when asked to identify what they had seen by feeling an assortment of hidden objects with their left hands, they readily selected the spoon. If the experimenter said, "Right!" the patient might reply, "What? Right? How could I possibly pick out the right object when I don't know what I saw?" It is, of course, the left brain doing the talking here, bewildered by what its nonverbal right brain quietly knows.

These experiments demonstrate that the right brain understands simple requests and easily perceives objects. In fact, the right brain is superior to the left at copying drawings, recognizing faces, perceiving differences, sensing and expressing emotion.

Although the left brain is adept at literal interpretations of language, the right brain excels in making subtle inferences. If "primed" with the flashed word *foot,* the left brain will be especially quick to then recognize the closely associated word *heel.* But if primed with *foot, cry,* and *glass,* the right brain will more quickly recognize another word that is distantly related to all three: *cut.* And if given a verbal problem—what word goes with *high, district,* and *house?*—the right brain more quickly than the left recognizes that the solution is *school.* As one patient explained after suffering right-brain stroke damage, "I understand words, but I'm missing the subtleties." Thus, the right brain helps us modulate our speech to make meaning clear—as when we ask "What's that in the road ahead?" instead of "What's that in the road, a head?"

Some split-brain surgery patients have temporarily been bothered by the unruly independence of their left hand, which might unbutton a shirt while the right hand buttoned it, or put groceries back on the shelf after the right hand put them in the cart. It was as if each hemisphere was thinking "I've half a mind to wear my green (blue) shirt today." Indeed, said Nobel laureate psychologist Roger Sperry, split-brain surgery leaves people "with two separate minds." (Reading these reports, I imagine a split-brain person enjoying a solitary game of "rocks, paper, and scissors"—left hand versus right.)

When the two minds are at odds, the left brain acts as the brain's press agent, doing mental gymnastics to rationalize unexplained actions. If the right brain commands an action, the left brain will intuitively justify it. If the right brain is commanded to laugh, the patient will respond with laughter. The left brain, when asked why the laughter, will rationalize, perhaps pointing to the "funny research." If a patient follows an order sent to the right brain ("Walk"), the left brain will offer a ready explanation ("I'm going into the house to get a Coke"). Michael Gazzaniga concludes that the left brain is an "interpreter" that instantly constructs theories to justify our behavior. We humans have a quick facility for constructing meaning.

Most of the body's paired organs—kidneys, lungs, breasts—perform identical functions, providing a backup should one side fail. Not so the brain's two halves. They are a biological odd couple, serving differing functions, each seemingly with a mind of its own. From simply looking at the similarly shaped hemispheres, who would suppose that they contribute so uniquely to the harmony of the whole? And not even Freud (who didn't anticipate the cool intelligence of the hidden mind) could have supposed that our brains are humming with so much resourceful activity outside our conscious awareness, and that our interpretive left brain, grasping at straws, can so speedily intuit false explanations for our behavior. Beneath the surface there is much intelligence, and above the surface there is much self-delusion.

IMPLICIT MEMORY

My ninety-three-year-old father recently suffered a small stroke that has had but one peculiar effect. His genial personality is intact. He is as mobile as before. He knows us, and while poring over family photo albums can reminisce in detail. But he has lost most of his facility for laying down new memories of conversations and everyday episodes. He cannot tell me what day of the week it is. He enjoys going out for a drive and commenting on what we're seeing, but the next day he cannot recall our going anywhere. Told repeatedly of his brother-in-law's death, he would still express surprise on learning the news.

Oliver Sacks tells of another such memory-loss patient, Jimmie, who thirty years after suffering brain damage in 1945 would still, when asked who is president, answer "Harry Truman." Sacks showed Jimmie a photo from *National Geographic*. "What is this?" he asked.

"It's the moon," Jimmie replied.

"No, it's not," Sacks answered. "It's a picture of the earth taken from the moon."

"Doc, you're kidding? Someone would've had to get a camera up there!"

"Naturally."

"Hell! You're joking—how the hell would you do that?" Jimmie's wonder was that of a bright young man from fifty-five years ago reacting with amazement to his travel back to the future.

Careful testing of these unique people reveals something even stranger: Although incapable of recalling new facts or anything they have recently done, Jimmie and other similarly amnesic people can learn. Once shown hard-to-find figures in pictures (*Where's Waldo?*), they can quickly spot them again later. They can learn to read mirror-image writing or do a jigsaw puzzle (after denying that they've ever seen the task before). They have even been taught complicated job skills. However, they do all these things with no awareness of having learned them.

These curious findings challenge the idea that memory is a single, unified system. Instead, we seem to have two systems operating in tandem. Whatever has destroyed conscious recall has left unconscious learning intact. These patients can learn *how* to do something —called *implicit memory* (or procedural memory). But they cannot know and declare *that* they know—called *explicit memory* (or declarative memory). Having read a story once, they will read it faster a second time, showing implicit memory. But there will be no explicit memory, for they cannot recall having seen the story before. After playing golf on a new course, they will forget the experience completely, yet the more they play the course, the more their game will improve. If repeatedly shown the word *perfume*, they will not recall having seen it. But if asked what word comes to mind in response to the letters *per*, they surprise themselves by saying *perfume*, readily displaying their learning. They retain their past but do not explicitly recall it. Intuitively, they know more than they are aware.

This dual explicit-implicit memory system helps explain "infantile amnesia": The reactions and skills we learned during infancy—how to walk, whether to trust or fear others—reach far into our future. Yet as adults we recall nothing (explicitly) of our first three years. Although benefiting from a legacy of collected intuitions—our perceptions of distance, our sense of good and bad, our preference for familiar foods, people, and places—our conscious minds draw a blank for those early years. Infantile amnesia occurs because we index so much of our explicit memory by words that nonspeaking toddlers have yet to learn, and also because a crucial brain region for laying down explicit memories (the hippocampus) is one of the last brain structures to mature. We are amnesic for much of our past. Yet some of what we don't explicitly recall we implicitly, intuitively remember.

KNOWING WITHOUT AWARENESS

On this much the old Freudians and new cognitive scientists agree: the mind is buzzing with influential happenings that are not reportably conscious. "Deep cognitive activation" is how psychologists Daniel Wegner and Laura Smart describe this subterranean world. The presumption of an unconscious mind has long had a credibility problem, however. How can we provide evidence for what we cannot report?

Freud's after-the-fact explanations of how unconscious dynamics explain one person's smoking, another's fear of horses, and another's sexual orientation fail to satisfy. If you feel angry over your mother's death, you illustrate the theory because "your unresolved childhood dependency needs are threatened." If you do not feel angry, you again illustrate the theory because "you are repressing your anger." As C. S. Lewis observed, "We are arguing like a man who should say, 'If there were an invisible cat in that chair, the chair would look empty; but the chair does look empty; therefore there is an invisible cat in it.'" After-the-fact interpretation is appropriate for some historical and literary scholars, which helps explain Freud's lingering influence on literary criticism. But in science as in horse racing, bets must be placed before the race is run.

Might our dreams, or how we project ourselves into Rorschach inkblots, provide a sort of psychological X-ray, a view beneath our mind's surface? (Freud called dreams "the royal road to the unconscious.") Critics say that it is time to wake up from Freud's dream theory, which he regarded as the most valuable of his discoveries but which actually is one of his greatest failures, with no proof that dreams express discernible unconscious wishes. Dream interpretation, the critics say, is a nightmare. Even Freud allegedly granted that "sometimes a cigar is just a cigar."

The much-cherished and oft-reviled Rorschach aims to reveal our unconscious feelings and conflicts. But researcher Lee Sechrest and his colleagues offer the "almost universal agreement among the scientific community" that the test lacks validity (and is "not empirically supported," as another set of experts recently concluded). Carnegie-Mellon University psychologist Robyn Dawes is blunter: "If a professional psychologist is 'evaluating' you in a situation in which you are at risk and asks you for responses to ink blots . . . walk out of that psychologist's office."

If the old psychoanalytic methods don't reliably reveal the unconscious mind's workings, the new cognitive science does. Consider, first, our capacity for divided attention. You surely are aware that your conscious attention is selective. It's in but one place at a time. If you doubt this, try (assuming you are right-handed) moving your right foot in a smooth counterclockwise circle while writing the number 3 repeatedly with your right hand. You can easily do either—but not at the same time. Or if you are musically trained, try tapping a steady three beats to the measure with your left hand while tapping four times with your right hand. Unless they become automatic with practice, such tasks require conscious attention, which can be in only one place at a time. Consciousness focuses us. If time is nature's way of keeping everything from happening at once, then consciousness is nature's way of keeping us from thinking everything at once.

Perceptions, too, come to us moment by moment, one perception being lifted from our mind's magic slate as the next appears. Because conscious attention is selective, we see the familiar reversible figure only one way at a time, before the perception flits away and the alternate replaces it.

Likewise, while reading this sentence you have been unaware of the pressure of the seat below, of your shoes pressing against your feet, or of your nose in your line of vision. But there they are (where did that nose come from?). At a cocktail party (or in a "dichotic listening" experiment in which headphones play separate messages to each ear) you can attend to one conversation or another. You can even bounce between two. But if you're paying attention to one, you won't perceive what is said in the other. Whatever has your attention has your undivided attention (which is why, for most of us, driving in Manhattan is best not done while talking on a cell phone).

But now things get really interesting, for it turns out that we can, nevertheless, process and be influenced by unattended information. Let someone from that hubbub of unattended party noise speak your name and instantly your attention shifts. You weren't listening to that speaker, but the downstairs laborers watching the radar screens noticed the blip—a signal amid the noise—and instantly alerted your mental CEO. In a dichotic listening experiment they will do the same when detecting an emotion-arousing word, such as one previously associated with electric shock. Likewise, in a "dichoptic viewing" experiment—with differing images seen by the two eyes—only one will be visible to you, though your brain's radar technicians will do a rudimentary scan of the other for any important information. Ergo, you are, right now, processing much information outside your awareness.

Or imagine yourself in this experiment, by social psychologist William Wilson. Through headphones, you listen to a prose passage played in one ear and repeat its words to check them against a written transcript. Because the task requires total attention, you pay no attention to some simple, novel tunes played in your other ear. The tunes are not subliminal. You *could* hear them, much as you can feel your shoes. But you are so unnoticing that when the experimenter later intersperses these tunes among new ones, you do not remember having heard them before. Although moments before you had been an earwitness, you cannot pick them out of the musical lineup. Nevertheless, when asked to rate how much you *like* each tune, you find yourself preferring the ones previously played. Your preferences reveal what your conscious memory cannot.

One clever experiment by Larry Jacoby and his colleagues piped unfamiliar names such as Adrian Marr and Sebastian Weisdorf into the unattended ear while people monitored strings of numbers piped into the attended ear. Afterward, the participants usually couldn't pick these names out of a lineup of unheard names. Yet they more often rated them as famous! By dividing attention and "making names famous without their being recognized," the researchers successfully demonstrated unconscious memory.

Or imagine, in another experiment, hearing in one ear an ambiguous statement such as "We stood by the bank." When a pertinent word (*river* or *money*) is simultaneously sent to your unattended ear, you don't consciously hear it. Yet the word "primes" your interpretation of the sentence. Priming experiments reveal how one thought, even outside of awareness, influences another thought or action. Priming is the awakening of associations. In yet another experiment, people asked to complete a sentence containing words like *old, wise,* and *retired* afterward walked more slowly to the elevator than those not primed—and without any awareness of walking slowly or of the high frequency of words related to aging.

The experiments have their counterparts in everyday life:

- Watching a scary movie alone at home can prime our thinking, activating emotions that cause us to interpret furnace noises as those of an intruder.
- For many psychology students, reading about psychological disorders primes how they interpret their own anxieties and gloomy moods. Reading about disease symptoms similarly primes medical students to worry about their congestion, fever, or headache.
- Ask people to pronounce the word spelled by S-H-O-P and then ask them (or ask yourself) what they do when they come to a green light. Many will answer "stop," and then will sheepishly grin when realizing their priming-induced error.

The take-home lesson: Although perception requires attention, unattended stimuli can subtly affect us. Moreover, implanted ideas and images can automatically—unintentionally, effortlessly, and without awareness—prime how we interpret and recall events.

In a host of new studies, the effects of priming surface even when the stimuli are presented subliminally—too briefly to be perceived. What's out of sight need not be out of mind. An electric shock, too slight to be felt, increases the perceived intensity of a later shock. An imperceptibly flashed word, *bread,* primes people to detect a related word, such as *butter,* more quickly than *bottle* or *bubble.* A subliminal color name facilitates speedier identification when the color itself appears on a computer screen, while an unseen wrong name delays color identification. In each case, an invisible image or word primes a response to a later question.

Picture yourself in yet another experiment, by Moshe Bar and Irving Biederman. If you are like their University of Southern California students, the chances are less than 1 in 7 that you could name a simple image (such as a hammer) after its presentation for 47 milliseconds. But what if you witness the image again in the same position as much as 15 minutes later and after intervening presentations of other images? The chances of your naming the hammer would now be better than 1 in 3. It is as if the second presentation, combined with the first presentation, sufficiently awakens the brain for some awareness.

The variety and subtlety of unnoticed influences is impressive:

- One experiment subliminally flashed emotionally positive scenes (such as kittens or a romantic couple) or negative scenes (such as a werewolf or a dead body) an instant before participants viewed slides of people. Although the participants consciously perceived only a flash of light, they gave more positive ratings to people whose photos had been associated with the positive scenes. People somehow looked nicer if their photo immediately followed unperceived kittens rather than an unperceived werewolf.
- Chinese characters, too, seem to imply something nicer if preceded by a flashed but unperceived smiling face rather than a scowling face.
- Graduate students evaluate their research ideas more negatively shortly after viewing the unperceived scowling face of their adviser—as if a sense of the adviser's disapproval was lurking in the unconscious mind.

- When shown subliminal pictures of spiders and then subjected to electric shocks, some students—those good at guessing their heart rates—could predict the impending shock. Although they never consciously saw the spider, these in-tune-with-their-body students had a gut feeling.

The striking and unavoidable conclusion: Sometimes we intuitively *feel* what we do not know we know.

The subliminal influence experiments further support the reality of unconscious information processing. Do the experiments also support the entrepreneurial claims of subliminal advertising and self-improvement tapes? Can "hidden persuasion" trespass on our minds? The research consensus is no. Although the hucksters claim that subliminal messages have a powerful, enduring effect on behavior, lab studies reveal but a subtle, fleeting effect on thinking and feeling. Moreover, experiments show that commercial subliminal tapes have no effect beyond that of a placebo—the effect of one's belief in them. Anthony Greenwald, a University of Washington psychologist who has conducted many studies of subliminal priming, conducted sixteen experiments with self-help tapes. His results were uniform: not one had any therapeutic effect. For example, students given a tape with subliminal messages aimed at improving their memory felt as though their memory was improving. But so did students who *thought* they were listening to the memory tape but who actually were given a self-esteem boosting tape. Likewise, students who thought they were getting subliminal self-esteem boosting messages perceived themselves receiving the benefits they expected. But tests administered before and after the therapy revealed that neither tape had any effect on self-esteem or memory.

As we will see again and again, such experiments are the scientific tool for sifting reality from fantasy, the facts of life from wishful thinking, bizarre ideas from those bizarre-sounding but true. Who would have guessed how the brain separates and then integrates the subroutines of vision. "Life is infinitely stranger than anything which the mind of man could invent," Sherlock Holmes rightly said in Arthur Conan Doyle's *Study in Scarlet*. To winnow the strange but true ideas from the make-believe, science offers a simple procedure: test them.

TWO WAYS OF KNOWING

We have seen that in psychological science as in pop psychology, intuition (by whatever name) is vibrantly alive. Our minds process vast amounts of information outside of consciousness, beyond language. Inside our ever-active brain, many streams of activity flow in parallel, function automatically, are remembered implicitly, and only occasionally surface as conscious words. "Thinking lite," this unconscious processing has been called—"one-fourth the effort of regular thinking." As the captain of the *Queen Mary 2* will depend on more than a thousand on-board staff, so we depend on our out-of-sight cognitive servants. Without them we would be challenged to get out of bed in the morning. Be thankful for intuitive knowing.

We have sampled but a few of the hundreds of 1990s experiments exploring the relative contributions of our two ways of knowing— automatic (unconscious) and controlled (conscious). When meeting and greeting people, when pondering and predicting their behavior, when screening and stereotyping strangers, to what extent are we guided by knee-jerk intuitions rather than by deliberate reasoning? To a great extent, surmises John Bargh, a leading researcher, "automatic, nonconscious processes pervade all aspects of mental and social life." As Galileo "removed the earth from its privileged position at the center of the universe," so Bargh sees automatic thinking research "removing consciousness from its privileged place." The purpose of consciousness, he theorizes, is *"to connect a parallel mind to a serial world"* (his italics). And the unconscious is less simpleminded and irrational than some researchers contend, argues Bargh. Unconscious, intuitive inclinations detect and reflect the regularities of our personal history. Thanks to a repository of experience, a tennis player automatically— and intelligently—knows just where to run to intercept the ball, with just the right racquet angle. As Venus Williams smacks the ball, conscious attention and unconscious perception and coordination integrate seamlessly. The result is her near-perfect intuitive physics.

University of Massachusetts psychologist Seymour Epstein also discerns two ways of knowing, experiential and rational. He sees one as intuitive, automatic, and nonverbal, and the other as rational, analytic, and verbal. Among their other differences are these:

Experiential knowing is	*Rational knowing is*
Rapid—enables immediate action	Slow—enables delayed action
Emotional—attuned to what feels good	Logical—based on what is sensible
Mediated by vibes from past experience	Mediated by conscious appraisal
Self-evident—"experiencing is believing"	Justified with logic and evidence
Generalized—conducive to stereotypes	Differentiated—discourages overgeneralization

Epstein and his students assess individuals' thinking styles with a questionnaire that invites people to report how much they "enjoy intellectual challenges," are good at "logical analysis," and enjoy "hard thinking" versus preferring "to rely on my intuitive impressions," "trusting my hunches," and "going by my instincts." But all of us engage both ways of knowing. And sometimes we live with their conflicting results. Rationally, we may know that flying is safer than driving (even after September 11, 2001), but experientially, emotionally, and immediately we may feel something different. We may know, rationally and deliberately, how we are *supposed* to feel toward members of some ethnic group. But our social intuitions, as we will see in the next chapter, may lead us in a different direction.

Social Intuition

*The best and most beautiful things in the world cannot be seen
or even touched. They must be felt with the heart.*
—Helen Keller

As Jackie Larsen left her Grand Marais, Minnesota, church prayer group one morning in April 2001, she encountered Christopher Bono, a short, clean-cut, well-mannered youth. Bono said that his car was broken down and that he was looking for a ride to meet friends in Thunder Bay. "I told him to come to my shop and I would look up his friends in the phone book and they could come for him," Larsen later recalled.

When he appeared before her, Larsen felt a pain in her stomach. Initially she thought he was a runaway, but something told her that something was very wrong. She insisted that they talk outside on the sidewalk. "I said, 'I am a mother and I have to talk to you like a mother. . . . I can tell by your manners that you have a nice mother.'" At the mention of his mother, Bono's eyes fixed on her. "I don't know where my mother is," he said.

As the conversation ended, Larsen directed Bono back to the church to talk with the pastor. She also called the police and suggested that they trace his car license plates. The car was registered to his mother in southern Illinois. When police went to her apartment, no one answered. Breaking in, they found blood all over and Lucia

Bono dead in the bathtub. Christopher Bono, sixteen, was charged with first-degree murder.

Jackie Larsen had a feeling. She intuitively sensed that something was not right. Such feelings often come quickly. After more than three decades of interviewing faculty candidates, I've learned that the impressions of our department secretary, after meeting candidates for just a minute, are remarkably predictive of the person's long-term collegiality. She is not alone. We've all had the experience of forming lasting impressions within a few moments of meeting someone and noting the person's animation, manner of speaking, and gestures.

READING "THIN SLICES"

Consider Nalini Ambady and Robert Rosenthal's discovery of the *speed* of our social intuitions. Mere "thin slices" of someone's behavior can reveal much. Ambady and Rosenthal videotaped thirteen Harvard University graduate students teaching undergraduate courses. Observers then viewed three thin slices of each teacher's behavior—mere ten-second clips from the beginning, middle, and end of a class—and rated each teacher's confidence, activeness, warmth, and so forth. These behavior ratings, based on thirty *seconds* of teaching from an entire semester, predicted amazingly well the average student ratings of the teachers at the semester's end. Observing even thinner slices—three two-second clips—yielded ratings that still correlated +.72 with the students' evaluations. (A correlation this large accounts for half the student-to-student variation in the end-of-term evaluations.) Some people's instant first impressions effectively predicted other people's lasting impressions.

In various experiments, the thin slices have been observed by viewing video clips (with or without audio), by watching from behind a one-way mirror as someone enters a room and greets someone, or by judging someone from a mere photo. After hearing people recite the alphabet, observers have been able to intuit, with some accuracy, their social assertiveness. After watching ninety seconds of people's walking and talking, observers could roughly estimate how others evaluated them. After a trifling glance at someone's photo, people gain some sense of the person's personality traits.

Even micro-thin slices tell us something. When John Bargh flashes an image of an object or a face for just 200 milliseconds, people instantly evaluate it. "We're finding that everything is evaluated as good or bad within a quarter of a second of seeing it," says Bargh. In the blink of an eye, before engaging any rational thought, we find ourselves loathing or liking a piece of abstract art, a Doberman, or the new neighbor.

There is ancient biological wisdom to this express link between perception and response. When meeting a stranger in the forest, one had to instantly assess whether that person was friend or foe. Those who could read a person accurately were more likely to survive and leave descendants, which helps explain why humans today can detect at a glance the facial expressions of anger, sadness, fear, or pleasure. Small wonder that the first ten seconds of a relationship tell us a great deal, or that our capacity for reading nonverbal cues crosses cultures. (A smile's a smile the world around—there is no culture where people express happiness by frowning.) Moreover, when people in China try to guess Americans' extraversion and agreeableness from their photos, they do so with fair consensus and accuracy, as do Americans when making the same intuitive judgments of photos of Chinese people. Our speedy social intuition packs enough insight to serve us well.

OUR DUAL ATTITUDE SYSTEM

In Chapter 1, I described our two ways of knowing (unconscious and conscious). The first is simple, reflexive, and emotional; the second complex, reflective, and rational. I also described our dual memory system (implicit and explicit). Some things we implicitly know without explicitly remembering. A third example of parallel information processing (one part intuitive, one part rational) is what Timothy Wilson and his colleagues call our dual attitude system. Wilson, a University of Virginia social psychologist, argues that the mental processes that *control* our social behavior are distinct from the mental processes through which we *explain* our behavior. Often, our gut-level attitudes guide our actions, and then our rational mind makes sense of them.

In nine experiments, Wilson and his co-workers found that expressed attitudes toward things or people usually predicted later behavior. However, if they first asked the participants to *analyze* their feelings, their attitude reports became useless. For example, dating couples' happiness with their relationship was a reasonably good predictor of whether they were still dating several months later. Other participants, before rating their happiness, first listed all the *reasons* they could think of why their relationship was good or bad. After doing so, their expressed attitudes were useless in predicting the future of the relationship. Dissecting the relationship apparently drew attention to easily verbalized factors that actually were less important than relationship aspects that were hard to put in words. Sometimes, wrote the poet Theodore Roethke, "Self-contemplation is a curse / That makes an old confusion worse."

In a later study, Wilson and his co-workers had people choose one of two art posters to take home. Those asked first to identify *reasons* for their choice usually preferred a humorous poster (whose positive features they could more easily verbalize). But a few weeks later they were less satisfied with their choice than were those who went by their gut feelings and generally chose the other poster. Intuitive first impressions can be telling, especially when feelings rather than reasons guide behavior.

Gut-level feelings not only predict some behaviors better than analyzed feelings, but they can also better predict the judgments of experts. Wilson and Jonathan Schooler discovered that college students' preferences for various strawberry jams best predicted expert judgments when the students responded without thinking too much. Students' instant preferences for college courses also better predicted experts' judgments than did rationally analyzed preferences. Wilson surmises that we're often unaware of why we feel as we do. Reflecting on the reasons for our feelings draws our attention to plausible but possibly erroneous factors. Sometimes the intuitionists are right: it pays to listen to our hearts.

Such findings illustrate our dual attitude system. Our automatic, *implicit* attitudes regarding someone or something often differ from our consciously controlled, *explicit* attitudes. Our likes and dislikes, our preferences and prejudices, are partly unconscious, partly conscious. From childhood, for example, we may retain a habitual, automatic fear or dislike of people for whom we now verbalize respect and appreciation. Although explicit attitudes may change with relative ease, notes Wilson, "implicit attitudes, like old habits, change more slowly."

ACADEMIC AND SOCIAL INTELLIGENCE

Today's research psychologists also contrast rational and intuitive knowing by distinguishing academic intelligence (as assessed by intelligence and academic aptitude tests) from what Nancy Cantor and John Kihlstrom call *social intelligence*—the know-how that enables us to comprehend social situations and manage ourselves in them. We all have known people who could blast the top off the SAT yet self-destruct for lack of social sensitivity and judgment. Indeed, as Seymour Epstein and Petra Meier note, if academic aptitude signifies social competence, then why are smart people "not, by a wide margin, more effective . . . in achieving better marriages, in successfully raising their children, and in achieving better mental and physical well-being?"

A critical part of social intelligence is what psychologists Peter Salovey and John Mayer term emotional intelligence—the ability to perceive, express, understand, and manage emotions. Emotionally intelligent people are self-aware. They cope with life without letting their emotions get hijacked by dysfunctional depression, anxiety, or anger. In pursuit of long-term rewards, they can delay gratification rather than letting themselves be overtaken by impulses. Their empathy enables them to read others' emotions and respond skillfully—knowing what to say to a grieving friend, when to encourage a colleague, how to manage conflicts. They are emotionally astute and thus often more successful in careers, marriages, and parenting than are those academically smarter but emotionally denser. One study, led by University of Delaware emotion researcher Carroll Izard, assessed five-year-olds' ability to recognize and label facial emotions. Even after controlling for verbal aptitude and temperament, the five-year-olds who could most accurately discern emotions became nine-year-olds who easily made friends, cooperated with the teacher, and effectively managed their emotions.

Mayer, Salovey, and David Caruso have advanced their research (which was popularized and more expansively defined in Daniel Goleman's *Emotional Intelligence*) by developing the Multifactor Emotional Intelligence Scale (MEIS), which assesses both overall emotional intelligence and its three components.

- *Emotion perception.* Items measure people's abilities to recognize emotions conveyed by various faces, musical excerpts, graphic designs, and stories.
- *Emotion understanding.* Items assess people's ability to recognize how emotions change over time, to predict differing emotions (for example, the emotions of a driver whose car hit a dog chasing a stick, and the emotions of the dog's owner), and to apprehend how emotions blend (sample item: "Optimism most closely combines which two emotions? pleasure and anticipation, acceptance and joy, surprise and joy, pleasure and joy?" Answer: pleasure and anticipation).
- *Emotion regulation.* People rate the strategies that they or others might use when facing various dilemmas.

Initial studies using the MEIS and its newer brief version indicate that emotional intelligence exhibits the reliability, coherence, and age-linked development of a genuine form of human intelligence.

In extreme cases, brain damage may diminish emotional intelligence while leaving academic intelligence intact. Antonio Damasio, a University of Iowa neuroscientist known for his registry of more than 2,000 brain-damaged patients, tells of Elliot, a man with normal intelligence and memory. Since the removal of a brain tumor, Elliot has lived without emotion. "I never saw a tinge of emotion in my many hours of conversation with him," Damasio reports. "No sadness, no impatience, no frustration." When shown disturbing pictures of injured people, destroyed communities, and natural disasters, Elliot shows—and realizes he feels—no emotion. Like Mr. Spock of *Star Trek,* and the human-appearing android Data of *Star Trek: The*

Next Generation, he knows but he cannot feel.* And lacking emotional signals, Elliot's social intelligence plummeted. Unable to adjust his behavior in response to others' feelings, he lost his job. He went bankrupt. His marriage collapsed. He remarried and divorced again. At last report, he was dependent on custodial care from a sibling and on a disability check.

THE BODY'S WISDOM

For most people, emotions are just there. We take them for granted. But where is "there"? No doubt you can recall times when you reacted emotionally to a situation before you had time to consciously interpret or think about it. How did you do it? How do we process threatening information in milliseconds, below the radar of our awareness? Have neuroscientists located social and emotional intuition in the brain? Although human abilities do not reside in any one place, researchers have identified pathways that explain why feeling sometimes precedes thinking.

Some of the brain's emotional pathways bypass the cortical areas involved in thinking. One such pathway runs from the eye via the thalamus, the brain's sensory switchboard, to the amygdala, a pair of emotional control centers in the brain's primitive core. This eye-to-amygdala shortcut, bypassing the cortex, enables your emotional response before your intellect intervenes.

The amygdala sends more neural projections up to the cortex than it receives. This makes it easier for our feelings to hijack our thinking than for our thinking to rule our feelings, note brain researchers Joseph LeDoux and Jorge Armony. After the cortex has further interpreted a threat, the thinking brain takes over. In the forest, we jump

---

*Star Trek's Data is the embodiment of cool, emotionless rationality. His brilliance and logic give him superhuman analytical intelligence. And yet he realizes that something is missing. He tries to write poetry, but without the passions of the heart it falls flat. Data's intellectual curiosity leads him to wonder about fear, anger, and joy, but he cannot create such feelings. He is all cognition, no emotion. In the film *A.I.*, Steven Spielberg created a different sort of robot, one programmed to give and receive love.

at the sound of rustling leaves, leaving the cortex to decide later whether the sound was made by a predator or just by the wind. Some of our emotional reactions apparently involve no deliberate thinking. The heart is not always subject to the mind.

The amygdala is a key part of our hard-wired alarm system, which was one aspect of the social intuition that enabled our ancestors instinctively to avoid predators and disasters and to know whom to trust. Another part, Damasio and his colleagues report, is an area of the frontal lobes lying just above our eyes. They studied six patients whose damage here spared their general intelligence but hampered the emotional memories that underlie effective intuition. They gave the patients, and ten normal individuals, a stash of phony money and four decks of cards, face down. The participants then turned 100 cards from the deck tops, hoping to find cards that brought cash rewards and to avoid cards that carried penalties. Two of the decks were "bad"; the cards usually gave rewards of $100, but sometimes they told participants to hand over large sums, resulting in an overall loss. The other decks were "good"; they carried rewards of only $50, but the penalty cards were less severe, resulting in an overall gain. Given this task—"designed to resemble life," with its uncertain risks and rewards—the unemotional patients showed minimal stress response when drawing the severe penalties, and they persevered longer in drawing from the bad decks. The normal individuals exhibited a more emotional response to the severe penalties and began to avoid the bad decks *well before they could articulate their reason for doing so.* Thanks to their emotional memories, they had a hunch, a gut-level intuition, that guided their choices. In many real-life situations, from the poker table to the board room, conscious reasoning likewise arises as an afterthought to the intuitive knowledge rooted in emotional memories. Sometimes "an ounce of intuition trumps a pound of pondering."

Classical ("Pavlovian") conditioning adds punch to the hunch. After Pavlov's hungry dogs repeatedly heard a tone before receiving food, their bodies intuitively knew to begin salivating in anticipation of the food. When researcher Michael Domjan turned on a red light just before presenting male quail with an approachable female, the males soon became sexually excited in response to the light, their body's intuitive wisdom preparing them for the impending rendezvous. Fears, too, get classically conditioned into our intuition. A year after being shot in the shoulder and ribs during the 1995 massacre of sixteen five-year-olds and their teacher in Dunblane, Scotland, Matthew Birnie still responded with terror to the sight of toy guns and the sound of balloons popping. The phenomenon has been brought to the laboratory in studies comparing abused with nonabused children. For abused children, an angry face on a computer screen produces brain waves that are dramatically stronger and longer lasting.

With conditioning, stimuli that are similar to naturally disgusting or appealing objects will, by association, evoke intuitive disgust or liking. Normally desirable foods, such as fudge, are unappealing when presented in a disgusting form, as when shaped to resemble dog feces. We perceive adults with childlike facial features (round face, large forehead, small chin, large eyes) as having childlike warmth, submissiveness, and naiveté. In both cases, people's emotional reactions to one stimulus intuitively generalize to similar stimuli.

The bottom line: Thanks to our neural shortcuts, our storehouse of emotional memories, and our conditioned likes and dislikes, our bodies accumulate and express our adaptive intuitions.

TESTING SOCIAL INTUITIONS

Other lines of social psychological research further explore our social intuitions. A quick look at each completes our survey of the powers of social intuition.

The mere exposure effect. Dozens of experiments pioneered by Robert Zajonc reveal that familiarity feeds fondness. Repeated exposure increases our liking of novel nonsense syllables, music, geometric figures, Chinese characters, faces, and even the letters of our own name. Richard Moreland and Scott Beach demonstrated the mere exposure effect by having four equally attractive women silently attend a 200-student class for zero, five, ten, or fifteen class sessions. At the course's end, students viewed slides of each woman and rated her attractiveness. The best looking? The ones they'd seen most. This familiarity-fondness link would not surprise the young Taiwanese man who wrote more than 700 letters to his girlfriend, urging her to marry him. She did marry—the mail carrier.

In hindsight, we can again see wisdom here. What our ancestors found familiar was usually safe and approachable. Things unfamiliar were more often dangerous. Zajonc surmises that evolution has therefore hard-wired us with an intuitive tendency to bond with those familiar and to be wary of those unfamiliar. Our gut-level preference for those familiar has a darker side, however—an intuitive, primitive, automatic prejudice against those unfamiliar.

Spontaneous trait inference. In observing others, we humans can't resist making judgments. We speedily, spontaneously, and unintentionally infer others' traits. In one experiment, John Darley and Paget Gross showed Princeton University students a videotape of Hannah, a fourth-grader, taking an oral achievement test in which she got some questions right and some wrong. Half the students, having previously seen Hannah videotaped in a depressed urban setting, unconsciously inferred low ability and recalled her as missing half the questions. The other half, having previously seen Hannah in an affluent suburban setting, inferred higher ability and recalled her as getting most questions right. This trait inference was subtle and unintentional, because students claimed to have been uninfluenced by having been exposed to lower- or upper-class Hannah.

People also have a peculiar tendency, when hearing someone say something good or bad about another, to associate the good or bad trait with the speaker. In several experiments, Lynda Mae, Donal Carlston, and John Skowronski have found that if we talk about others' gossipiness, people may unconsciously associate "gossip" with *us*. Call someone a dolt or a jerk and folks may later construe *you* as one. Describe someone as sensitive and compassionate and *you* will seem more so. Even bearers of bad news get intuitively disliked, as do strangers who remind us of a disliked person.

Moral intuition. Are your moral judgments and actions more a matter of reasoned discernment, or of rapid intuitions? Under the influence of the psychologist Lawrence Kohlberg and the philosopher John Rawls, academics have favored the rationalist model. But building on the new research on dual processing—our two ways of knowing—University of Virginia social psychologist Jonathan Haidt has shown that the mind makes many moral judgments in the way it makes aesthetic judgments—quickly and automatically. Later, we rationalize our immediate feelings. As we feel intuitive disgust when seeing people engaged in degraded or subhuman acts, so we feel "elevation"—a tingly, warm, glowing feeling in the chest—when seeing people display exceptional generosity, compassion, or courage. We also feel inspired to follow their example.

One woman in Haidt's research recalled driving through her snowy neighborhood with three young men as they passed "an elderly woman with a shovel in her driveway. I did not think much of it, when one of the guys in the back asked the driver to let him off there. . . . When I saw him jump out of the back seat and approach the lady, my mouth dropped in shock as I realized that he was offering to shovel her walk for her." Witnessing this unexpected goodness triggered elevation: "I felt like jumping out of the car and hugging this guy. I felt like singing and running, or skipping and laughing. I felt like saying nice things about people. . . . I went home and gushed about it to my suite-mates, who clutched at their hearts. And, although I have never seen this guy as more than just a friend, I felt a hint of romantic feeling for him at this moment."

In Haidt's "social intuitionist" account of morality, first come the feelings, then comes the rationalization. "Could human morality really be run by the moral emotions," he wonders, "while moral reasoning struts about pretending to be in control?" Indeed, he surmises, "moral judgment involves quick gut feelings, or affectively laden intuitions, which then trigger moral reasoning." Moral reasoning aims to convince others of what we intuitively feel.

The social intuitionist explanation of morality finds additional support from a study of moral paradoxes. Imagine a runaway trolley headed for five people. All will certainly be killed unless you throw a switch that diverts the trolley onto another track, where it will kill one person. Should you throw the switch?

Most say yes. Kill one, save five. Now imagine the same dilemma, except that your opportunity to save the five requires pushing a large stranger onto the tracks, where he will die as his body stops the trolley. Kill one, save five?

Although the logic is the same, most say no. Seeking to understand why, a Princeton research team led by a philosophy graduate student, Joshua Greene, used brain imaging to spy inside people's skulls as they contemplated such dilemmas. Only when given the personal (body-pushing) type of moral dilemma did their brains' emotion areas—those active when someone is sad or frightened—light up. Although engaging identical logic, the personal dilemma engages emotions that feed moral intuitions. Moral judgment is more than thinking; it's also gut-level feeling.

Contagious moods. To sense what others are feeling, let your body and face mirror their expressions. In experiments, such imitation evokes empathy. Actually, you hardly need try. Observing others' faces, postures, and voices, we naturally and unconsciously mimic their moment-to-moment reactions. We synchronize our movements, postures, and tones of voice with theirs. Doing so not only helps us intuit their feelings, it also makes for "emotional contagion." No wonder it's fun to be around happy people and depressing to be around depressed people. No wonder one study of British nurses and accountants found "mood linkage"—shared up and down moods—within various work groups. And no wonder Desmond Tutu reports that the trauma that South Africa's Truth and Reconciliation Commission experienced while listening to accounts of horrific happenings was even more keenly felt by "our interpreters, because they had to speak in the first person, at one time being the victim and at another being the perpetrator." Echoing the words and body language of the suffering caused them to suffer.

Emotional contagion is automatic. We're generally unaware that we're grimacing as another expresses pain and smiling with those who smile, and we're certainly not forcing these expressions (which sometimes are measurable only as subtle muscle movements). Imagine yourself participating in an experiment reported by Tanya Chartrand and John Bargh, working alongside a confederate who occasionally either rubs her face or shakes her foot. Would you—like their participants—be more likely to rub your face when with a face-rubbing person and shake your foot when with a foot-shaking person? If so, you almost certainly would engage in this chameleon behavior without conscious intentions. But doing so would help you intuit what the other person is feeling, and it would help the other person sense your empathy. Unconscious mimicry smoothes social interaction.

Carl Rogers' client-centered therapy makes emotional mimicry—called active listening—into an intentional empathic art. What the client expresses, verbally and nonverbally, the counselor echoes and restates. So perhaps it shouldn't surprise us that on the Myers-Briggs Type Indicator, 70 percent of counselors, psychologists, and psychiatrists describe themselves as "intuiting" types, nearly triple the 25 percent in the general population.

Empathic accuracy. Some people seem especially skilled at reading others' thoughts, feelings, and intentions. They possess, it seems, some of the intuitive power of the Harry Potter stories' magic mirror: "I show not your face but your heart's desire." To study "empathic accuracy," William Ickes and his colleagues have videotaped many interactions between two people (sometimes strangers, sometimes friends or spouses or client and therapist). Then they have each conversation partner watch the tape, stopping at whatever points they had a specific thought or feeling (and recording what it was). Then the tape is replayed again and an observer (sometimes the other conversation partner) is asked to guess what the first person was thinking or feeling at each of those moments.

What predicts accuracy in mind reading? Our intuitions are most accurate when reading the mind of friends rather than strangers. After thirty-eight years of marriage, I know how to read that look in my wife's eye, that tone in her voice. Know someone well and you may recognize that the fixed smile while everyone else sings "Happy Birthday" is really covering embarrassment at being the center of attention. But some people are generally easier to read. And some people are better readers—they have greater empathic accuracy. With videotaped person after person they exhibit sensitivity and skill in discerning thoughts and feelings. Curiously, however, there is little correlation between how accurate people *think* they were in reading minds and how accurate they actually were. Yet people can learn. When given feedback, Ickes reports, their empathic accuracy improves. Given the importance of social intuition not only for therapists but also for negotiators, teachers, diplomats, personnel directors, police officers, judges, salespeople, parents, and lovers, that is encouraging news.

Detecting lies. Few of us, however, have learned accuracy in detecting deception. The bottom line from hundreds of experiments over the last quarter century is that most people just aren't very good at detecting lies. I've made this phenomenon into a class demonstration. Inspired by a clever experiment, I invite ten volunteers to talk about a specific life experience (a favorite vacation, a surprising talent, their earliest memory, and so forth). Before telling their story, each draws a slip out of a hat, five of which say "tell a lie" and five of which say "tell the truth." After each one tells a true story or spins a yarn, class members guess whether they've heard truth or a lie. The common result: near 50 percent (chance) accuracy in picking up lies.

But a few exceptional people have developed skill in detecting deceit. Psychologists Paul Ekman and Maureen O'Sullivan showed this after videotaping university students. As the students watched either a nature film or an upsetting gruesome film, they talked all the while as if they were enjoying the nature film. Telltale signs of lying, such as raised vocal pitch, enabled the researchers to detect 86 percent of the time whether a participant was lying or truth-telling. They also challenged 39 college students, 67 psychiatrists, 90 polygraphers, 110 court judges, and 126 police officers to spot the liars. All five groups' guesses were near chance. Only a sixth group of experienced crowd scanners—U.S. Secret Service agents—beat chance, with 64 percent correct.

In a follow-up study, the Ekman team found three more groups of skilled lie-catchers. When viewing videotapes of people stating their opinions on issues such as capital punishment—or the opposite of their opinions—federal law officers (mostly CIA agents) spotted the liars 73 percent of the time. Clinical psychologists interested in lying research guessed with 68 percent accuracy, and street-smart Los Angeles County sheriff's interrogators scored a similar 67 percent. With experience and training, it seems, people as well as computers can often catch the liar's microexpressions of guilt, despair, and fear.

Why are most of us such poor detectors of lies? Ekman believes it's because we receive so little corrective feedback about who's conning us and who's telling the truth, and also because we rely too much on what people say and not enough on the momentary expressions that are the facial counterpart of Pinocchio's nose. People who are unusually skilled in identifying "micromomentary" facial expressions are also more accurate in judging lying. And, remarkably, people with brain damage that renders them less attentive to speech are *more* accurate at attending to face, body, and voice clues, and thus at spotting deception. In one recent study, aphasic stroke victims were able to spot liars 73 percent of the time when focusing on facial expressions; nonaphasic people did no better than chance. As the intuitives have told us, it seems that most of us have unrealized potential for improving our social intuitions.

WOMEN'S AND MEN'S INTUITION

On May 15, 1995, a news story broke that allowed me to experience first-hand how easily we mistake lies for truth. Not many months before, I had had a fascinating conversation with John Bennett, creator of the Foundation for New Era Philanthropy. We both served on the advisory board of another foundation, and during the coffee break he explained that his foundation was funded by seven mega-wealthy individuals—"people like John Templeton and Laurance Rockefeller," he said gesturing toward these two men across the room, "but not them." Wanting to encourage others' philanthropy, these donors were anonymously matching donations from other individuals, some of them solicited by nearly 400 organizations, ranging from the University of Pennsylvania and the Philadelphia Orchestra to Christian charities such as World Vision and Fuller Theological Seminary. Institutions could park their newly raised money with New Era for six months and receive double back; the interest funded New Era's operating costs. After the six-month escrow, individuals (among them former Treasury Secretary William Simon and singer Pat Boone) could likewise have their contributions to selected charities doubled.

Learning this first hand, I felt moral elevation. I went home to tell my wife and friends this amazing story, a story that turned out to be even more amazing when I learned that I was in the ranks of those who had fallen for John Bennett's lie. There were no anonymous donors. Thanks to the suspicions and diligence of a college accountant, the house of cards on this biggest-ever Ponzi scheme collapsed after taking in nearly $356 million. One wonders what would lead a man to concoct a scheme that was bound to fail, leaving himself and his family in the rubble. (Most of the money was returned after the pyramid's winners and losers agreed to cooperate, and Bennett went to prison.)

One also wonders how so many folks got led astray by trusting their intuition. I jested afterward that, had he invited me to participate, I would have become skeptical. But in my heart I knew that he could have flimflammed me, too. Was it a coincidence that Jackie Larsen, who saw through Christopher Bono in this chapter's opening story, was a woman, and that most of those suckered by John Bennett were men (or was it just that men tended to control the money he was after)? Is women's intuition, as so many believe, indeed superior to men's? In my experience, no question about intuition is asked more often.

Gender and empathy. When surveyed, women are far more likely to describe themselves as empathic, as being able to rejoice with those who rejoice and weep with those who weep. To a lesser extent, the gender gap in empathy extends to observed behavior. Women are somewhat more likely to cry or report feeling distressed at another's distress. The empathy difference helps explain why both men and women report their friendships with women to be more intimate, enjoyable, and nurturing than are their friendships with men. When seeking empathy and understanding, both men and women usually turn to women.

Gender and decoding emotions. One explanation for the gender empathy gap is women's skill at reading others' emotions. In her analysis of 125 studies of sensitivity to nonverbal cues, Judith Hall discerned that women generally surpass men at decoding emotional messages. Shown a two-second silent film clip of the face of an upset woman, women guess more accurately whether she is criticizing someone or discussing her divorce. Although boys average 45 points higher on the rational 200- to 800-point SAT math test, girls surpass boys in reading facial expressions. In other experiments, women's nonverbal sensitivity has given them an edge in spotting lies. Women also have surpassed men in discerning whether a male-female couple is a genuine romantic couple or a posed phony couple, and in discerning which of two people in a photo was the other's supervisor.

Women's sensitivity helps explain their somewhat greater emotional responsiveness in both depressing and joyful situations. It may also play a role in women's skill at *expressing* emotions nonverbally. This is especially so for positive emotion, report Erick Coats and Robert Feldman. When observers viewed five-second silent video clips of men and women recalling times they had been happy, sad, and angry, women's happiness was more easily discerned.

Gender and "ways of knowing." The gender intuition gap is easily overstated. Some men are more empathic and sensitive to nonverbal messages than is the average woman. But the gap appears to be real, and it has become celebrated by some feminists as one of "women's ways of knowing." Women, it is said, more often than men base knowledge on intuitive and personal grounds. Witness the ten winners and fourteen runners-up on the *Skeptical Inquirer* list of outstanding twentieth-century rationalist skeptics—all men. In the "science and the paranormal" section of the spring-summer 2001 catalogue for Prometheus Books, the leading publisher of skepticism, I counted 110 male and 4 female authors.

For the sake of comparison, my assistant and I checked the gender of authors of intuition titles, including those mentioned in this book's Introduction (52 percent were female). Then we checked the authors of two sections containing 253 New Age books at our local Barnes and Noble superstore; 37 percent are female. Skepticism, it seems, is culturally masculine, intuition and spirituality more feminine. "Activating intuition always starts with a shift into softness and silence," explains Penney Peirce in *Intuition Magazine*. She encourages her readers to "tune down" the "'masculine mind,' the kind of awareness both men and women must use to achieve concrete results. We're in our linear, left-brained masculine mind so often, we've come to identify it as normal. We forget there is an equally powerful, complementary state of consciousness that is quiet, unhurried, and tension-free: the 'feminine mind.' The feminine mind is not goal-oriented; it simply observes, includes, appreciates, and is present with whatever it notices.'"

Whoa! say other scholars, including some feminists. Is this gender gap really intrinsic to gender, or is it the social sensitivity of subordinates? People low in social power (female or male) learn to attune to the boss's nuanced expressions. When they become bosses, those same people may tune out their subordinates' subtle mood shifts. A similar phenomenon surfaces with speaking styles: Men are more likely to act as powerful people often do—talking assertively, intrusively interrupting, touching with the hand, staring more, smiling less. Stating the results from a female perspective, women's influence style tends to be more indirect—less interruptive, more sensitive, more polite, less cocky. So, should women stop feigning smiles, averting their eyes, tolerating interruptions, and tuning in to subtle messages, and instead look people in the eye, speak assertively, and take them at their word? Judith Hall thinks not. She values women's less autocratic communication style, noting that "whenever it is assumed that women's nonverbal behavior is undesirable, yet another myth is perpetuated: that male behavior is normal and that it is women's behavior that is deviant and in need of explanation."

Evolutionary psychologists add that the genetic and cultural origins of gender—nature and nurture—"co-evolve." Evolutionary pressures may have selected women with skills at decoding children's and potential mates' nonverbal expressions (while the testosterone-loaded men were out hunting and providing). Over generations, surmise Tiffany Graham and William Ickes, "this small-but-reliable gender difference became increasingly noticeable" and got incorporated into folk wisdom about how women and men differ. At the end of this gene-culture co-evolution, "women were not just seen as *more likely to be* better nonverbal decoders than men: they were *expected to be, assumed to be,* and—by implication—*supposed to be* better nonverbal decoders than men."

For whatever reason, western tradition has a history of viewing rational thinking as masculine and intuition as feminine, notes feminist historian Evelyn Fox Keller. "Women's ways of knowing," argue Mary Belenky and her colleagues, give greater latitude to personal knowledge, to subjective knowledge, to intuition's inner voice. Women, she contends, winnow competing ideas less through hostile scrutiny than by getting inside another's mind, often in friendly conversation, so that they can know and experience that way of thinking. Belinky and her cohorts may overstate the gender difference, but their argument finds some support from the gender gap in nonverbal sensitivity and self-reported empathy. Moreover, Rosemary Pacini and Seymour Epstein found a gender difference on their scales assessing rationality (for example, "I enjoy intellectual challenges") and experientiality ("I like to rely on my intuitive impressions"). "The men," they report, "were more likely than the women to identify themselves as rationally capable, and the women were more likely than the men to identify themselves as engaging in experiential processing and as being good at it." Likewise, on the popular Myers-Briggs (no relation) test, nearly six in ten men score as "thinkers" (claiming to make decisions objectively using logic) and three in four women score as "feelers" (claiming to make decisions subjectively based on what they feel is right).

As I was finishing this book, my friend Mary Pipher solicited my thoughts on her new book manuscript, *The Middle of Everywhere: The World's Refugees Come To Our Town*. My way of understanding the experience of refugees in America would likely have been to assemble research, digest surveys, and study migration, employment, and health data. Mary's was to engage and befriend refugee families from eastern Europe, Africa, the Americas, and Asia and to give voice to their emotions and experiences. By becoming a classroom assistant and counselor to such people and by sharing meals, camping holidays, and visits to immigration service centers, she gained empathy and understanding, and she allows us to do so as well. Belenky would not be surprised that a majority of Mary Pipher's audience are women. Without explaining or exaggerating the gender difference—women can be adversarial skeptics and men can be sensitive and intuitive—the two ways of knowing perhaps have something to offer each other. Perhaps rationalist skeptics should open themselves to other ways of knowing, and perhaps intuitives should sharpen their critical thinking.

I wondered whether the seeming gender difference in openness to nonrational ways of knowing carries over to participation in faith communities. Analyzing data (I can't help it) from more than 40,000 people responding to National Opinion Research Center surveys since 1972, I found that 23 percent of men and 33 percent of women reported attending religious services at least weekly. I also wonder: Is the apparent gender difference in skepticism and spirituality some-how related to women's greater self-reported empathy and connect-edness to others? Women spend more time caring for both preschool-ers and aging parents. Compared with men, they buy three times as many gifts and greeting cards, write two to four times as many per-sonal letters, and make 10 to 20 percent more long distance calls to friends and family. Asked to provide photos that portray who they are, women include more photos of parents and of themselves with others. Women and men are more alike than different. But it's the small differences that capture our fascination, one of which is wom-en's seeming more empathic, more sensitive to nonverbal cues, and more relational.

Intuitive Expertise and Creativity

Suddenly, unexpectedly, I had this incredible revelation.
—Andrew Wiles, on discerning the proof of Fermat's last theorem

As the mushrooming mountain of evidence plainly indicates, we have two minds—two ways of knowing, two kinds of memory, two levels of attitudes. One is above the surface, in our moment-to-moment awareness; the other is below, operating the autopilot that guides us through most of life. We see the work of those downstairs cognitive laborers in the social intuitions they slip into our awareness, and also in our developing expertise and creative inspirations. Through experience we gain practical intuition—subtle, complex, ineffable knowledge that aids our problem solving.

INTUITIVE EXPERTISE

From your two eyes your brain receives slightly differing images of an object. In a microsecond, the brain analyzes these differences and infers the object's distance. Even with a calculator at hand, your conscious mind would be hard pressed to make the same computation. No matter, your intuitive mind already knows. Indeed, we know much that is too complex for our conscious minds to understand.

Nonconscious learning. What you know, but don't know you know, affects you more than you know. That's the bottom line of more than

300 experiments on our powers of unconscious learning (or "non-conscious learning, as cognitive scientists often prefer to call it, lest their concept be confused with Freud's idea of a seething unconscious mind). Some of these experiments have been financed by more than $1 million of National Science Foundation grants to Pawel Lewicki and his colleagues at the University of Tulsa's Nonconscious Information Processing Laboratory. The multitasking nonconscious mind is not just tending to housekeeping details, Lewicki's experiments reveal. It is quick, agile, perceptive, and surprisingly capable of "detecting complex patterns of information."

An example: You know which of these two phrases sounds better—"a big red barn" or "a red big barn"—but your conscious mind struggles to articulate the rule that you intuitively know. Likewise, say Lewicki, Thomas Hill, and Maria Czyzewska, the "seemingly simple act" of recognizing an object's shape and size and placing it "in three-dimensional space requires a set of sophisticated geometrical transformations and calculations that go far beyond what most perceivers could articulate or even comprehend." Don't bother to ask chess masters to explain their next move, or poets where the image came from, or lovers why they're in love. "All they know is that they just do it."

The Tulsa experiments reveal that people's nonconscious learning can anticipate patterns "too complex and too confusing to be consciously noticed." In one study, some students watched (others didn't) as the numeral "6" jumped around a computer screen, from quadrant to quadrant. Although it seemed like a random order—no one consciously detected any rule—those who had seen the earlier presentations were quicker to find the next 6 when it was hidden among a screen full of numbers. Without knowing how it happened, they saw their ability to track the number improve. When the numbers' movement became truly random, performance declined.

Lewicki repeated the experiment with his quick-witted psychology professor colleagues, who knew that he was studying nonconscious learning. They too gained speed in locating the target's next position, and they too didn't know why. When the experimenters switched to a random sequence and performance declined, the professors conjectured reasons for the decline (threatening subliminal messages, perhaps?). To students who had displayed unconscious learning, Lewicki even offered $100 if they could uncover the pattern. Some spent hours trying to decipher the sequence. None succeeded.

Nonconscious learning, though surprisingly sophisticated, can be stubbornly rigid. In another experiment, Lewicki showed students computer-altered faces—some lengthened, some normal, some shortened—and told the students that some of these people were professors who were fair graders, while others were unfair graders. After viewing some "unfair" professors with lengthened faces and "fair" professors with shortened faces, the students estimated the fairness

of twenty new faces. Although unaware of their nonconscious learning—the students said they were "just guessing"—they continued to infer fairness from facial proportions, guessing that the long-faced professors were unfair and the short-faced ones were fair. In real life, too, initial impressions, formed on limited evidence, can persevere in the absence of supportive evidence. Once born, stereotypes live on.

In one of his early experiments, with University of Warsaw students, Lewicki showed how quickly we form nonconscious associations that influence our behavior. When some students simply rated which of two pictured women (labeled A or B) looked friendlier, half picked each woman. Other students, having interacted with a warm, friendly experimenter who resembled woman A, chose woman A by a 6-to-1 margin. In a follow-up study, the experimenter acted *unfriendly* toward half the subjects. When these subjects later had to turn in their data to one of two women, they *avoided* the one who resembled the experimenter. (Perhaps you can recall a time when you intuitively reacted, positively or negatively, to someone who reminded you of someone else.)

Learned expertise. In 1998, world checkers champion Ron "Suki" King of Barbados set a record by simultaneously playing 385 players in 3 hours and 44 minutes. While his opponents often could leisurely plot their moves, King could devote only about 35 seconds to each game—barely more than a glance at the board for each move. Yet he still managed to win all 385 games. How did he do it? And how are car mechanics, physicians, and swimming coaches (all of whom have been subjects of study) often able to instantly diagnose problems?

Compared to novices, experts know much more. In a classic study, William Chase and Herbert Simon found that chess experts, unlike the rest of us, could often reproduce a chess board layout after a mere five-second glance. Unlike a poor chess player who has few patterns stored in memory, a good player has 1,000, and a chess master has roughly 50,000. A chess master may also perceive the board in several chunks—clusters of positions that they have seen before. A quick look at the board is therefore all it takes to recognize many layouts—unless the pieces are placed randomly, in which case the experts' memory becomes slightly *worse* than novices'. Chess masters can therefore play by intuition at five to ten seconds a move, without time for analysis of alternatives, without much performance decline. In *Mind Over Machine,* a book about the power of human intuition, philosopher Hubert Dreyfus and engineering professor Stuart Dreyfus report challenging one international chess master, Julio Kaplan, to add numbers while playing five-second-a-move chess against a slightly weaker but master-level player. "Even with his analytic mind completely jammed by adding numbers, Kaplan more than held his own against the master in a series of games." Just as you can recognize thousands of faces, so Kaplan could recognize and respond to thousands of chess positions.

Physicians and mechanics likewise can often make spot diagnoses, as if thinking, "This reminds me of symptoms I've seen before, when the problem was X." The diagnosis isn't dictated by logic—other ailments could produce the same symptoms. But it's quick and usually right.

Even quicker and more astoundingly accurate are professional chicken sexers. Poultry owners once had to wait five to six weeks before the appearance of adult feathers enabled them to separate cockerels (males) from pullets (hens). Egg producers wanted to buy and feed only pullets, so they were intrigued to hear that some Japanese had developed an uncanny ability to sex day-old chicks. Although even poultry farmers can't tell male from female organs in a newly hatched chick, the Japanese experts could do it at a glance. Hatcheries elsewhere then gave some of their workers apprenticeships under the Japanese experts, with feedback on their accuracy. After months of training and experience, the best Americans and Australians could almost match the Japanese, by sexing 800 to 1,000 chicks per hour with 99 percent accuracy. But don't ask them how they do it. The sex difference, as any chicken sexer can tell you, is too subtle to explain.

Individuals with savant syndrome vividly demonstrate what University of Alberta psychologist Carolyn Yewchuk calls "intuitive excellence amidst general deficit." Despite their subnormal intelligence scores, savants may be able to tell you the day of the week on which any date has occurred or will occur, compute square roots quicker than mechanical calculators, or draw scenes from memory with minute detail—all without awareness or the ability to explain how they do it. One teen-age calendar calculator simply explained, "Use me brain." They know without knowing how.

When experienced gourmet cooks say they "just use experience and intuition" in mixing ingredients, they are stating "the theory of expert performance that has emerged in recent years," noted Simon. "In everyday speech, we use the word *intuition* to describe a problem-solving or question-answering performance that is speedy and for which the expert is unable to describe in detail the reasoning or other process that produced the answer. The situation has provided a cue; this cue has given the expert access to information stored in memory, and the information provides the answer. Intuition is nothing more and nothing less than recognition." Although we don't know what they're sensing, chicken sexers are intuitively recognizing subtle indicators of sex.

Experts' knowledge is also more organized than novices', in ways that enable them to access it efficiently. Novices see information in isolated pieces; experts see large, meaningful patterns. Medical students may know the typical features of different diseases, but experts see connections among diseases with similar symptoms. Each of us is an expert in something, with organized knowledge that enables us to creatively integrate information.

Armed with organized knowledge, experts take time to define a problem precisely. Then they often work both backward from the goal to the current state of affairs, and forward from the current state. Yet their expertise is selective. Cardiologists beat surgeons and psychiatrists at diagnosing cardiac problems. But none of them are very good at selecting candidates for internships and residents. Personnel selection is beyond their domain of expertise.

Where we have expertise, however, we may have genius. Until 1997, Garry Kasparov could beat IBM's Deep Blue computer, which was programmed with thousands of classic chess games (giving it access to the best moves played over the last century) and able to calculate 200 million moves per second. It was, one person noted, like playing Scrabble against an opponent having access to the *Oxford English Dictionary*. With intuitive calculation and creativity, Kasparov affirmed the mind's magnificence.

Tacit knowledge. Academic intelligence and motivation help explain why some people succeed in life and work. But streets smarts— "practical intelligence"—also matters, notes Yale psychologist Robert Sternberg. Much intuitive expertise and practical know-how is acquired as "tacit knowledge." Managerial success, for example, depends less on the academic smarts assessed by an intelligence test score (assuming the score is average or above) than on a shrewd ability to manage one's tasks, other people, and oneself. Much of this knowledge is unarticulated and not directly taught. It is tacit rather than explicit. "We know more than we can tell," noted the physical chemist-turned-philosopher Michael Polanyi.

Tacit knowledge is implicit knowledge, learned by experience but without intention. Tacit knowledge, says the *Dictionary of Philosophy of Mind*, is "not ordinarily accessible to consciousness"—it is intuitive. Tacit knowledge is procedural. Unlike explicit knowledge—"knows *that*"—tacit knowledge "knows *how*." From their studies of managers, sales people, teachers, and military officers, Sternberg and his associates, Richard Wagner and Joseph Horvath, have gleaned some of the unverbalized knowledge that makes for success. They have, for example, developed a test of practical managerial intelligence that assesses one's tacit knowledge about how to write effective memos, how to motivate people, when to delegate, how to read people, and how to promote one's own career. Executives who score high on this test tend to earn higher salaries and receive better performance ratings than do their lower-scoring colleagues.

Hubert and Stuart Dreyfus note how the accumulation of experienced-based tacit knowledge has served Japanese companies, which they regard as

> often better managed than American ones. Japanese workers employed by large corporations typically stay with one company throughout their career, rise through the ranks, and, should they reach the top levels of management, are thoroughly familiar with all aspects of the company they manage. American managers, on the other hand, frequently change jobs in order to hasten their climb up the corporate ladder. What does the typical American manager bring with him when he changes companies? Not, unfortunately, much of the know-how he presumably acquired on the bases of concrete experience in his previous job. No two companies are exactly alike in personnel, problems, or philosophy.

Physical genius. A little exercise: Say the words *bad* and *dad*. Can you notice the difference in how your mouth forms the beginning of each? Easy, yes? But what about the difference between *bad* and *pad*? Could you instruct someone how to do it? Before I asked, were you even aware? Are you aware now?

The difference between the *b* and *p* sounds is partly one of subtle timing (controlled by the cerebellum, which looks rather like a small cauliflower hanging off the back of your brain). To make the *b* sound you open your lips as you vibrate your vocal cords. To make the *p* sound your lips burst open for about a thirtieth of a second before you vibrate your vocal cords. The difference is minuscule. But intuitively —effortlessly, instantly, thoughtlessly—you do it (unless cerebellar stroke damage has messed up your timing, in which case when you mean to say *pot* you may say *bot,* but never *dot*).

Or consider the intricate ease of our natural smiles. Our bodies intuitively know how to smile (replete with raised cheeks). Yet when asked to smile for a camera we may force a plastic, stretched-mouth smile—not the warm, genuine smile with which we greet a friend. How ironic that an effortless act we perform many times daily becomes, as every portrait photographer knows well, difficult to produce voluntarily.

These are modest examples of intuitive physical genius. Athletes, as we will see in Chapter 7, exhibit a remarkable intuitive understanding of physics and mathematics. As Michael Jordan would shoot a basketball, he unconsciously and instantly made complex calculations about force, motion, gravitational effects, parabolic curves, and aerodynamic drag. He knew how to read the complex motions of nine other players and to intuit where to go and when, and to whom to deliver the ball.

As skilled violinists sight-read a piece, their body and fingers intuitively know how to process and respond to incoming visual, aural, and manual information. My accomplished violinist colleagues Mihai and Deborah Craioveanu explain that, with years of practice, one can visualize a particular pitch and, by "acquired intuition," know just where to place the fingers on the string, when to move them, how much pressure to apply, at what angle and pressure to apply the bow, and how to move the body to maintain balance and release energy. All this happens simultaneously, without time for discrete conscious decisions about each element, and with virtually perfect accuracy (99 percent isn't good enough). The violinist's intuition is hard-earned. It is natural, graceful automatic processing wrought from thousands of hours of practice.

CREATIVITY

Pierre de Fermat, a seventeenth-century mischievous genius, challenged mathematicians of his day to match his solutions to various number theory problems. He jotted his most famous challenge—his so-called last theorem, after mathematicians solved all his others—in a book alongside Pythagoras' formula: $a^2 + b^2 = c^2$. The equation has infinite integer solutions, such as $a = 3$, $b = 4$, $c = 5$, but no solutions, said Fermat, for a family of similar equations, $a^n + b^n = c^n$, where n represents any whole number greater than 2. "I have a truly marvelous demonstration of this proposition, which this margin is too narrow to contain."

For more than three centuries the puzzle baffled the greatest mathematical minds, even after a $2 million prize (in today's dollars) was offered in 1908. Like countless others, Princeton mathematician Andrew Wiles had pondered the problem for more than thirty years, and he had come to the brink of a solution. Then, one morning, out of the blue, the "incredible revelation"—the fix to the one remaining difficulty—struck him. "It was so indescribably beautiful; it was so simple and so elegant. I couldn't understand how I'd missed it and I just stared at it in disbelief for twenty minutes. Then during the day I walked around the department, and I'd keep coming back to my desk looking to see if it was still there. It was still there. I couldn't contain myself, I was so excited. It was the most important moment of my working life."

Wiles' creative moment illustrates what Robert Sternberg and Todd Lubart have discerned as the five components of creativity—the production of novel and valuable ideas.

The first component is *expertise*. "Chance favors only the prepared mind," observed Louis Pasteur. The more ideas and images each of us has gained through accumulated learning, the more chances we have to combine the building blocks in creative ways. Wiles' well-developed base of knowledge put other mathematical theorems and methods at his disposal.

The second component is *imaginative thinking skills*. In moments of creativity we see things in new ways, recognize patterns, make connections. Having mastered the basic elements of a problem, we redefine or explore it in a new way. Copernicus first developed expertise regarding the solar system and its planets, and then he defined the system as revolving around the sun, not the earth. Wiles' imaginative finale combined two important but incomplete solutions.

The third component is a *venturesome personality*. The idea is summed up in Sternberg and Lubart's title for their creativity book, *Defying the Crowd*. The creative person tolerates ambiguity and risk, perseveres in overcoming obstacles, and seeks new experiences. Inventors often persist after failures—Thomas Edison tried countless substances in quest of his lightbulb filament. Wiles says he labored on the Fermat problem in isolation from the mathematics community partly to stay focused and avoid distraction.

The fourth component is *intrinsic motivation*. Creativity researchers Teresa Amabile and Beth Hennessey explain: "People will be most creative when they feel motivated primarily by the interest, enjoyment, satisfaction, and challenge of the work itself—rather than by external pressures." In Amabile's experiments, students produced the most creative artwork when *not* told beforehand that experts would evaluate their creations. In the real world, creative people focus less on extrinsic motivators—meeting deadlines, impressing people, making money—and more on their work's intrinsic pleasure and challenge. "I was so obsessed by this problem," Wiles recalled later, "that for eight years I was thinking about it all of the time—when I woke up in the morning to when I went to sleep at night."

The fifth component is a *creative environment*. Novel and valuable ideas are often sparked, supported, and refined by relationships. After studying the careers of 2,026 prominent scientists and inventors, psychologist Dean Keith Simonton noted that the most eminent were seldom lone geniuses. They were mentored, challenged, and bolstered by others. Many had the emotional intelligence needed to network effectively with peers. Even Wiles, a relative loner, stood on the shoulders of others while supported by the collaboration of his former student, Richard Taylor.

Creativity's intuitive dimension stems from unconscious processing. Wiles' downstairs cognitive workers chewed long hours on his problem. "You have to really think about nothing but that problem—just concentrate on it. Then you stop. Afterwards there seems to be a kind of period of relaxation during which the subconscious appears to take over, and it's during that time that some new insight comes." The same was true of Isaac Newton, noted John Maynard Keynes. "His peculiar gift was the power of holding continuously in his mind a purely mental problem until he had seen straight through it. I fancy his preeminence is due to his muscles of intuition being the strongest and most enduring with which a man has ever been gifted."

Wiles' insights popping into his mind in times of relaxation illustrates the effortlessness of many moments of insight. Archimedes stepped into the bath and exclaimed "Eureka!" as he realized that a crown of pure gold would displace less water than would silver. Kekule's dream of intertwined snakes led him to see the benzene ring. In explaining how he arrived at concepts such as his theory of relativity, Einstein reported that "words and language . . . do not seem to play any part in my thought process." In one survey, seventy-two of eighty-three Nobel laureates in science and medicine implicated intuition in their success. "We felt at times there was almost a hand guiding us," said Michael Brown, winner of the 1985 prize for medicine. "We would go from one step to the next, and somehow we would know which was the right way to go, and I really can't tell how we knew that."

Bach likewise spoke of musical ideas appearing effortlessly: "The problem is not finding them, it's—when getting up in the morning and getting out of bed—not stepping on them."

Wordsworth wrote in *Lines Composed a Few Miles Above Tintern Abbey:* "While with an eye made quiet by the power / Of harmony, and the deep power of joy / We see into the life of things."

"Painting is stronger than I am," said Picasso. "It makes me do what it wants." At the start of any work, he explained, "there is someone who works with me."

Larry Gelbart, who wrote ninety-seven episodes of $M^*A^*S^*H$, similarly explains his creative process: "It's like your brain is somebody else, just using your body as an office."

Do insights really arrive in the unconscious mind before they surface in conscious awareness? We have all experienced our mind's unconscious workings when we have set a mental alarm at bedtime, and then—thanks to our mental clock—awakened five minutes before our bedside alarm was to rouse us for that early flight. Or when, unable to call up a person's name or the PIN for our bank account, we move on to other things, until, unbidden, like a website's pop-up ad, the missing information erupts into consciousness. It feels as if unconscious activity blossoms forth with conscious answers.

Poets, novelists, composers, and artists readily recognize intuition's role in creativity. "You get your intuition back when you make space for it, when you stop the chattering of the rational mind," counsels writer Anne Lamott.

> So try to calm down, get quiet, breathe, and listen. Squint at the screen in your head, and if you look, you will see what you are searching for, the details of the story, its direction—maybe not right this minute, but eventually. If you stop trying to control your mind so much, you'll have intuitive hunches about what this or that character is all about. It is hard to stop controlling, but you can do it. If your character suddenly pulls a half-eaten carrot out of her pocket, let her. Later you can ask yourself if this rings true. Train yourself to hear that small inner voice."

In an experiment with German second-graders, Robert Siegler cleverly demonstrated that insights can indeed arrive first in the unconscious. Give children a simple math problem ($18 + 24 - 24$) and they can tell you how they solved it. "Inversion problems" of this sort ($A + B - B$) nearly always take young children more than eight seconds to solve by computation but less than four seconds by insight (seeing that the answer is simply A). Given a series of such problems, children move from computation (taking eight or more seconds) to unconscious shortcut (taking less than four seconds but not being able to verbalize the shortcut) to, about five problems later, being able to state the shortcut. Between the transition from conscious computation to conscious shortcut are typically about four trials of unconscious insight—solving the problem with a speed that demands the shortcut while consciously thinking they had used addition and subtraction. "It is by logic that we prove," said mathematician Henri Poincaré. "It is by intuition that we discover."

The Perils of Intuition

Intuitions About Our Past and Future

You don't know your own mind.
—*Jonathan Swift,* Polite Conversation, *1738*

Thanks to the three pounds of wet neural tissue folded and jammed into our skulls, we are the world's greatest wonder. With circuitry more complex than the planet's telephone networks, we process boundless information, consciously and unconsciously. Right now your visual system is disassembling the light striking your retina into millions of nerve impulses, distributing these for parallel processing, and then reassembling a clear and colorful image. From ink on the page to a perceived image to meaning, all in an instant. Our species, give us credit, has had the inventive genius to design cell phones and harvest stem cells; to unlock the atom and crack and map our genetic code; to travel to the moon and tour the sunken *Titanic*. Not bad, considering that we share 90 percent of our DNA with a cow. Just by living, we acquire intuitive expertise that makes most of life effortless. Understandably, Shakespeare's Hamlet extolled us as "noble in reason! . . . infinite in faculties! . . . in apprehension how like a god!" We are rightly called *Homo sapiens*—wise humans.

But as Pascal taught 300 years ago, no single truth is ever sufficient, because the world is complex. Any truth, separated from its complementary truth, is a half-truth. It's true that our intuitive information-processing powers are impressive for their efficiency, yet it is also true that they are prone to predictable errors and misjudgments. With remarkable ease, we form and sustain false beliefs. Perhaps T. S. Eliot was right to call us the "hollow men . . . headpiece filled with straw." We wise humans are sometimes fools.

If our capacity for misleading intuition (explored here and in the next two chapters) proves shocking, remember that our thinking is generally adaptive. "Cognitive errors . . . exist in the present because they led to survival and reproductive advantages for humans in the past," note evolutionary psychologists Martie Haselton and David Buss. Illusory intuitions typically are by-products of our mind's efficient shortcuts. They parallel our perceptual intuitions, which generally work but sometimes run amok. And as perception researchers study visual illusions for what they reveal about our normal perceptual mechanisms, so other psychologists study other illusory intuitions for what they reveal about normal information processing. These researchers aim to chart a map of everyday social thinking, with the hazards clearly marked. In their own way they are like novelists, who also portray both the sublime and the ridiculous. Science, literature, and liberal education aim to cultivate our appreciation of human nature but also to illuminate our limitations. The mental chart makers work in hopes of helping us think smarter, even as we recall our past, explain our present, and predict our future.

CONSTRUCTING MEMORIES

For the things you are designed to remember—voices, sounds, and songs; tastes, smells, and textures; faces, places, and happenings—your memory capacity is staggering. Imagine viewing more than 2,500 slides of faces and places for only 10 seconds each. Later you see 280 of these slides one at a time, paired with a previously unseen slide. If you are like the subjects in this experiment by Ralph Haber, you would recognize 90 percent of those you saw before. Little wonder that 85 percent of college students in one survey agreed that "memory can be likened to a storage chest in the brain into which we deposit material and from which we can withdraw it later if needed." As a 1988 ad in *Psychology Today* put it, "Science has proven the accumulated experience of a lifetime is preserved perfectly in your mind."

Actually, and with due credit to our memory feats, science has essentially proven the opposite. Remember a time when you lay basking in the sun on a beach. Tell yourself what you "see." If you see yourself, perhaps lying there on a blanket, you are not remembering a scene that you observed through your eyes. As this illustrates, memories are not copies of experiences that remain on deposit in a memory bank. Rather, like scientists reconstructing dinosaurs from bone remnants, we construct memories as we withdraw them from storage.

Revising our life histories. As a fourteen-year-old, how concerned were you about preserving the natural environment? How often would you have said your parents had spanked you as a child? What attitudes would you have reported toward gays and lesbians? If you are now considerably older than fourteen, you might be shocked at your misrecall of the person you used to be. Several research teams have asked questions of students, and then many years later asked them to recall how they answered the questions. One team, led by Northwestern University psychiatrist Daniel Offer, interviewed 73 suburban Chicago ninth-grade boys in 1962, and then in the late 1990s traveled to 24 states to reinterview 67 of the survivors. When asked how they had reported their father's discipline, how much they reported enjoying intellectual activities, and how they felt about high school students having sex, the men's recollections were astonishingly inaccurate. Nearly half believed they had said it was acceptable to start having sex during high school, though only 15 percent had given that answer. Only one in three now recalled receiving physical punishment, though as ninth-graders 82 percent said they had.

In several experiments, social psychologists have likewise found that people whose attitudes have changed insist that they've always felt as they do now. In one University of Michigan study, a national sample of high school seniors reported their attitudes toward minorities, the legalization of marijuana, and equality for women. Nearly a decade later their attitudes had changed, but they now recalled earlier attitudes akin to their current sentiments. As George Valliant noted after following adult development through time, "It is all too common for caterpillars to become butterflies and then to maintain that in their youth they had been little butterflies. Maturation makes liars of us all."

Are you in a love relationship right now? Looking back, were you able early on in the relationship to see clues to how it would now be going? Social psychologists Cathy McFarland and Michael Ross had university students rate their steady dating partners. Two months later, they rated them again. Looking back, those now more in love than ever recalled love at first sight. Those who'd broken up were more likely to misrecall having recognized their partner's selfishness and bad temper early on. Ditto when Diane Holmberg and John Holmes surveyed newlyweds, then two years later resurveyed them. Those whose marriages had soured misrecalled things as always having been bad. The eerie result can be a downward spiral, note Holmberg and Holmes. "The worse your current view of your partner is, the worse your memories are, which only further confirms your negative attitudes."

Intuitions about our more recent past can also err. Are women more depressed, tense, and irritable during the two or three days before menstruating? Many think so—enough to have persuaded the American Psychiatric Association to include severe PMS (renamed premenstrual dysphoric disorder) in its manual of disorders, despite objections from its own Committee on Women. Ask women to recall their fluctuating emotions and many will report stereotypic PMS, which, according to *Parade* magazine's medical columnist, "plagues most women of childbearing age." (He attributes this plague of womanhood to "female hormones" that "reduce the level of serotonin, an important mood-altering chemical.") But what do they say if asked how they feel right now, and if asked again tomorrow and the next day? Several studies have engaged Canadian, American, and Australian women in keeping daily mood diaries. Although many women *recalled* feeling out of sorts just before their last period, their own day-to-day self-reports typically revealed little fluctuation across the menstrual cycle (at least much less than the "raging hormones" view would lead one to expect). Moreover, women who said they suffered PMS didn't differ in mood fluctuations from those who didn't. (Our theories guide our interpretations. Given the popular PMS theory, a crabby mood early in the cycle may be discounted, a late-cycle bad mood attributed to PMS.)

Believe it or not, even our memories of how much pain we've

experienced may be demonstrably distorted. Daniel Kahneman and his co-researchers discovered this when they asked people to immerse one hand in painfully cold water for sixty seconds, and the other hand in the same painfully cold water for sixty seconds followed by an additional, but slightly less painful, thirty seconds. Curiously, when asked which trial they would prefer to repeat, 69 percent preferred more pain to less—they preferred the longer trial, with more net pain, but less pain at the end. Our stored snapshots for pain, it seems, record its peak moment and its end moment, but overlook its duration. They are snapshots without a stopwatch. When medical patients recalled colon exam pain a month later, their memories were similarly dominated by the final (and the worst) moments, not by the duration. The medical implication of this pain misrecall is clear: Better to taper down a painful procedure than switch it off. When this has been done in colon exams, people given the taper-down treatment later recall the lengthened discomfort as *less* painful.

Emotional memories for positive events often become more positive over time. Months after Bill Clinton's first election, Democrats remembered experiencing greater joy than they actually did at the time. Students who have done well on an exam later remembered feeling even happier than they actually were. In other studies, college students on a three-week bike trip, older adults on a guided tour of Austria, and undergraduates on vacation have all reported enjoying their experiences as they had them. But they later *recalled* these experiences even more fondly, by minimizing the unpleasant or boring aspects and remembering the high points. Thus, the pleasant times during which I have sojourned in Scotland I now idealize as bliss. The midges and drizzle have faded, the beauty and serenity live on. With most positive experiences, some of the pleasure resides in the anticipation, some in the actual experience, and some in the "rosy retrospection." Travel writer Paul Theroux agrees: "Travel is glamorous only in retrospect."

Dubious testimonials. The unreliability of recall makes patients' memories a questionable way to evaluate how much they've changed with therapy. People readily construct memories that support their current views. If their present view is that they've improved, they will likely misrecall their past as more *un*like the present than it actually was. "The speed, magnitude, and certainty" with which people revise their own histories is "striking" reported Clark University attitude researchers D. R. Wixon and James Laird.

Memory construction helps resolve a puzzling pair of findings. Those who participate in psychotherapy and self-improvement programs for weight control, smoking cessation, and exercise show only modest improvement on average. Yet they often claim considerable benefit. Michael Conway and Michael Ross explain why: Having expended so much time, effort, and money on self-improvement, people may think, "I may not be perfect now, but I was worse before; this did me a lot of good."

Moreover, by diminishing our old selves we can believe "I'm a better person than I used to be." Most of us believe ourselves to be more competent, socially skilled, tolerant, and interesting than we used to be, and that we've improved more than our friends and relatives. Chumps yesterday, champs today. At age fifty-nine, I find that even my basketball game is maturing—my instincts honed, my shot more practiced. The farther we move from our past, the more we underestimate our old self-ratings, report Anne Wilson and Michael Ross. This disparagement of our old selves pays dividends. No longer do we need feel guilt or take blame for that different self, that former me.

Malleable memories are one reason why most psychologists greeted with skepticism Robert Spitzer's massively publicized study of "200 Subjects Who Claim to Have Changed Their Sexual Orientation from Homosexual to Heterosexual."* Given the ambiguity of after-the-fact testimonials (one can collect such for consumers of snake oil, homeopathy, and therapeutic touch), researchers who evaluate therapeutic effectiveness now routinely turn to the most powerful tool for winnowing wishful thinking from reality: the controlled experiment. If you want to know how likely someone is to be helped by a given therapy (such as for sexual reorientation), then a) evaluate some volunteers (with self-report and physical sexual response measures in the case of homosexuals), b) randomly assign half to receive the

*Spitzer himself acknowledged that he had "great difficulty" finding 200 such people in the United States. Upon seeing his work misportrayed, he cautioned that "I suspect the vast majority of gay people would be unable to alter by much a firmly established sexual orientation."

treatment, the others to a wait-list control group or to various alternative therapies, and c) at some point after the treatment, reassess the two groups. Before and after assessments are credible; hindsight recollections are not.

Mood and intuitions. Our sense of our own past is influenced by our current views, and also by our current moods. Depressed moods prime negative associations, which sour memories. If put in a buoyant mood—a World Cup soccer victory for the German participants in one study—people suddenly view their past and present through rose-colored glasses. They judge themselves competent, others benevolent, life wonderful.

We've all experienced the phenomenon. Our passions infiltrate our intuitions. When in a bad mood, we read someone's neutral look as a glare; in a good mood, we intuit the same look as interest. Social psychologists have played with the effect of emotions on social intuitions by manipulating the setting in which someone sees a face. Told a pictured man was a Gestapo leader, people will detect cruelty in his unsmiling face. Told he was an anti-Nazi hero, they will see kindness behind his caring eyes. Filmmakers have called this the "Kulechov effect," after a Russian film director who similarly showed viewers an expressionless man. If first shown a bowl of hot soup, their intuition told them he was pensive. If shown a dead woman, they perceived him as sorrowful. If shown a girl playing, they said he seemed happy. The moral: our intuitions construe reality differently, depending on our assumptions. "We don't see things as they are," says the Talmud, "we see things as we are."

In some studies, depressed people have recalled their parents as rejecting, punitive, and guilt-promoting; when not depressed they described their parents more positively. The same is true of adolescents: as their moods swing, so do their ratings of their parents. When teens are down, their intuitions tell them that their parents are jerks. As their mood brightens, their parents morph from devils into angels.

The misinformation effect. In her now-famous experiments involving more than 20,000 participants, University of Washington memory researcher Elizabeth Loftus has explored how we construct memories. In her typical experiment, people witness an event. Then some witnesses receive misleading information about the event (for example, by being asked whether they saw a nonexistent yield sign). When she later tests their recollections, her oft-repeated finding has been "the misinformation effect." People readily incorporate misinformation into their memories. They recall a yield sign as a stop sign, hammers as screwdrivers, a *Vogue* magazine ad as from *Mademoiselle,* Dr. Henderson as Dr. Davidson, breakfast cereal as eggs, and a clean-shaven man as mustached.

So powerful is the effect of misinformation that people often have difficulty discriminating between their memories of real and suggested events. Intuitively, false memories feel real, much as perceptual illusions feel real. The felt reality of false memories was strikingly apparent among those who three years later misrecalled where they were when hearing the news of the space shuttle *Challenger*'s explosion. Shown their own handwritten accounts from the day after the explosion, some felt so sure of their false memories that they insisted their original version must have erred. One woman clearly recalled a student running from her dorm, screaming, "The space shuttle blew up." Actually, she had heard about it from friends over lunch.

Children, too, may experience unreal memories as real. In a provocative study, Cornell University researchers Stephen Ceci, Maggie Bruck, and their colleagues had a child choose a card from a deck of possible happenings, which an adult then read. For example, "Think real hard, and tell me if this ever happened to you. Can you remember going to the hospital with a mousetrap on your finger?" After ten weekly interviews, with the same adult repeatedly asking each child to think about several real and fictitious events, a new adult asked the same question. The stunning result: 58 percent of preschoolers produced false (often vivid) stories regarding one or more events they had never experienced. Here is one from a boy who initially had denied the mousetrap incident:

My brother Colin was trying to get Blowtorch [an action figure] from me, and I wouldn't let him take it from me, so he pushed me into the wood pile where the mousetrap was. And then my finger got caught in it. And then we went to the hospital, and my mommy, daddy, and Colin drove me there, to the hospital in our van, because it was far away. And the doctor put a bandage on this finger.

Experiments with young adults have produced similar findings. It's little wonder that Loftus, Ceci, and Bruck have all worried about therapists who have nudged children and adults to recall past sexual abuse. "Spend time imagining that you were sexually abused," counseled Wendy Maltz in *The Sexual Healing Journey*. "As you give rein to your imagination, let your intuitions guide your thoughts."

To see how far our intuition will go in creating a fiction, Richard Wiseman and his University of Hertfordshire colleagues staged eight seances, each with twenty-five curious attendees. During the supposed seance, the medium (actually a professional magician-actor) asked everyone to concentrate on the moving table. Although it never moved, he suggested it had: "That's good. Lift the table up. That's good. Keep concentrating. Keep the table in the air." When questioned two weeks later, 34 percent of the participants recalled having actually seen the table levitate.

Some memory errors arise from our attributing an experience to the wrong source. Ronald Reagan's occasional "source misattributions" illustrated how imagined fictions can become remembered facts. During his three presidential campaigns, he told and retold a story of heroic sacrifice. A terrified World War II gunner was unable to eject from his seat when his plane was hit by anti-aircraft fire. "Never mind, son," said his commander, "we'll ride it down together." With misty eyes, Reagan would conclude by telling how the brave commander received the Congressional Medal of Honor posthumously. A curious journalist checked the 434 medal recipients and found no such story. Digging further, he found the episode—in the 1944 movie *A Wing and a Prayer.*

Are memories intuitions? Are they (recalling intuition's definition) direct, immediate apprehensions without rational analysis? They often seem so. Regardless, our hunches about our memories surely are intuitions, and they, too, demonstrably err. In experiments on eyewitness testimony, for example, researchers have repeatedly found that the most confident eyewitnesses are the most persuasive, but often not the most accurate. Eyewitnesses, whether right or wrong, intuitively feel similar self-assurance. Often that self-assurance is exaggerated. In a representative recent study by Brian Bornstein and Douglas Zickafoose, Louisiana State University students felt 74 percent confident in their later recollections of a classroom visitor but were correct only 55 percent of the time.

MISREADING OUR OWN MINDS

"Know thyself," admonished Socrates. We try. We constantly explain ourselves, to ourselves and others. But how well do we really know ourselves?

Very well, argued C. S. Lewis: "There is one thing, and only one in the whole universe which we know more about than we could learn from external observation." That one thing, he said, is ourselves. "We have, so to speak, inside information."

It's a wonder, then, that when influences upon us are subtle, we may intuitively dismiss factors that matter and inflate those that don't. In studies, people have misattributed their rainy day gloom to life's emptiness and their excitement while crossing a wobbly suspension bridge to their response to an attractive passerby. In one 1960s experiment, Richard Nisbett and Stanley Schachter asked Columbia University students to receive an increasingly intense series of electric shocks. Beforehand, some took a fake pill that supposedly would produce heart palpitations, breathing irregularities, and stomach butterflies—the typical responses to being shocked. Nisbett and Schachter expected that those given the pill would think that their response to shock was caused by the pill and would therefore tolerate more shock. They were right; in fact, the effect was gigantic. People given the fake pill withstood four times the shock. But when asked why they withstood so much shock, they didn't mention the pill. When told the predicted pill effect, they granted that others might be influenced but denied its influence on them. "I didn't even think about the pill," was a typical reply.

Social psychologists have since accumulated a list of classic demonstrations of our intuition failing to recognize things that matter.

- Bibb Latané and John Darley's famous studies of bystander inaction showed that others' presence can dramatically suppress people's responsiveness to emergencies. If a woman in an adjacent room falls in distress, if someone over an intercom has an apparent seizure, or if smoke fills a room in which a group completes a questionnaire, people are much less responsive if others are present. (Others' presence lifts some of the burden of responsibility for action, and their inaction may lead one to interpret the situation as a nonemergency.) Yet nearly everyone denied being influenced by others' presence. "Other people may have been affected, but not me. I would have reacted just the same if they weren't there."

- Hundreds of studies of television, videogames, and pornography reveal the media's significant influence on our sensitivities, perceptions of reality, and behaviors. Most folks agree that the media affect the culture but deny their effect on them. Many parents will recall hearing this from their children: "Don't worry, Mom. Watching this stuff doesn't affect me." This "media affect others more than me" phenomenon is so robust that researchers have given it a name—the third person effect. Others, more than us, we think, are affected by ads, political information, media violence, and sexual scripts. *We* are not slaves to fads, fashions, and opinions; we are true to ourselves. The research, however, unveils our hubris; we have met the "others," and they are us.

- Several conformity experiments reveal that someone who punctures a group's unanimity deflates its social power. Faced with others' erroneous perceptions or opinions, individuals will nearly always voice their own convictions if just one other person has already done so. Later they may recall feeling warm toward their nonconforming ally. Yet they deny that the ally influenced them: "I would have answered just the same if he weren't there."

- People of the other sex have been judged more sexually attractive if pictured with retouched larger pupils. Yet those looking at the photos had no awareness of being influenced by pupil size.

The shocking lesson of these and other studies is unavoidable: *often we don't know why we do what we do.* As the split-brain patients (Chapter 1) remind us, once we have acted we're adept at inventing reasons for our behavior. We instantly fill in the gaps. But when the influences are subtle or hidden (as when the nonverbal right hemisphere compels an action), our intuitions may be radically mistaken.

There are many other thought-provoking demonstrations of what we might call the "you don't know your own mind effect" (echoing Jonathan Swift's words at this chapter's outset). Some come from studies in which for several weeks people each day recorded their moods, the weather, the day of the week, how much they'd slept, and so forth. At the end they judged how much each factor had affected their moods. Remarkably, in view of the study's directing their attention to their moods, there was little relationship between their intuitive estimate of how well a factor predicted their daily mood and how well it actually did so. In judging what shapes our moods we seem hardly better than we are at judging our blood pressure. (One study asked hypertension patients, "Can people tell when their blood pressure is high?" Eighty percent gave the medically correct response: "No." But asked whether they could intuit their own blood pressure— "What about *you? Can you* tell?"—88 percent said yes.)

MISPREDICTING OUR OWN FEELINGS

Many of life's big decisions require intuiting our future feelings. Would marrying this person lead to lifelong commitment? Would entering this profession make for enduring satisfaction? Would going on this vacation produce happy memories? Or would the likelier results be divorce, burnout, and disappointment?

Sometimes our intuitions are on target. We know how we will feel if we fail that exam, win that big game, or soothe our tensions with a three-mile jog. We know which situations will be exhilarating, and which will elicit anger or boredom. We know, said one anonymous wag, that "Heaven is a place with an American house, Chinese food, British police, a German car, and French art," and that "Hell is a place with a Japanese house, Chinese police, British food, German art, and a French car."

Our intuitions more often fail in predicting an emotion's intensity and duration. In recent studies, people have mispredicted the durability of their emotions after a romantic breakup, losing an election, winning that game, and being insulted. To introduce this "durability bias," Harvard psychologist Daniel Gilbert and his colleagues invite us to "imagine that one morning your telephone rings and you find yourself speaking with the King of Sweden, who informs you in surprisingly good English that you have been selected as this year's recipient of a Nobel prize. How would you feel and how long would you feel that way?" Might you not expect a "sharp and lasting upturn" in your well-being? Now imagine that the telephone call is from your college president, "who regrets to inform you (in surprisingly good English) that the Board of Regents has dissolved your department, revoked your appointment, and stored your books in little cardboard boxes in the hallway. How would you feel and how long would you feel that way?" Most people facing this personal catastrophe, say Gilbert and his colleagues, would expect the emotional wounds to be enduring.

Such expectations are often wrong. Gilbert, Timothy Wilson, George Loewenstein, and David Schkade offer examples:

- When shown sexually arousing photos, then exposed to a passionate date scenario in which their date asks them to "stop," many male youths admit that they might not stop. If not first aroused by the pictures, however, they more often deny the possibility of sexual aggression. When not aroused, one easily mispredicts how one will feel and act when sexually hot—a phenomenon that leads to professions of love during lust, to unintended pregnancies, and to repeat offenses among sex abusers who have vowed "never again."
- Researchers have documented what obstetricians know—that women in labor sometimes reverse their stated preference for anaesthetic-free delivery. When we mispredict intensity, pain as well as pleasure can hijack our intentions. As George Macdonald wrote in 1886, "When a feeling was there, they felt as if it would never go; when it was gone, they felt as if it had never been; when it returned, they felt as if it had never gone."
- Shoppers do more impulse buying when hungry than when shopping after dinner. When hungry, one mispredicts how gross those deep-fried doughnuts will seem when one is sated.

When sated, one mispredicts how yummy a doughnut might be with a late-night glass of milk.

- People also mispredict their preferences for variety. If asked to pick weekly snacks for several weeks ahead, people choose variety. But if asked week by week, they tend to choose their favorite each time. (Reading this research, while huddled at Russ's restaurant savoring my umpteenth midafternoon strawberry shortcake, I smile sheepishly.)
- Only one in seven occasional smokers (those who smoke less than a cigarette per day) predict that they will be smoking in five years. Even most of those who've smoked for twenty years or tried quitting ten or more times think that they'll successfully quit within the next year. But they underestimate the addictive power of nicotine.
- In various studies, people have overestimated how much their well-being would be affected by warmer winters, relocations, football victories, gaining or losing weight, more television channels, or extra free time. Even extreme events—winning a state lottery or suffering a paralyzing accident—affect long-term happiness less than most people suppose. Recently, I talked with Chris, a former student of mine who lives with cerebral palsy so severe that he cannot feed himself, care for himself, talk, or walk more than a few agonizing steps. Through a talking computer, operated with his left foot, he explained to me that, like anyone else, he gets sad and mad. Yet because disability is all he has ever known, he has adapted to his challenges with support from his family and faith. Chris reports experiencing what I've sensed from him—a quite normal day-to-day happiness. "My mother says I have always been a happy person," he adds. Without denying the challenges of disability (I am losing my hearing), I take some comfort in knowing of our human capacity to adapt. We needn't trivialize the enduring consequences of a disability, a divorce, or a death to acknowledge our resilience.

Our intuitive theory seems to be: We want. We get. We are happy. If that were true, this chapter would be shorter. In reality, note Gilbert and Wilson, we often "miswant." People who imagine an idyllic desert island holiday with sun, surf, and sand may be disappointed when they discover "how much they require daily structure, intellectual stimulation, or regular infusions of Pop Tarts." We think that if our candidate or team wins we will be delighted for a long while. But study after study reveals that the emotional traces of good tidings evaporate more rapidly than we expect. Attention shifts, and within hours, days, or weeks (depending on the extremity of the good or bad happening) the feelings subside and we recalibrate our ups and downs around the new reality.

Such was the experience of the fictional Count Alexei Vronsky, after gaining his heart's desire, the beautiful and well-bred Anna Karenina. Gilbert quotes Tolstoy: "Vronsky, meanwhile, although what he had so long desired had come to pass, was not altogether happy. He soon felt that the fulfillment of his desires gave him only one grain of the mountain of happiness he had expected. This fulfillment showed him the eternal error men make in imaging that their happiness depends on the realization of their desires."

But it is after negative events that we're especially prone to durability bias—to mispredicting the durability of emotions. When people being tested for HIV predict how they will feel five weeks after getting the results, they expect to be feeling misery over bad news and elation over good news. Yet five weeks later, the bad news recipients are less distraught and the good news recipients less elated than they had anticipated. And when Gilbert and his colleagues asked assistant professors to predict their happiness a few years after achieving tenure or not, most believed that a favorable outcome was important for their future happiness. "Losing my job would crush my life's ambitions. It would be terrible." Yet when surveyed several years after the event, people who had been denied tenure were about as happy as those who had received it.

Let's make this personal. Gilbert and Wilson invite us to imagine how we might feel a year after losing our nondominant hand. Compared to today, how happy would you be?

In thinking about this, you perhaps focused on what the calamity would mean: no clapping, no shoe tying, no competitive basketball, no speedy keyboarding. Although you likely would forever regret the loss, your general happiness some time after the tragedy would be influenced by "two things: a) the event, and b) everything else." In focusing on the negative event, we discount the importance of everything else that matters, and so overpredict our enduring misery. "Nothing that you focus on will make as much difference as you think," concur fellow researchers David Schkade and Daniel Kahneman.

Moreover, say Gilbert and Wilson, people neglect the speed and power of their "psychological immune system," which includes their strategies for rationalizing, discounting, forgiving, and limiting trauma. Being largely ignorant of this emotional recovery system, we accommodate to disabilities, romantic breakups, exam failures, tenure denials, and personal and team defeats more readily than we would expect. "Weeping may tarry for the night, but joy comes in the morning," reflected the Psalmist.

MISPREDICTING OUR OWN BEHAVIOR

How would you respond if someone in your community called, asking you to volunteer three hours to an American Cancer Society drive? In an eye-opening little study, social psychologist Steven Sherman did just this with a sample of Bloomington, Indiana, residents, asking them to predict how they would respond. Seeing themselves as helpful people, half predicted that they would agree to help. Meanwhile, Sherman was also calling an equivalent sample of their neighbors, asking them to actually volunteer the time. Only 4 percent agreed to do so.

Imagine again: As you arrive at a psychological laboratory for an experiment, the researcher directs you to a table with three others. Your small group receives a list of fifteen men and fifteen women from different occupations, and you all must agree on which twelve of the thirty would be best suited for survival on a deserted island. During the discussion, one of the male group members injects three sexist statements. Responding to someone's nominating an athlete/ trainer, he says, "Yeah, we definitely need to keep the women in shape." In his turn to nominate, he muses, "Let me see, maybe a chef? No, one of the women can cook." Later he nominates a female musician, noting, "I think we need more women on the island to keep the men satisfied."

Hearing these sexist words, what would you do? Would you say nothing, perhaps seeing how others respond? Or would you comment on their inappropriateness? When Janet Swim and Lauri Hyers put these questions to Pennsylvania State University students, only 5 percent predicted they would fail to respond; 48 percent said they'd comment on inappropriateness. But when they put comparable other students in this situation, how did they actually respond? Fifty-five percent (not 5 percent) said nothing, and 16 percent (not 48 percent) criticized the man (who was actually a confederate working for Swim and Hyers). (The rest mostly asked questions or joked.)

As this illustrates, our intuitions about our future behavior are prone to error. If asked whether they would obey demands to deliver severe electric shocks to a hapless "learner," everyone told Stanley Milgram "not me." But when Milgram put comparable people under actual social pressure to do so in his most famous of social psychological experiments, 65 percent obeyed.

Predicting our everyday behavior. These clever experiments simulate real-life experiences, but they're not real life. Are our intuitions about our everyday futures similarly flawed? To find out, Sidney Shrauger had college students predict the likelihood of their experiencing dozens of different events during the ensuing two months (becoming romantically involved, being sick, and so forth). Surprisingly, the students' self-predictions were hardly more accurate than predictions derived from the average person's experience.

In fact, report Nicholas Epley and David Dunning, one can sometimes better predict people's future behavior by asking them to predict *others'* actions than by asking them to predict their own. Five weeks ahead of Cornell University's annual Daffodil Days charity event, students were asked to predict whether they would buy at least one daffodil for charity, and also to predict what proportion of their fellow students would do so. More than four in five predicted they would buy a daffodil, but only 43 percent actually did—close to their prediction of 56 percent by their peers. In a laboratory game played for money, 84 percent predicted that they would cooperate with another for their mutual gain, though only 61 percent did (again, close to their prediction of 64 percent cooperation by others). In further studies of giving and volunteering, students as a group likewise over-estimated their own behavior, which actually was close to their on-target predictions of others. In every study, students *expected* that their moral concerns would override their self-interest, but they were wrong. If Lao Tzu was right that "he who knows others is learned. He who knows himself is enlightened," then most people, it would seem, are more learned than enlightened.

With negative behaviors, such as when one is likely to cry or lie, self-predictions become more accurate than predictions by one's mother or friends. Nevertheless, the surest thing we can say about your individual behavior is that it's often hard for even you to predict. "Between the idea and the reality, between the motion and the act, falls the shadow." When predicting your own behavior, the best advice is therefore this: consider your past behavior in similar situations.

Illusory optimism. "The optimist," noted H. Jackson Brown, "goes to the window every morning and says, 'Good morning, God.' The pessimist goes to the window and says, 'Good god, morning.'" Optimism pays dividends. Without initial blindness to the limits of our competence, how many new ventures would we undertake? Compared to helpless-feeling pessimists, optimists enjoy not only greater success, but also better health and greater happiness.

Many of us, however, have what Rutgers University psychologist Neil Weinstein calls an "unrealistic optimism about future life events." College students, for example, perceive themselves as far more likely than their classmates to get a good job, draw a good salary, and own a home, and as far less likely to experience negative events, such as developing a drinking problem, having a heart attack before age forty, or being fired. (This makes a great class demonstration: if everyone in a class perceives themselves as more likely than their average class-mate to experience life's blessings and less likely to experience calami-ties, then at least half their intuitions must be wrong.)

Illusory optimism has health consequences. Most smokers per-ceive themselves as less vulnerable than other smokers to tobacco's ravages. In Scotland and the United States, most older adolescents say that they are much less likely than their peers to become infected by HIV. Sexually active undergraduate women who don't consistently use contraceptives have perceived themselves, compared with other women at their university, as *less* vulnerable to unwanted pregnancy. After experiencing the 1989 earthquake, students in the San Francisco Bay area did lose their optimism about being less vulnerable than their classmates to injury in a natural disaster, but within three months their illusory optimism had rebounded.

Believing ourselves less vulnerable than others to misfortune, we may cheerfully shun seat belts, smoke cigarettes, and stumble into unhealthy relationships. When buying clothes, many people favor snug fits ("These will fit just right when I drop a few pounds"); virtually no one predicts weight gain ("Most people my age are putting on pounds, so I'd better allow room for expansion"). Like pride, blind optimism may go before a fall.

Many people also exhibit illusory optimism, and therefore complacency, about their relationships. Dating couples see their future through rose-colored glasses. By focusing on the current positives, lovers often feel sure that they will always be lovers. Their friends and family often know better, report Tara MacDonald and Michael Ross, from their studies with University of Waterloo students. These less optimistic predictions of their parents and roommates proved more accurate than the students' own intuitions. (Many a parent, having seen an offspring lunge confidently into an ill-fated relationship against all advice, nods agreement.) In one survey, 137 marriage license applicants accurately estimated that half of marriages end in divorce, yet most assessed their chance of divorce as *zero* percent.

Although optimism beats pessimism for promoting self-confidence, health, and well-being, a dash of realism—or what Julie Norem calls "defensive pessimism"—can save us from the perils of unrealistic optimism. Self-doubt can energize students, most of whom (especially those destined for low grades) exhibit excess optimism about upcoming exams. (Shortly before getting the exam back, the illusory optimism disappears as students brace for the worst.) Students who are overconfident tend to underprepare. Their equally able but more anxious peers, fearing that they are going to bomb on the upcoming exam, study furiously and get higher grades. The moral: success in school and beyond requires enough optimism to sustain hope and enough realism to motivate diligence.

So, despite our impressive capacity for thinking without awareness, for social intuitions, and for intuitive expertise and creativity, our intuitions sometimes mislead us as to what we have experienced, how we have changed, what has influenced us, and what we will feel and do. "There are three things extremely hard," said Benjamin Franklin. "Steel, a Diamond, and to know one's self."

That being so, we need psychological science. If the researchers whom we've met in this chapter had relied on people's intuitions, they would never have made their surprising discoveries about memories, moods, and misinformation, or about misguided self-predictions and optimism. Subjective personal reports are suggestive but not definitive —often powerfully persuasive, but sometimes powerfully misleading. Asking people to explain their past actions or to guess their future actions sometimes gives us wrong answers. By being mindful of the limits on our self-knowledge we can restrain our gullibility and motivate ourselves to think critically, to check our own and others' intuition against reality, and to replace illusion with understanding.

Intuitions About Our Competence and Virtue

Nothing is so difficult as not deceiving oneself.
—Ludwig Wittgenstein

At the center of our worlds, more pivotal for us than anything else, are we ourselves. Whatever we do, whatever we perceive, whatever we conceive, whomever we meet will be filtered through our self. When we think about something in relation to ourselves, we remember it better. If asked whether specific words, such as *outgoing,* describe us, we later remember those words better than if asked whether they describe someone else. If asked to compare ourselves with a character in a short story, we remember the character better. Two days after a conversation with someone, we best recall what the person said about us. Ergo, memories form around our primary interest: ourselves.

From our self-focused perspective, we also overestimate our conspicuousness. We often see ourselves as responsible for events in which we have been a minor player. We also tend to see ourselves at center stage, intuitively overestimating the extent to which others' attention is aimed at us.

Thomas Gilovich, Victoria Medvec, and Kenneth Savitsky explored this "spotlight effect" by having individual Cornell University students don embarrassing Barry Manilow T-shirts before entering a room with other students. The self-conscious T-shirt wearers guessed that nearly half their peers would notice the shirt. But only 23 percent actually did. What's true of our dorky clothes and bad hair is also true of our emotions—our anxiety, irritation, disgust, deceit, or attraction: fewer people notice than we presume. Keenly aware of our own emotions, we often suffer an illusion of their transparency. We presume that our feelings are leaking out when actually we're opaque. Ditto for our social blunders and public mental slips. What we agonize over, others may hardly notice and soon forget. For better or worse, others just aren't as focused on us as we are.

Intuition also is prone to err when we evaluate our own knowledge and abilities. This is most strikingly evident in three robust phenomena: hindsight bias, self-serving bias, and overconfidence bias. To anticipate and illustrate these phenomena, you can ask someone (or ask yourself) to offer seat-of-the-pants answers to a few questions:

- Imagine someone tells you that "social psychologists have found that whether choosing friends or falling in love, we are most attracted to people whose traits differ from our own. As the old saying goes, 'Opposites attract.'" Why might this be true? Any ideas? Would you find this result surprising or unsurprising?
- At what age would you guess you will die?
- How would you rank your driving ability in comparison with other drivers? And, honestly now, how would you rank your handwriting? Your jumping ability? Your social skills?
- Let's also audition you for *Who Wants to Be a Millionaire?* You probably will feel unsure of the answers to these questions, but maybe your intuition can help. Which is longer, the Panama Canal or the Suez Canal? How confident of your answer are you (between it's a 50/50 tossup and 100 percent certain)? Another question: in the United States, which claims more lives each year, homicide or suicide? Again, how confident are you? Final question: There's a lot of debate these days about nuclear power as a response to both global warming and the energy crisis. At the turn of the millennium, how many nuclear power plants were operating in the world? Give me a range big

enough that you'd intuitively feel 98 percent sure includes the true answer.

HINDSIGHT BIAS ("I KNEW IT ALL ALONG")

While reading this book, have you sometimes felt as though you knew it all along? Sometimes you probably have. Having spent your lifetime observing people, you have surely glimpsed some of what psychologists have uncovered in their observations and experiments. As Yogi Berra once said, "You can observe a lot by watching." So does psychology simply formalize what any amateur psychologist already knows?

The Atlantic's managing editor, Cullen Murphy, has thought so: "Day after day social scientists go out into the world. Day after day they discover that people's behavior is pretty much what you'd expect." He contends that "far too often" psychology and sociology merely discern the obvious or confirm the commonplace. But there is a problem with intuitive common sense: we commonly invoke it after we know the facts. A series of experiments by Paul Slovic, Baruch Fischhoff, and others confirms that events become "obvious" and predictable in hindsight. When people learn the outcome of an experiment, that outcome suddenly seems less surprising than it is to people who are simply told about the experiments and its possible outcomes. How easy it is to seem wise when drawing the bull's-eye after the arrow has struck.

In everyday life, too, we often don't expect something to happen until it does. We then see the forces that brought it about and regard the event as inevitable. As Dr. Watson said to Sherlock Holmes, "Anything seems commonplace, once explained." After an election, armchair politicians have no trouble explaining the outcome. "Gore blew it by not capitalizing on the economic boom and by being overbearing in the first debate and timid in the second debate." Had a few additional Florida African-Americans been allowed to vote, the commentators would have been explaining the inevitable Gore victory. If the stock market drops, it was "due for a correction." Although history may seem in retrospect like a series of inevitable events, the actual future is seldom foreseen. No one's diary recorded, "Today the

Hundred Years' War began." As Kierkegaard put it, "Life is lived forwards, but understood backwards."

If this knew-it-all-along phenomenon (a.k.a. the hindsight bias) is pervasive, you may suddenly be feeling that, yawn, you already knew it. Indeed, almost any conceivable psychological science result can seem like common sense—*after* you know it. Did you find "opposites attract" an unsurprising result? When I have posed the question as I did above, nearly everyone has. But—hold the phone—people respond similarly if given an *opposite* result: "Social psychologists have found that, whether choosing friends or falling in love, we are most attracted to people whose traits are similar to our own. As the old saying goes, 'Birds of a feather flock together.'" After explaining this result, virtually everyone finds *this* unsurprising. (In fact, it is these folks who are right: similarity breeds content. With the possible exception of the blissful union of a sadist and masochist, birds that flock together usually *are* of a feather. Smart birds flock together. So do rich birds, Protestant birds, tall birds, pretty birds, happy birds, and birds that share similar attitudes, values, and personalities.)

Indeed, we can draw on many a proverb to help us understand many a result. If we should discover that separation intensifies romance, well then, of course "absence makes the heart grow fonder." Should separation instead weaken attraction, John or Judy Public may still roll their eyes: "My grandmother could have told you that 'out of sight is out of mind.'" As the philosopher Alfred North Whitehead once remarked, "Everything important has been said before." Mark Twain had the same idea when jesting that Adam was the only person who, when saying a good thing, knew that nobody had said it before. No matter what we discern as more often true—that too many cooks spoil the broth or that two heads are better than one, that the pen is mightier than the sword or that actions speak louder than words, that you can't teach an old dog new tricks or that you're never too old to learn—someone will have foreseen the "obvious" result.

Karl Teigen must have had a few chuckles when asking University of Leicester students to evaluate actual proverbs and their opposites. When given the proverb "Fear is stronger than love," most believed it to be true. But so did students who were given its reversed form, "Love is stronger than fear." Likewise, the genuine proverb "He that is fallen cannot help him who is down" was rated highly; but so too was "He that is fallen can help him who is down." My favorites, however, were these two highly rated proverbs: the authentic "Wise men make proverbs and fools repeat them" and its made-up counterpart, "Fools make proverbs and wise men repeat them."

The hindsight bias experiments show us the impossibility, once we know an outcome, of simply reverting to our former state of mind. It's rather like viewing the dalmatian in the classic photo by R. C. James. Can you see it sniffing the ground near the center? Once your mind has it, the knowledge controls your interpretation to such an extent that it becomes difficult to return to your prior state and *not* see the dog.

Our inability to see the world minus our current knowledge has been called the "curse of knowledge." Teachers, technology developers, and authors often mistakenly assume that what's clear to them will be clear to others. They realize that others lack their expertise, yet they underestimate how confusing their explanations and instructions can be.

A little demonstration: How long do you think it takes the average person to solve anagrams such as these two: *wreat* (water) and *grabe* (barge)?

Perhaps, like participants in experiments by Colleen Kelley and Larry Jacoby, you found it hard to appreciate—once I gave you the solutions—how difficult they are. The participants guessed that people would need about ten seconds for each. But give these two to a friend and see whether the friend solves them as quickly as you expected. Or when you have three minutes, try a similar one yourself: ochsa.

Some of us have been astonished at others' dim-wittedness when playing "Name That Tune." If, for example, we tap the rhythm to "Happy Birthday" or "Mary Had a Little Lamb" on a friend's arm, we are amazed (while hearing the tune in our mind) at how difficult our friend finds this seemingly easy task. When you know a thing, it's hard to mentally simulate what it's like not to know. Such is the curse of knowledge.

We therefore readily blame ourselves for our past foolishness in love, in the stock market, in our parenting. "I should have known better!" And we blame others for what in hindsight seem like stupid mistakes:

- Physicians told both a patient's symptoms and a pathologist's report on cause of death sometimes wonder how an incorrect diagnosis could ever have been made. (Juries, too, decide malpractice awards from the perspective of hindsight.) Other physicians, given only the symptoms, don't find the diagnosis nearly so obvious.
- President Carter's ill-fated attempt to rescue American hostages in Tehran, thwarted when a sand storm disabled half the helicopters, was "doomed from the start" said journalists *after* they knew it had failed. Were it not for the wind in the desert that night, journalists might well have celebrated the president's courage and eventual reelection.
- And was the FBI's assault on the Branch Davidian complex a "debacle"—a "blunder" for which "heads should roll"—or rather an unfortunate tragedy? Psychologist Robyn Dawes ar-

gues that if the assault in Waco was a reasonable decision, given the information available at the time, it's unreasonable to judge the decision makers with hindsight, based on an unpredictable outcome.

So do we conclude that intuitive common sense is usually wrong? Sometimes it is. Common sense once told us that the earth was flat and the sun revolved around us. Common sense, supported by medical experience, assured doctors that bleeding was an effective treatment for typhoid fever, until someone in the middle of the nineteenth century bothered to experiment—to divide patients into two groups—one bled, the other given mere bed rest.

Other times, conventional intuition is right. Love *does* breed happiness. Sometimes intuition falls on both sides of an issue. Does additional happiness come more from knowing the truth or from preserving healthy illusions? From restraint or catharsis? From making others happy or enjoying our enemies' misery? From being with others or enjoying peaceful solitude? Opinions are a dime a dozen.

The point, then, is not that commonsense intuitions are predictably wrong. Rather, they are right *after the fact.* We therefore easily deceive ourselves into thinking that we know and knew more than we do and did. And that is why (excuse this word from our sponsor) we need psychological science—to help us sift reality from illusion, sensible predictions from easy hindsight, and true insights from false intuitions.

SELF-SERVING BIAS

"No man, deep down in the privacy of his heart, has any considerable respect for himself," supposed Mark Twain, anticipating the late twentieth-century self-esteem movement. One of the movement's architects, humanistic psychologist Carl Rogers, agreed. When disputing the religious doctrine that humanity's problems often arise from excessive self-love (pride), Rogers wrote that, to the contrary, most people he knew "despise themselves, regard themselves as worthless and unlovable." "All of us have inferiority complexes," echoed John Powell. "Those who seem not to have such a complex are only pretending." As Groucho Marx lampooned, "I don't want to belong to any club that would accept me as a member."

Actually, most of us have a good reputation with ourselves. In studies of self-esteem, even low-scoring people respond in the mid range of possible scores (by saying "somewhat" or "sometimes" to statements such as "I am fun to be with" and "I have good ideas"—statements that most people readily agree with). Moreover, one of social psychology's most provocative and repeatedly confirmed conclusions concerns the potency of "self-serving bias."

People accept more responsibility for good deeds than for bad, and for successes than for failures. In dozens of experiments, people readily accept credit when told they've succeeded on some task, but they frequently attribute supposed failure to external factors, such as bad luck or an impossible situation. Similarly, in explaining their victories, athletes commonly credit themselves, but they attribute losses to bad breaks, bad refereeing, or the other team's super effort or dirty play. Such blame-shucking has a long tradition: "The woman whom you gave to be with me, she gave me fruit from the tree, and I ate."

On insurance reports, drivers have offered countless self-serving explanations: "An invisible car came out of nowhere, struck my car, and vanished." "As I reached an intersection, a hedge sprang up, obscuring my vision." "A pedestrian hit me and went under my car."

In a classic demonstration of self-serving bias, Michael Ross and Fiore Sicoly found that young married Canadians typically took more responsibility for house cleaning and child care than their spouses credited them for. The phenomenon has been observed many times since. Ask a wife and a husband to estimate what percentage of the time they each do the dishes, walk the dog, turn out the lights, or shop, and their estimates will usually sum to more than 100 percent. The same is true of people working on group projects, of athletes on teams, and of debaters.

Self-serving intuitions about responsibility contribute to marital discord, worker dissatisfaction, and bargainer stalemate. Most divorcing people blame their breakup on their underperforming partner. Most managers blame poor performance on workers' inability or indolence. (The workers more often blame something external—excessive workload, difficult co-workers, ambiguous assignments.) And people evaluate pay raises as fairer when receiving more rather than less than most others. Seldom do managers hear, "That's not fair! You're paying me too much." "What have I done to deserve this?" is something we ask about our difficulties, not our successes (those we assume we deserve).

Students exhibit the self-serving bias. When receiving a good exam grade, they accept credit and regard the exam as valid. When receiving a poor grade, they often fault the exam. Teachers are not immune from this bias—they tend to accept some credit for students' achievements but to blame failure on the students. "With my help, Gillian graduated with honors. Despite my help, George flunked out."

Most people see themselves as better than average. Our intuitions do not insult us. Nine in ten managers rate themselves as superior to their average peer, as do nearly nine in ten Australians when rating their job performance. In three surveys, nine in ten college professors rated themselves as superior to their average colleague. And most drivers—even most drivers who have been hospitalized after accidents—believe themselves safer and more skilled than the average driver. "The one thing that unites all human beings, regardless of age, gender, religion, economic status or ethnic background," observes Dave Barry, "is that deep down inside, we all believe that we are above average drivers."

Compared with their average peer, most people also believe themselves to be more intelligent, better looking, and less prejudiced. In a 1997 Gallup Poll, 44 percent of white Americans rated *other* whites as having high prejudice against blacks (5 or higher on a 0 to 10 scale). Yet only 14 percent rated themselves as similarly prejudiced.

We're also more ethical than others. In national surveys, most business people see themselves as more ethical than the average business person. Even social psychologists, who know about self-serving bias, regard themselves as more ethical than most other social psychologists. (Those of us who research or teach these phenomena are not automatically exempt from them.)

Los Angeles residents have viewed themselves as healthier than most of their neighbors, and most college students believe that they will outlive their actuarially predicted age of death by about ten years. In one poll of baby boomers, three in four thought they looked younger than their peers, and four in five said they had fewer wrinkles than other people their age. In another poll, 12 percent of people acknowledged feeling old for their age, while five times as many—66 percent—thought they were young for their age. Every community, it seems, is like Lake Wobegon, where "all the women are strong, all the men are good-looking, and all the children are above average." All this calls to mind Freud's joke about the husband who told his wife, "If one of us should die, I think I should go live in Paris."

And what happens when we die? Asked by *U.S. News and World Report* who was at least "somewhat likely" to go to heaven, 19 percent of Americans thought that O. J. Simpson was likely to be welcomed at the pearly gates. As of the poll date, 1997, they were more optimistic about Bill Clinton (52 percent), Princess Diana (60 percent), and Michael Jordan (65 percent). The second closest person to a perceived heavenly shoo-in was Mother Teresa (79 percent). And who do you supposed topped Mother Teresa? At the head of the class, with an 87 percent perceived heavenly admission rate, people placed *themselves.*

Self-serving bias is most apparent on socially desirable, subjective dimensions—for example on "driving ability" and "social skills" rather than the less subjective and necessary "handwriting" and "jumping ability." (Did you, too, rank your driving ability and social skill higher than your handwriting and jumping?) Students are more likely to rate themselves superior in "moral goodness" than in "intelligence." And community residents overwhelmingly see themselves as *caring* more than most others about the environment, about hunger, and about other social issues, though they don't see themselves as *doing* more with their time and money. If it's subjective and if it's good, it's us.

Subjective dimensions give us leeway in defining them to suit our skills. Assessing our "leadership ability" allows us each to conjure up an image of an effective leader whose style is like our own. Rating our "athletic ability" we may ponder our swimming or golfing, and not the agonizing P.E. classes where we struck out time and again. In one College Entrance Examination Board survey of 829,000 high school seniors, 0 percent (that is not a typo) rated themselves below average in the subjective and valued "ability to get along with others," 60 percent rated themselves in the top 10 percent, and 25 percent saw themselves among the top 1 percent. With apologies to Elizabeth Barrett Browning, "How do I love me? Let me count the ways!"

False consensus and uniqueness. We further shore up our self-image by misperceiving the extent to which others think and act as we do. On matters of opinion, we find support for our positions by overestimating the extent to which others agree. If we're for it, we presume that others will be, too. And those who harbor negative ideas— for example, about another racial group—will presume that many others share their views. How we perceive others reveals something of ourselves.

When we behave badly or fail in a task, we can reassure ourselves by thinking such lapses common. After one person lies to another, the liar begins to perceive the other as dishonest. "Okay, I lied. But doesn't everyone?" Those who smoke, or cheat on their spouses or income taxes, will likely overestimate the number of others doing likewise. *Penthouse* publisher Bob Guccione may have been illustrating this "false consensus effect" when commenting on a national survey in which 83 percent of adults reported zero or one sexual partner in the previous year: "Positively, outrageously stupid and unbelievable. I would say five partners a year is the average for men."

False consensus occurs partly because, lacking other information, we impute our knowledge and responses to others. One professor asked his class to guess what percentage of the class had cell phones. Not knowing, they tended to impute their choices to others. Those who had cell phones guessed that 65 percent did; those who didn't guessed that 40 percent did (the truth was in between). Also, it's easy to overestimate relatively infrequent negative behaviors. If 20 percent of people lie, there is lots of room for overestimating the number of liars. Also, we're more likely to associate with people who share our attitudes and behaviors, and then to judge the world from those we know. Perhaps this is why Pamela Anderson Lee could say that "everybody says I'm plastic from head to toe. Can't stand next to a radiator or I'll melt. I had [breast] implants, but so has every single person in L.A."

Concerning matters of *ability* or instances when we behave *well,* however, we more often intuit a false uniqueness effect. Though our failings seem normal, our talents and virtues seem special. Thus those who drink heavily but use seat belts *over*estimate (false consensus) the number of other heavy drinkers and *under*estimate (false uniqueness) the commonality of seat belt use. Who we are affects our social intuitions. And "how little we should enjoy life if we never flattered ourselves!" mused the French wit La Rochefoucauld.

THE OVERCONFIDENCE PHENOMENON

We are all what psychologists Dacher Keltner and Robert Robinson call naive realists. We intuitively assume that as we see and remember the world, so it is. We assume that others see it as we do (false consensus). And if they obviously don't, we assume that the bias is at their end.

Our naiveté extends to our self-confidence. The "cognitive conceit" that appears in our judgments of past knowledge ("I knew it all along") surfaces again in estimates of our current knowledge and future behavior. We know that we have muffed things in the past, but we're confident we will do better in the future at meeting deadlines, nurturing relationships, and following that exercise routine. And we certainly don't lack for confidence in our hunches and judgments.

To explore this "overconfidence phenomenon," researchers have given people all sorts of factual questions and then asked them to state their confidence: Is absinthe a liqueur or a precious stone? Which is longer, the Panama Canal or the Suez Canal? In the United States, which claims more lives each year, homicide or suicide? The routine result: When tasks are challenging, people are usually more confident than correct. When 60 percent of folks answer a question correctly, they, on average, feel 75 percent sure. Even when people feel 100 percent certain they err about 15 percent of the time. (The answers, by the way, are a liqueur; the Suez, which is twice as long as the Panama; and suicide, which takes nearly twice as many lives.)

Other studies have invited people to answer factual questions with a wide enough range to surely include the actual answer. "I feel 98 percent certain that the population of New Zealand is more than _____ but less than _____" or that "the number of operating nuclear power plants is more than _____ but less than _____." Psychologists Daniel Kahneman and Amos Tversky, two Magellans of the mind who specialized in "debugging human intuition," reported that nearly one-third of the time people's estimates, made with 98 percent confidence, failed to include the correct answer (3.7 million New Zealanders and 438 plants at the end of 2000). Although very sure of themselves, they were often wrong. Moreover, warnings ("Be honest with yourselves!" "Admit what you don't know!") and admonitions ("Spread out those distributions!") hardly reduced the typical over-confidence.

But these are almanac-type questions. Can we more accurately calibrate our confidence in our social intuitions? To find out, psychologist David Dunning and his associates simulated a little game show. They asked Stanford students to guess a stranger's answer to such questions as, "Would you prepare for a difficult exam alone or with a small study group?" and "Would you pocket $5 found at a local campus eatery or turn it in?" Knowing the type of question, but not the actual questions, the participants were first given a chance to interview the target person about academic interests, hobbies, family, aspirations, astrological signs—anything they guessed might be helpful. Then the target person answered twenty of the two-choice questions while the interviewers predicted the target's answers and rated their own confidence.

The result? The interviewers were "markedly overconfident." Although they guessed right 63 percent of the time, they felt, on average, 75 percent sure. When guessing their own roommates' responses to the questions, they became a bit more accurate (68 percent). But their 78 percent confidence again exceeded their accuracy. Moreover, the most confident people tended to be the most *over*confident. Overconfidence has also reigned in studies of people's intuitive lie detection abilities. On average, participants have been 57 percent accurate but 73 percent sure. Again, the most confident people were not more accurate.

So, our judgments are better than chance (two cheers for social intuition) but generally not as good as we think. In the previous chapter we saw that even our self-predictions are imperfect. But can we accurately calibrate our confidence in our self-predictions? To find out, Robert Vallone and his colleagues had university students predict in September whether they would drop a course, declare a major, elect to live off campus next year, and so forth. Although the students felt, on average, 84 percent sure of these self-predictions, they erred nearly twice as often as they expected. Even when feeling 100 percent sure they erred 15 percent of the time (just as we noted on the almanac questions).

Other studies show that people are similarly overconfident in predicting how they're going to change—to lose weight, to study harder, to quit smoking, to exercise regularly. For most, the typical pattern is to start well and then to regress to old habits. (One of psychology's maxims is that the best predictor of future behavior is past behavior, not present intentions.) We then blame ourselves, feel a bit guilty and depressed, and eventually make a new resolution or seek a new self-help program. Change can happen, but it's most likely for those who realistically appreciate the challenge and the discipline and mental energy required. Without this appreciation, inflated promises and unrealistic expectations breed a "false-hope syndrome," note University of Toronto psychologists Janet Polivy and Peter Herman. This syndrome entails "disappointment, discouragement, and perception of oneself as a failure."

Psychologist Roger Buehler, of Wilfrid Laurier University, and his colleagues report that most students will confidently underestimate how long it will take to complete papers and other major assignments. They have much company. Planners routinely underestimate project time and expense (as Bostonians awaiting their new submerged highway can verify). In 1969, Montreal Mayor Jean Drapeau proudly announced that a $120 million stadium with a retractable roof would be built for the 1976 Olympics. The roof was completed in 1989; it alone cost $120 million.

At its worst, overconfidence breeds folly (see box) and catastrophe. It was an overconfident Hitler who invaded the countries of Europe. It was an overconfident Lyndon Johnson who sent the U.S. Army to salvage democracy in South Vietnam. It was an overconfident Saddam Hussein who marched his army into Kuwait. It was an overconfident Slobodan Milosevic who proclaimed that he would never allow peacekeeping troops in Kosovo.

In *The Lost Japan*, Hasegawa Nyozekan explains that the "war was

FROM THE ANNALS OF OVERCONFIDENCE

It ain't so much the things we don't know that get us into trouble.

It's the things we know that just ain't so.

—Artemus Ward

Regarding the atomic bomb:
"That is the biggest fool thing we have ever done. The bomb will never go off, and I speak as an expert on explosives."
Admiral William Leahy to President Truman, 1945

"We don't like their sound. Groups of guitars are on their way out."
Decca Records, in turning down a recording contract with the Beatles in 1962

"The 'telephone' has too many shortcomings to be seriously considered as a means of communication. The device is inherently of no value to us."
Western Union memo concerning Alexander Graham Bell's patent in 1876

"The telephone may be appropriate for our American cousins, but not here, because we have an adequate supply of messenger boys."
British expert group evaluating the invention of the telephone

"The horse is here to stay but the automobile is only a novelty—a fad."
Michigan banker advising Henry Ford's lawyer not to invest in the fledgling Ford Motor Company

"They couldn't hit an elephant at this dist—."
General John Sedgwick's last words, uttered during a U.S. Civil War battle, 1864

started as the result of a mistaken intuitive 'calculation' which transcended mathematics. We believed with a blind fervor that we could triumph over scientific weapons and tactics by means of our mystic will. . . . The characteristic reliance on intuition by Japanese had blocked the objective cognition of the modern world."

People sustain overconfidence by seeking information that confirms their decisions, and also—when failure can't be denied—by recalling their mistaken judgments as times they were almost right.

Phillip Tetlock observed this after inviting various academic and government experts to project—from their viewpoint in the late 1980s—the future governance of the Soviet Union, South Africa, and Canada. Five years later communism had collapsed, South Africa had become a multiracial democracy, and Canada remained undivided. Experts who had felt more than 80 percent confident were right in predicting these turns of events less than 40 percent of the time. Yet, in reflecting on their judgments, those who erred felt that they were still basically right. I was "almost right," said many. "The hardliners almost succeeded in their coup attempt against Gorbachev." "The Quebecois separatists almost won the secessionist referendum." "But for the coincidence of de Klerk and Mandela, there would have been a lot bloodier transition to black majority rule in South Africa." Among political experts—and stock market forecasters, mental health workers, and sports prognosticators—overconfidence is hard to dislodge.

Columbia University psychologist Janet Metcalfe summed up research on human overconfidence with these humbling words:

> People think they will be able to solve problems when they won't; they are highly confident that they are on the verge of producing the correct answer when they are, in fact, about to produce a mistake; they think they have solved problems when they haven't; they think they know the answers to information questions when they don't; they think they have the answer on the tip of their tongue when there is no answer; they think they produced the correct answer when they didn't, and furthermore, they say they knew it all along; they believe they have mastered learning material when they haven't; they think they have understood, even though demonstrably they are still in the dark.

Ouch. All this research is humbling, and encourages us not to be intimidated by others' preening confidence. Yet we must also remember the complementary truths about our great capacity for intelligence without awareness, about the speed of our social intuition, and about the potentials of our intuitive expertise. And let's also recognize the adaptiveness of self-confidence. Failing to appreciate our potential for error when making business, political, or military decisions can have devastating consequences. But so can a lack of confidence. People who err on the side of overconfidence live more happily and make tough decisions more easily. "Life is the art of being well deceived," mused William Hazlitt.

Still, we also do well to keep our confidence and optimism in touch with reality. Part of wisdom is to know oneself. And what is it to know oneself? Said Confucius 2,500 years ago, "When you know a thing, to hold that you know it; and when you do not know a thing, to allow that you do not know it; this is knowledge."

Intuitions About Reality

The greatest obstacle to discovery is not ignorance—
it is the illusion of knowledge.
—Daniel Boorstin, Librarian of Congress, 1984

Let's begin with another little intuition checkup. Quick and easy now, starting with some gut checks on your intuitive physics:

1. The diagram shows a curved tube, lying flat on a table. A BB is shot into the opening and out the other end. With your finger on the page, draw the BB's path through the tube and after it shoots out the tube.

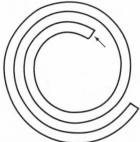

2. While flying at a constant speed, a plane drops a bowling ball. Draw the path the ball will follow (ignoring wind resistance) and show where the plane will be as the ball hits the ground. If a BB were dropped at the same time as the bowling ball, which would hit the ground first?

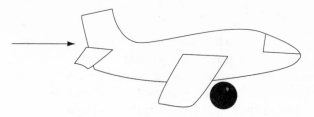

Ground

3. Water is about to be poured from a glass into a bowl resting on a table below. Draw a line in the glass, representing the water's surface (starting at the designated point)

How's your arithmetic?

4. The Brownsons drive to Kalamazoo at an average speed of 60 mph but on their return are stuck in slow traffic and average only 30 mph. What was their average speed for the round-trip?
5. A farmer bought a horse for $60 and sold it for $70. Then the farmer bought the horse back for $80 and sold it again, for $90. How much money did the farmer make on this horse trading?

Finally, let's check your intuitive understanding of probabilities:

6. The people in your city have a 1 percent risk of having bone cancer. Everyone is therefore invited to take a test that is 90 percent reliable (it spots the cancer in 90 percent of those who have it, and 10 percent of the time gives a false positive report). You take the test and are given the bad news: a positive report. What is the probability you have bone cancer?
7. I shuffle a deck of 80 black and 20 red cards. As I turn the cards up (after replacing and reshuffling the last card), you receive $1 each time you guess correctly whether black or red is about to appear. To pocket the most money, what percent of the time should you say "black" and "red"?
8. I toss two coins, promising that if at least one of them comes up heads I will tell you. I look at both coins and volunteer that at least one is indeed a head. What's the probability that the other is also a head?
9. Suppose you are on Monty Hall's old *Let's Make a Deal* television show and are given the choice of three doors. Behind one is a car; behind the others, goats. You pick door number 1. The host, who knows what's behind the doors, opens number 3, which has a goat. He then says to you, "Do you want to switch to door number 2?" Should you switch, or does it not matter?

Ready to check your intuitive physics, arithmetic, and probabilities? The answer key:

1. The BB exits in a straight line. About half of Johns Hopkins students, when queried in Michael McCloskey's studies of intu-

itive theories of motion, presumed the BB would continue a
curved path.

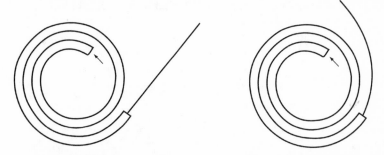

2. The ball will drop in a forward curve, with the plane directly
   above it as it hits the ground. Forty percent of McCloskey's
   Hopkins students intuited arcs resembling the actual path (A).
   And contrary to Aristotle's idea that heavy objects fall faster, a
   BB and a bowling ball would reach earth simultaneously.
   Though wrong, the Aristotelian idea intuitively felt right
   enough to have lasted for centuries.

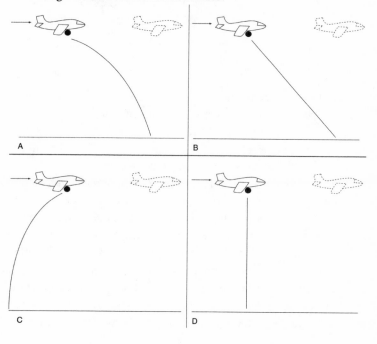

3. On the "water-level task" devised by Jean Piaget, up to 40 percent of the population incorrectly intuits that the water would deviate from horizontal (indicated by the dotted line).

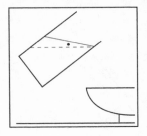

4. The Brownsons averaged 40 mph. If they had a sixty-mile drive each way, it would have taken them one hour going and two hours returning—thus three hours to drive 120 miles.
5. The farmer made $20. Most people, including most German banking executives (a German colleague tells me), answer $10. But let's do the accounting:

	Buying price (amount paid)	Selling price (amount received)
Deal 1	$60	$70
Deal 2	$80	$90
Total	**$140**	**$160**

If this isn't convincing, reread the question with this second sentence: "Then the farmer bought some bricks for $80 and sold them for $90." (Should it matter whether the second deal was bricks or a horse?) If still in doubt, get out some Monopoly money and go through the transactions.
6. With a 90 percent reliable test, the probability (given your alarming positive result) is 92 percent that you *don't* have cancer. If 1,000 people show up for the test and 1 percent—ten people—actually have the bone cancer, the test will spot it in about nine of them. So far so good. But what about the other 990? A 10 percent misdiagnosis rate would yield 99 false positives (92 percent of the 108 people who were given a true or false positive outcome). Studies show that most physicians fail to comprehend these elementary mathematics.

7. You should say black 100 percent of the time, which would earn you about $80. Saying black 80 percent of the time would yield about $68 ($64 on correct guesses when black turned up and $4 for the 20 percent of the time you correctly guessed red).

8. Can we agree that there are four equally likely outcomes to the two coin tosses: TT, HH, TH, and HT? Because I've revealed that the first didn't happen, I've ruled out TT. Of the three remaining possibilities, only one has a second heads. So the odds are one out of three (not 50/50) that the second coin is a head.

9. Finally, the mother of all beguiling mental puzzles, the Monty Hall Dilemma (which in a different format was introduced by Martin Gardner in a 1959 *Scientific American* column). When a reader posed the dilemma to *Parade* columnist Marilyn vos Savant, she answered, "Yes, you should switch." That set off a storm of more than 10,000 letters, nine in ten disagreeing, and a series of articles in statistical journals, newspapers, and magazines. Nevertheless, when the dust settled it was clear from both logical analysis and empirical simulations that vos Savant was right. Think of it this way: The chances are 1 in 3 that you initially picked the right door, and 2 in 3 that it's one of the other two. When the host eliminates one of those two (the host always opens the unchosen door that isn't the prize door), there still are 2 chances in 3 that the correct door is *not* the one you picked. (Since your original guess would be wrong two out of three times, the *other* door—the door you switch to, if you switch—must be the right one two out of three times.) When more than 70,000 folks played the game (as you can at National Public Radio's *Car Talk* website—cartalk.cars.com/ About/Monty) 33.1 percent of "stickers" and 66.7 percent of "switchers" were indeed winners.

Let's not go overboard. Some unschooled intuitions hit the mark. As I noted in Chapter 1, even babies have an innate counter and a head for elementary physics. If accustomed to a Daffy Duck puppet jumping three times on stage, they show surprise if it jumps only twice. (They stare longer—as if doing a double-take.)

Yet these little brain teasers illustrate that intuition, even when informed by experience and observation, sometimes misses the mark. As K. C. Cole writes, "Math—that most logical of sciences—shows us that the truth can be highly counterintuitive and that sense is hardly common."

Okay, maybe math and physics never were our best subjects. Surely we do better when it comes to judging people, politics, and practicalities. As La Rochefoucauld observed, people may complain about their memory, but never their judgment. Indeed, thanks to our intuitive efficiency and accuracy, we generally navigate life quite well. If we had to analyze every judgment, we'd never get through the day. As Robert Ornstein writes, "There has never been, nor will there ever be, enough time to be truly rational." But on judgments that really matter, and where quick and rough intuitive approximations may stray from reality, critical thinking can help.

THE FUNDAMENTAL ATTRIBUTION ERROR

In his autobiography, Auschwitz commandant Rudolf Höss reported feeling anguished by the results of his actions. But as a "good SS officer" he hid any display of "feminine" emotions: "My pity was so great that I longed to vanish from the scene; yet I might not show the slightest trace of emotion." However, when observing his Jewish inmates similarly showing little emotion, even when leading others to the gas chambers, he presumed that their stoicism reflected an uncaring "racial characteristic." He was stoic because of the demands of the situation, they because of their callous dispositions.

Höss exhibited what social psychologists know as the "fundamental attribution error." A classic experiment by David Napolitan and George Goethals illustrates the phenomenon. The researchers had college students talk individually with a young woman who, in accordance with the researchers' instructions, acted either aloof and critical or warm and friendly. Beforehand, they informed half of the students that the woman had been instructed to act in a given way (either friendly or aloof). They told the other half that she was acting spontaneously. The effect of being informed that the woman was just playing a role? Nil. If she acted friendly, they inferred that she really was a warm person. If she acted unfriendly, they inferred that she really was a cold person. They discounted the situation that mandated her behavior and instead attributed her warmth or coldness to her inner disposition—in other words, they made the fundamental attribution error.

In another classic experiment, people's knowing that a debater had been *assigned* a pro- or anti-Castro position did not prevent their attributing corresponding attitudes to the debater. They seemed to think, "Yeah, I know he was assigned that position, but I think he really believes it."

Observing Cinderella cowering in her oppressive home, her family and neighbors infer that she is timid; dancing with her at the ball, the prince perceives a suave, glamorous woman. Cinderella knows better: depending on the situation, she is both. This bias—to underestimate the situation and overestimate inner dispositions when explaining others' behavior—is almost irresistible, especially for those of us socialized in individualist western countries. I recall being shocked when meeting a student actor who had convincingly played a bitter old woman. I had assumed that this unfortunate young woman had been typecast, but she was, I discovered, a delightful person. (I failed to attribute her play behavior to her assigned role.) Leonard Nimoy of *Star Trek* fame understands. He titled one of his books *I Am Not Spock*.

Everyday examples of the fundamental attribution error abound. I used to think that only introverts signed up for my 8:30 a.m. classes, when glassy stares would greet me each morning, and that the bubbly extraverts gravitated to the 7 p.m. class, which felt like party time. Now I see that I was committing the fundamental attribution error; I attributed to their dispositions what I should have attributed to their situations. Occasionally I read of police breaking up campus bashes and invariably wonder who those students are. Never any of mine, I am always sure; in class and in my office, they all seem so sober and sensible.

Students, in turn, may assume that professors are all outgoing because they see us in class situations that require us to act that way. Catch us in a different situation, hiding in the corner at a party, perhaps, and we seem less professorial. Outside their assigned roles, presidents seem less presidential, judges less judicious, and servants less servile. We professors, seeing ourselves in varied situations, are less inclined to think ourselves extraverts and more inclined to say, "Me, outgoing? Well, it all depends on the situation. In class, yes; at conventions, I'm rather bashful." And if you think we're smart because we so often know the answers, remember that in class *we* get to choose the topic and ask the questions. Put us in a different situation and we may seem clueless. In quiz-game experiments, those randomly assigned to ask the questions seem smarter than those assigned to play contestant. Even Regis Philbin might seem dim-witted if he were sitting in the other chair.

When the situation demands it, villains can act pleasant and ordinary people can behave like villains. After spending less than two hours with Russian President Vladimir Putin, George W. Bush thought he had the Russian leader all sized up. "I looked the man in the eye," President Bush reported. "I found him to be very straightforward and trustworthy. . . . He loves his family. We share a lot of values." Putin, as *Washington Post* writer Richard Cohen noted, is a "trained liar"—a former KGB agent who headed his country's domestic intelligence service and who has restricted civil liberties, tapped telephones, and prosecuted academics on sham charges as in the communist days of old. On the other side of the coin is Stanley Milgram's famous experiment, in which subjects were instructed to give apparently traumatizing electric shocks to an innocent person. Nearly two-thirds of them complied with the researcher's instructions, despite the (feigned) screams of the person supposedly receiving the shocks.

Though we fail to take the power of the situation into account in judging the behavior of others, we tend to make the opposite error in explaining our own behavior. If *I'm* crabby it's because I've had a rotten day; if *you're* crabby, it's because of your rotten disposition. Indeed, when explaining ourselves, we typically use action verbs ("I get annoyed when . . ."). Referring to someone else, we more often describe what the person *is* ("He can be nasty"). In court, the defendant may argue, "I was a victim of the situation. Under the circumstance anyone would have done the same." "No," the prosecution replies, "You're to blame. You chose to do this."

Why are we so vulnerable to the fundamental attribution error? It's because, in part, we find explanations wherever we focus our attention. Where we're looking, we instantly and effortlessly see causes. When *we're* doing something, our attention focuses on the situation to which we're reacting. When we're observing the actions of others, we focus on *them.* Reverse the perspectives of actor and observer—have each view a videotape replay from the other's perspective—and the explanations get reversed. By seeing the world through others' eyes, we better appreciate their situation. By seeing ourselves as others do, we better appreciate our own peculiar personality. The passage of time can also cause perspectives to change. When we are looking back, our focus may shift and enable us to become more empathic, more understanding of another's difficult situation. Seeing ourselves in life's rear-view mirror, we may be able to acknowledge that "yes, I have been rather a jerk."

ILLUSORY CORRELATION

Imagine yourself participating in a pioneering study of how people associate events. Psychologists William Ward and Herbert Jenkins show you the results of a hypothetical fifty-day cloud seeding experiment. They tell you for each day whether clouds were seeded and whether it rained. The information is a random mix: sometimes it rained after seeding, sometimes not. If you *believe* that cloud seeding works, might you be more likely to notice and recall days with both seeding and rain? In Ward and Jenkins' experiment, and in many others since, people have become convinced that they really did see precisely what they expected. An overstated Chinese proverb has the idea: "Two-thirds of what we see is behind our eyes."

"Illusory correlations"—perceiving relationships where none exist—help explain many a superstition, such as the presumption that more babies are born when the moon is full or that infertile couples who adopt become more likely to conceive. Salient coincidences, such as those who conceive after adopting, capture our attention. We focus on them and are less likely to notice what's equally relevant to assessing correlation—those who adopt and never conceive, those who conceive without adopting, and those who neither adopt nor conceive. Only when given all this information can we discern whether parents who adopt have elevated conception rates.

Such illusory intuitions help explain why for so many years people believed (as many still do) that sugar made children hyperactive, that cell phones cause brain cancer, that getting cold and wet caused colds, and that weather changes trigger arthritis pain. Physician Donald Redelmeier, working with Amos Tversky, followed eighteen arthritis patients for fifteen months. The researchers recorded their subjects' pain reports, as well as each day's temperature, humidity, and barometric pressure. Despite patients' beliefs, the weather was uncorrelated with their discomfort, either on the same day or up to two days earlier or later. Shown columns of random numbers labeled "arthritis pain" and "barometric pressure," even college students saw an illusory correlation. We are, it seems, eager to detect patterns, even when they're not there.

Likewise, stories of positive-thinking people experiencing cancer remission impress those who believe that positive attitudes counter cancer. Emotions do, we now know, influence health. Mind and body are an integrated system. But to assess whether positive attitudes help defeat cancer we need four bits of information. We need to know how many positive and not-positive thinkers were and were not cured. Without all the data, positive examples tell us nothing about the actual attitudes-cancer correlation.

Shortly after I wrote this, a journalist called, seeking help with a story on why so many famous people (Bill Clinton, Hillary Clinton, Jimmy Carter) have embarrassing brothers. Do they? I responded. Or is our attention just drawn to the salient conjunctions of famous people and boorish brothers? Is boorishness less frequent among men with unfamous siblings, or just less memorable? If we easily deceive ourselves by intuitively seeing what is not there, the remedy is simple: Show me the evidence. Gather and present the comparison data.

Illusory correlations can also fuel misleading stereotypes. Stereotypes assume a correlation between group membership and individuals' characteristics ("Italians are emotional," "Jews are shrewd," "Accountants are perfectionists"). Even under the best of conditions, our attentiveness to unusual occurrences can lead our intuition astray.

Because we are sensitive to distinctive events, the co-occurrence of two distinctive events is especially noticeable. Thus Rupert Brown and Amanda Smith found that British faculty members overestimated the number of (relatively rare, though noticeable) female senior faculty at their university.

David Hamilton and Robert Gifford demonstrated illusory correlation in a classic experiment. They showed students slides on which various people, members of Group A or Group B, were said to have done something desirable or undesirable. For example, "John, a member of Group A, visited a sick friend in the hospital." Twice as many statements described members of Group A as Group B, but both groups did nine desirable acts for every four undesirable behaviors. Since both Group B and the undesirable acts were less frequent, their co-occurrence—for example, "Allen, a member of Group B, dented the fender of a parked car and didn't leave his name"—was an unusual combination that caught people's attention. The students therefore overestimated the frequency with which the "minority" group (B) acted undesirably and judged Group B more harshly.

Remember, Group B members actually committed undesirable acts in the same proportion as Group A members. Moreover, the students had no preexisting biases for or against Group B, and they received the information more systematically than daily experience ever offers it. Although researchers debate why it happens, they agree that illusory correlation helps fuel racial stereotypes.

The mass media reflect and feed this phenomenon. When former mental patients like Mark Chapman and John Hinckley, Jr., shoot John Lennon and President Reagan, respectively, the person's mental history commands attention. Assassins and mental hospitalization are both relatively infrequent, making the combination especially newsworthy. Such reporting adds to the illusory intuition of a large correlation between violent tendencies and mental hospitalization.

BELIEF PERSEVERANCE

"We hear and apprehend only what we already half know," commented Henry David Thoreau. Experiments suggest how right Thoreau was. In one experiment, students in favor of and opposed to capital punishment were shown the findings of two research studies, one confirming and the other disconfirming their preexisting beliefs about capital punishment's supposed deterrent effect. Both groups readily accepted the evidence that confirmed their view but sharply criticized the evidence that challenged it. The result: showing the two sides an *identical* body of mixed evidence increased their *disagreement*. In a follow-up study, pleas to be as *"objective* and *unbiased* as possible" did nothing to reduce the biased evaluation of evidence. Once a belief forms, we filter information in ways that sustain it.

While watching presidential debates, have you not similarly come away more convinced than ever of your candidate's virtues? By nearly a 10-to-1 margin, those already favoring one candidate have perceived that candidate as having won the debate. Most people also find the arguments supporting their views to be more persuasive and thus, after the debate, are even more convinced of their predebate preference.

In human relationships, viewing others through the lens of our expectations can have self-fulfilling effects. In a now-classic study of "behavioral confirmation," social psychologists Mark Snyder, Elizabeth Tanke, and Ellen Berscheid had University of Minnesota men students talk by phone with women they thought (from having been shown a picture) were either attractive or unattractive. Analysis of the women's part of the conversations revealed that the supposedly attractive women spoke more warmly than the supposedly unattractive women. The men's erroneous beliefs had become a self-fulfilling prophecy by leading them to act in a way that influenced the women to fulfill their expectation that beautiful people are desirable. Other experiments show that if we think someone likes us, we may treat them in ways that indeed make them like us. Assume someone is nice or good or smart, and they may confirm your beliefs.

We also actively seek information that confirms our ideas, a phenomenon known as "confirmation bias." Peter Wason demonstrated our preference for confirmation bias in a famous experiment with British university students. He gave students the three-number sequence 2–4–6 and asked them to guess the rule he'd used to devise the series. First, however, he invited them to test their hunches by generating their own three-number sequences. Each time Wason told them whether their sets conformed to his rule. (Stop: If Wason walked in on you right now, what three numbers might you try out on him? If he answered "yes," what additional three numbers might you put to him?) Once they had tested enough to feel certain they understood the rule, they were to announce it.

The result? Often wrong but seldom in doubt. Only one in five of these confident people correctly discerned the rule, which was simply any three ascending numbers. Typically, Wason's students formed a wrong idea ("counting by two's?") and then searched only for confirming evidence, for example by testing 6–8–10, 31–33–35, and so forth. (Perhaps you, too, would have tested your hunch by seeking to confirm rather than disconfirm it?) Experiments on our preference for belief-confirming evidence would not have surprised Francis Bacon, whose 1620 *Novum Organum* anticipated our modern understanding of the limits of intuition: "The human understanding, when a proposition has been once laid down . . . forces everything else to add fresh support and confirmation."

Try another of Wason's classic little problems, one that has been the subject of much research and debate: Which cards must you turn over to determine whether this rule is true or false: "If there is a vowel on one side, then there is an even number on the other side."

Like everyone else responding to this problem, you probably first wanted to turn over the A. So far, so good. Some stop there, but we need to turn over one more card. Most folks, seeking to confirm the rule, want next to turn over the 2. But if there's a consonant on the other side, this card would be irrelevant to the rule ("If there is a *vowel* on one side . . ."). Only 4 percent of people correctly turn over the 7. (If there's a vowel on the other side, the rule is false; if not, it's irrelevant.) Our confirmation bias on these tasks suggests that natural human reasoning is flawed, or at least better suited to assessing probabilities than to executing logic.

What if our initial intuition or belief is disconfirmed, even shown to be utterly groundless? What if its basis is demolished? Still, the belief may survive. In another provocative experiment, Craig Anderson, Mark Lepper, and Lee Ross asked people to consider whether risk-taking or caution makes for a better firefighter. Then they told half the people about a risk taker who was an excellent firefighter and about a cautious person who was a mediocre firefighter. Given these stories, the participants surmised that risk takers tend to be better firefighters. Asked to explain why, one person reasoned that "risk takers are braver." Other participants, given two cases suggesting the opposite conclusion, were more likely to explain that "cautious people think before they act. They're less likely to make foolish mistakes."

The researchers then demolished the foundation for the beliefs by truthfully disclosing that the cases were simply made up for the experiment. Did pulling the legs out from under their new belief erase it? Not by much, because the participants still retained their explanations for why it *might* be true. The evidence was gone but their theory survived, and thus they walked away from the experiment continuing to believe that risk takers (or cautious people) really do make better firefighters.

These disturbing studies don't show that we never change our belief. Rather, they show that the more we examine our intuitions and beliefs and explain how they *might* be true, the more closed we become to challenging information. Once beliefs form it can take more compelling evidence to change them than it did to create them. Once we consider why O. J. Simpson was (or wasn't) guilty, once we explain why another country is hostile (or friendly), once we form a philosophy that justifies our theism (or atheism), we're inclined to welcome confirming evidence and to discount contrary evidence. Beliefs therefore persevere. "To begin with," said Freud, "it was only tentatively that I put forward the views I have developed . . . but in the course of time they have gained such a hold upon me that I can no longer think in any other way."

Is there a remedy for this "belief perseverance"—for the resilience of a belief even when its foundation is discredited? There is: *explain the opposite*. Imagining and explaining why an opposite theory might be true—why a cautious rather than risk-taking person might be a better firefighter—reduce or eliminate belief perseverance. To open people to a different idea, don't just argue your point. Instead, get them to imagine why someone else might hold an opposite view. Indeed, mindful of our fallibility, perhaps we would all do well to recall Oliver Cromwell's 1650 plea to the Church of Scotland: "I beseech ye in the bowels of Christ, consider that ye may be mistaken."

HEURISTICS: FAST AND FRUGAL THINKING

Each day we make countless instant decisions on the fly. Will I need an umbrella? Is that unkempt person someone I should worry about? Am I safer if driving or flying to Chicago? Usually, we just follow our intuition. After interviewing government, business, and education policymakers, the late social psychologist Irving Janis concluded that they, too, "often do not use a reflective problem-solving approach. How do they usually arrive at their decisions? If you ask, they are likely to tell you . . . they do it mostly by the *seat of their pants.*"

It's little wonder, say evolutionary psychologists. Our distant ancestors evolved thinking strategies that helped them gather fruit, survive, and reproduce. They (and we) had minds designed to instantly decide whether there might be a lion behind those rustling leaves, or just a bird. The mind works "to do or die, not to reason or to know why," observes Robert Ornstein. It was never developed to intuit stock market fluctuations, optimum welfare policies, or the relative safety of driving versus flying. Jumping quickly to conclusions may therefore work better in the situations that our species has come from than those it's now in.

Many of our seat-of-the-pants decisions are facilitated by the mind's "heuristics"—simple rules in our cognitive toolbox for making what Berlin psychologists Gerd Gigerenzer and Peter Todd call the "fast and frugal" decisions that make us intuitively smart. Others might instead call heuristics the "quick and dirty" mental shortcuts that sometimes err. Most, however, would agree that heuristics are like perceptual cues that usually work well but occasionally trigger illusions or misperceptions. Our brains intuitively assume that fuzzy-seeming objects are farther away than clear objects, and usually they are. But on a foggy morning that car ahead may be closer than it looks.

The representativeness heuristic. Some more fun and games:

- A stranger tells you about someone who is short, slim, and likes to read poetry, and then asks you to guess whether this person is more likely an Ivy League classics professor or a truck driver. Let you intuition guide you: which would be the better guess?
- Here's a description of someone that University of Oregon students were told was drawn at random from a sample of thirty engineers and seventy lawyers: "Twice divorced, Frank spends most of his free time hanging around the country club. His clubhouse bar conversations often center around his regrets at having tried to follow his esteemed father's footsteps. The long hours he had spent at academic drudgery would have been better invested in learning how to be less quarrelsome in his relations with other people." *Question:* What is the probability that Frank is a lawyer rather than an engineer?
- Finally, consider Linda, who is thirty-one, single, outspoken, and very bright. She majored in philosophy in college. As a student she was deeply concerned with discrimination and other social issues, and she participated in antinuclear demonstrations. Based on this description which would you say is most likely?
  a) that Linda is an insurance salesperson
  b) that Linda is a bank teller
  c) that Linda is a bank teller and active in the feminist movement

We use the "representativeness heuristic" when we judge the likelihood of something in terms of how well it represents, or matches, a particular prototype. If you are like most folks, you answered "professor" to the first question, because this person seems more *representative* of—better fits your prototypical image of—classics professors than of truck drivers. If so, the heuristic enabled you to make a fast and frugal snap judgment. But if it led you to ignore other relevant information, such as the total number of classics professors and truck drivers, it may have also been quick and dirty. When I have helped people think more deeply about this question, their reasoning usually leads them to an answer that contradicts their earlier intuition. My questioning goes like this:

> *Question:* First, let's figure out how many professors fit the description. How many Ivy League universities do you suppose there are?
>
> *Answer:* Oh, about ten, I suppose.
>
> *Question:* How many classics professors would you guess there are at each?
>
> *Answer:* Maybe four.
>
> *Question:* Okay, that's forty Ivy League classics professors. What fraction of these are short and slim?
>
> *Answer:* Let's say half.
>
> *Question:* And, of these twenty, how many like to read poetry?
>
> *Answer:* I'd say half—ten professors.
>
> *Question:* Okay, now let's figure how many truck drivers fit the description. How many truck drivers do you suppose there are?
>
> *Answer:* Maybe 400,000.
>
> *Question:* What fraction are short and slim?
>
> *Answer:* Not many—perhaps 1 in 8.
>
> *Question:* Of these 50,000, what percentage like to read poetry?
>
> *Answer:* Truck drivers who like poetry? Maybe 1 in 100—oh, oh, I can see where this is going—that leaves me with 500 short, slim, poetry-reading truck drivers.
>
> *Question:* Yup. So, although the person I've described may be much more representative of classics professors than of truck drivers, this person is still (even if we accept your stereotypes) fifty times more likely to be a truck driver than a classics professor.

Ruth Beyth-Marom and Shlomit Dekel offer a variant of this question that also makes an effective class demonstration: "Judy is a beautiful young woman. She takes care of herself and her figure is slim and sexy. She always wears fashionable clothes and is frequently seen in beauty parlors, coffee houses, and clothing boutiques. What is the probability that Judy is a fashion model?" Beyth-Marom and Dekel report that a typical answer is about "seventy percent." However, when other students are asked what is the probability that she is an actress or a cosmetics distributor or a salesperson in a boutique, they, too, give high probabilities. Very soon the sum of the probabilities, all distorted by the representativeness heuristic (with disregard for base rate populations of models, acting professionals, and so forth), far exceed 100 percent. Whoops. Something is awry, the students quickly realize.

Asked to guess Frank's occupation, the University of Oregon students surmised he was about 80 percent likely to be a lawyer rather than an engineer. I suspect something like that was true of you as well, and that's entirely reasonable. But how do you suppose their estimates changed when the researchers, Baruch Fischhoff and Maya Bar-Hillel, changed the sample to say that 70 percent were engineers? Not in the slightest. In their minds, the "base rate" of engineers and lawyers didn't matter, because Frank was more *representative* of lawyers, and to them that was all that mattered.

On the classic "Linda problem," first offered by the late Amos Tversky and Daniel Kahneman, most people think c (feminist bank teller) is most likely, because Linda represents their image of feminists. But a moment's reflection tells us that our heuristics-guided intuition has once again led us astray. Is there a better chance that Linda is *both* a bank teller *and* a feminist than that she's a bank teller, whether feminist or not? (All feminist bank tellers are bank tellers! And might not at least a few other bank tellers have been activist philosophy majors?) As Tversky and Kahneman remind us, the conjunction of two events can't be more likely than either event alone.*
The irrationality of most people's responses, note Seymour Epstein and his colleagues from their studies, "suggests that people are even more nonrational than there had been previous reason to suspect."

*If you don't see the illogic of answering c, consider a parallel finding: Many people think there are more seven-letter words ending in -ing than with i as the fifth letter. Not so! Seven-letter words ending in -ing are easier to imagine ("banking," "morning," etc.), but every such word *has* an i as the fifth letter, as do some other words (check this chapter's title, for one).

Even when rational solutions are accessible, they note, we seem to prefer intuitive heuristics.

The availability heuristic. Question time again: 1) In English words, does *k* appear more often as the first or third letter? 2) Which has more people—Cuba or Venezuela? You can't mentally retrieve and search all the books, articles, billboards, and labels you've ever read, and you can't count the people, so just let your fast and frugal intuition be your guide.

For most people, words beginning with *k* come more readily to mind, and so they assume that *k* occurs more frequently in the first position. Actually, *k* appears two to three times more often in the third position. (So far in this chapter, words such as *knowing, key,* and *Kalamazoo* are outnumbered fifty-one to fifteen by words such as *take, likely,* and *ask.*) Ergo, our use of the "availability heuristic"—judging the likelihood of things by their availability in memory—has produced an intuitive error. Likewise, many people find Cuba and Cubans easier to picture, and so they guess there are more Cubans. Actually, the 24 million people in Venezuela are double the 12 million folks in Cuba.

The availability heuristic is easy to demonstrate in both the classroom and laboratory. In one study, Stuart McKelvie read a list of famous people of one sex (Mother Teresa, Jane Fonda, Tina Turner) intermixed with an equal-size list of unfamous people of the other sex (Donald Scarr, William Wood, Mel Jasper). Later he asked them how many men's and women's names they had seen. The gender of the famous names was more available to recall and therefore seemed more frequent.

Often, events that come quickly to mind *are* more common. But not always, and the occasional misjudgments are not always cute and harmless. Vivid, easy-to-imagine events seem more likely than harder-to-picture events that actually occur more often. We fear homicide more than pneumonia, which actually kills three times as many people. When Ruth Hamill and her co-workers presented folks with a single vivid but atypical welfare abuse case (in which a long-term recipient had several unruly children sired by different men) it did more to shape opinions of welfare recipients than did statistical evidence indicating a different reality. Images feed beliefs.

Fictional happenings in novels, television, and films also leave images that later penetrate our judgments. Oliver Wendell Holmes, Jr., was right: "Most people reason dramatically, not quantitatively." Because we tend to accept as real the images seared in our minds, a powerful story or picture can be worth a thousand numbers. Thanks to the availability heuristic, people are remarkably quick to infer general truth from a vivid (and therefore readily available) narrative. After hearing and reading news stories of rapes, robberies, and beatings (but without any data to indicate whether these were atypical or not), nine out of ten Canadians overestimated—usually by a considerable margin—the percentage of crimes that involve violence. No wonder congressional lobbyists depend more on horror stories told at hearings than on presenting more representative but boring statistics. As U.S. trade office executive Charlene Barshefsky remarked, "All the statistics in the world about export-related jobs don't offset one picture of a closed factory whose loss is blamed on foreign competition."

At a meeting to plan a church survey, my friend Sandy is skeptical: "I don't get much from statistics. You can say anything with statistics. I'm more impressed by real-life stories." Yes, I reply, stories *are* powerful. Stories form the heart of our memories and our collective consciousness. "But the trouble with any story, or anecdote, is that it may be atypical. Don't think statistics, think people, because behind those numbers are all our people, each one given a voice."

We social scientists are continually challenged by the power of vivid, available stories ("Yes, but I know a person who . . ."). In a radio interview, developmental psychologist Sandra Scarr recalls describing eight research studies summarizing evidence from thousands of families in four countries, all indicating that mothers' employment does not harm children. On the other NPR microphone was an author offering "intuitive evidence" by recounting several anecdotes of family stress in homes of working mothers. For the show's host and callers, the evidence and the stories were, at best, a draw. And so it goes, as the slaughter of teens at Columbine High School led people to believe that teen violence was exploding during the late 1990s, when actually it was subsiding (although still well above a half century earlier). Moreover, while the horror of twelve teens dead caused Americans to wonder "What has happened to America?" we could ask that question daily, given that twelve American children dead by gunshot represents an average day. In the past two decades, some 80,000 American children have been killed by firearms. Should we weep for the great loss of Cassie Bernall and her friends in the Columbine school library but not for the "mere statistics"—the other 79,988 dead kids? Perhaps Bertrand Russell was right to suggest that "The mark of a civilized human is the ability to look at a column of numbers, and weep."

Acknowledging the power of stories and the truth of numbers, consider finally, that little girl, Jessica McClure, who in 1987 fell into a Texas well. During her three-day entrapment, hundreds of millions of people worldwide were riveted on Jessica and her rescue. We worried: would a child's life be lost? During those same three days, more than 100,000 invisible children—a mere column of numbers on some World Health Organization spreadsheet—died of preventable starvation, diarrhea, and disease. One hundred thousand Jessica McClures died, and few of us wept. Fundraisers for the world's sick and hungry understand. Don't solicit for something abstract, like millions of starving people. People won't weep over that. Instead tell the story of one real, hungry child.

FRAMING

Another check on our rationality asks whether the same question, framed in two different but logically identical ways, elicits the same answer. Dr. Jones tells his patient, John, that 10 percent of people die while undergoing a contemplated surgery. Meanwhile, down the hall, Dr. Smith is telling her patient, Joan, that while undergoing that surgery 90 percent survive. Given the same information, will John and Joan be equally open to the surgery? If they react like participants in research studies, John will intuitively be more apprehensive after learning that 10 percent *die*. Even doctors have been found more likely to recommend an operation with a 93 percent survival rate than a 7 percent mortality rate.

We've long known that the wording of survey questions can influence answers. In one poll, 23 percent of Americans thought their government was overspending on "assistance to the poor." But 53 percent thought the government was overspending on "welfare." Most people favor cutting "foreign aid" and increasing spending "to help hungry people in other nations." "Forbidding" something may be the same as "not allowing" it. But in 1940, 54 percent of Americans said we should "forbid" anti-democracy speeches, while 75 percent said we should "not allow" them.

Do these wordings have subtly different meanings? In more recent experiments on the "framing effect," alternate wordings are synonymous. Consumers are intuitively more accepting of ground beef that is "75 percent lean" rather than "25 percent fat." People express more surprise when a "1 in 20" event occurs than when an equivalent "10 in 200" event occurs, and they would rather pay money for their chance on a 10 in 100 draw than on a 1 in 10 draw. Nine in ten collegians rate a condom as effective if it has a "95 percent success rate" in stopping HIV transmission; but only 4 in 10 rate it effective, given its "5 percent failure rate."

Have you noticed how framing affects everyday consumer behavior? Some stores (and most airlines) put huge markups on their "regular" prices so they can offer huge savings on their frequent "sale prices." Store X's $200 CD player marked down from $300 can seem like a better deal than Store Y's same item regularly priced at $200. People may accept a 5 percent pay raise during a time of 12 percent inflation, yet protest if given a 7 percent pay cut during a time of zero inflation. My dentist doesn't charge extra if we pay later; she offers a 5 percent discount for immediate cash payment. She is smart enough to understand that a fee framed as a forfeited discount intuitively irritates us less than one framed as a surcharge, though they add up to the same thing.

Our flip-flopping judgments remind us again of the limits of our intuition. Intuitive responses are fast and frugal, but sometimes irrational. People who understand the power of framing can therefore use it to influence decisions. A young monk found himself rebuffed when he asked if he could smoke while he prayed. Ask a different question, advised an understanding friend. Ask if you can pray while you smoke.

EVIDENCE OF INTUITION'S POWERS

- *blindsight* and *prosopagnosia*—brain-damaged persons' "sight unseen" as their bodies react to things and faces not consciously recognized
- *everyday perception*—the instant parallel processing and integration of complex information streams
- *automatic processing*—the cognitive autopilot that guides us through most of life
- *young children's intuitive learning*—of language and physics
- *right-brain thinking*—split-brain persons displaying knowledge they cannot verbalize
- *implicit memory*—learning *how* to do something without knowing *that* one knows
- *divided attention* and *priming*—unattended information processed by the mind's downstairs radar watchers
- *thin slices*—detecting traits from mere seconds of behavior
- *dual attitude system*—as we have two ways of knowing (unconscious and conscious)

and two ways of remembering (implicit and explicit), we also have gut-level and rational attitude responses
- *social and emotional intelligence*—the intuitive know-how to comprehend and manage ourselves in social situations and to perceive and express emotions
- *the wisdom of the body*—when instant responses are needed, the brain's emotional pathways bypass the cortex; hunches sometimes precede rational understanding
- *social intuitions*—our effortless spontaneous trait inferences, moral intuitions, contagious moods, and empathic accuracy
- *intuitive expertise*—phenomena of nonconscious learning, expert learning, tacit understandings, and physical genius
- *creativity*—the sometimes spontaneous appearance of novel and valuable ideas
- *heuristics*—those mental shortcuts or rules of thumb, that normally serve us well enough

INTUITION'S DOZEN DEADLY SINS

- *memory construction—* influenced by our present moods and by misinformation, we may form false memories and offer dubious testimonials
- *misreading our own minds—* often we don't know why we do what we do
- *mispredicting our own feelings—*we badly mispredict the intensity and duration of our emotions
- *mispredicting our own behavior—*our intuitive self-predictions often go astray
- *hindsight bias—*looking back on events, we falsely surmise that we knew it all along
- *self-serving bias—*in various ways we exhibit inflated self-assessments
- *overconfidence—*our intuitive assessments of our own knowledge are routinely more confident than correct

- *fundamental attribution error—*overly attributing others' behavior to their dispositions by discounting unnoticed situational forces
- *belief perseverance* and *confirmation bias—*thanks partly to our preference for confirming information, beliefs are often resilient, even after their foundation is discredited
- *representativeness* and *availability—*fast and frugal heuristics become quick and dirty when leading us into illogical and incorrect judgments
- *framing—*judgments flip-flop depending on how the same issue or information is posed
- *illusory correlation—* intuitively perceiving relationships where none exist

THE POWERS AND PERILS OF INTUITION

Much more could be said about intuition's powers and pitfalls. But these six chapters have been enough, I trust, to authenticate two huge ideas from contemporary psychological science—that, more than we've realized, *our lives are guided by subterranean intuitive thinking* and that *our intuitions, though speedily efficient, often err in ways we need to understand.* Ergo, intuition—our capacity for di-

rect, immediate knowledge prior to rational analysis—has both surprising potency and surprising perils. The human mind has offered us remarkable displays of its subtle, ineffable powers, but also of why Madeline L'Engle was right when she said, "The naked intellect is an extraordinarily inaccurate instrument."

Respecting both the powers and perils of our inner knowing, what then shall we conclude? When forming judgments and making decisions—in business, politics, sports, religion, and other everyday realms—discerning people will welcome the powers of their gut wisdom yet know when to restrain it with rational, reality-based, critical thinking. Most of the time, our autopilot's perceptions and intuitions are good enough, and they probably exist because they enabled our ancestors to survive and reproduce. But sometimes in the modern world accuracy really matters. When it does, reason should rule. The Statue of Liberty holds up the torch of reason. Freedom thrives under reason.

As we next evaluate popular claims about intuition in sports, the professions, investing, risk assessment, gambling, and spirituality, let us remember: wisdom comes both from illusions lost and knowledge gained. "To free a man of error is to give, not to take away," said Schopenhauer. "Knowledge that a thing is false is a truth." From sports to spirituality, sifting intuition's powers from its perils will prepare us to think and act smarter.

By checking our intuitions—our hunches, our gut feelings, our voices within—against available evidence we *can* think smarter. In the chapters to come we will sift reality from illusion as we put testable beliefs to the test. If they find support, so much the better for them. If they crash against a wall of observation, so much the worse for them.

Practical Intuition

Sports Intuition

The human understanding supposes a greater degree of order . . .
in things than it really finds.
—*Francis Bacon,* Novum Organum, *1620*

In sports, as in other realms of life, weird things happen. Random events sometimes produce bizarre, unforgettable results.

- Eight golfers witnessed Todd Obuchowski's hole-in-one on the Beaver Brook golf course in Massachusetts. His shot soared over the green, onto a highway, hit a passing Toyota, and ricocheted back to the green and into the cup.
- In July 2000, David Howard of Brookings, South Dakota, an average golfer (45 for nine holes) and 210 bowler, sank his first hole-in-one and then, hours later, bowled a 300 game.
- In August 2001, Scott Hatteberg of the Boston Red Sox hit into a rare triple play. On his next at-bat he redeemed himself with a grand slam.
- Ron Vachon was sitting among thousands of fans at a September 1990 baseball game in Boston when Oakland A's outfielder Rickey Henderson hit two foul balls right to him, on successive pitches. (He dropped them both.)

That Ron Vachon should be hit two foul balls on successive pitches was incredibly unlikely. That something like this would sometime happen in some sport was not. An event that happens to but one in a billion people in a day happens 2,000 times a year to someone. That much we can understand without inventing needless explanations. The problem comes with curiously streaky patterns, which seduce us into perceiving order and phenomena that do not exist.

Nature abhors a vacuum, human nature abhors chaos. Show us randomness and we will find order, pattern, clusters, and streaks. "The tendency to impute order to ambiguous stimuli is simply built into the cognitive machinery we use to apprehend the world," notes Thomas Gilovich in *How We Know What Isn't So*. That's the up side of our yen for order—our skill at detecting real patterns, making connections, forming scientific theories. But there's a down side as well. It shows up in our illusory coherence, superstition, and folly. The last is demonstrably true of sports fans, coaches, players, and announcers. We may know that basketball players sometimes get in a "zone," and that every baseball batter endures slumps and enjoys streaks. We know to pass to the shooting guard with the hot hand, and to pitch around the second baseman with the hot bat. But, surprise! We may be misinterpreting player streaks. To see why, consider the realities of randomness.

RANDOM SEQUENCES ARE OFTEN STREAKY

The key to more discerning sports intuition is understanding this simple fact of life: Random sequences seldom look random, because they contain more streaks than people expect. Many, many years ago, some people excelled at perceiving rainfall patterns, game-at-the-water-hole patterns, crop cycle patterns. We are the descendants of these skilled pattern-detectors. True to our legacy, we look for order, for meaningful patterns—even in random data.

Consider a random coin flip: If someone flipped a coin six times, which of the following sequences of heads (H) and tails (T) would seem most likely: HHHTTT or HTTHTH or HHHHHH?

Daniel Kahneman and Amos Tversky report that most people believe HTTHTH would be the most likely random sequence. (Ask someone to predict six coin tosses and they will likely tell you a sequence like this.) Actually, all are equally likely (or, you might say, equally unlikely). To demonstrate this phenomenon for myself (as you can do), I flipped a coin fifty-one times, with these results: HTTTHHHHTTTTTHHTTHTTTHHTTTHTTTTHTH**TTTTTTTHTTTHT**H**HHHHTHH**TTTT Looking over the sequence, patterns jump out: Underlined tosses 10 to 22 provided an almost perfect pattern of pairs of tails followed by pairs of heads. On the boldfaced tosses, 30 to 38, I had a "cold hand," with only one head in nine tosses. But my fortunes shortly thereafter reversed with a hot hand—six heads out of seven tosses.

Why these patterns? Was I exercising paranormal control over my coin? Did I snap out of my tails funk and get in a heads groove? No such explanations are needed, for *these are the sorts of streaks found in any random sequence.* Comparing each toss outcome to the next, twenty-four of the fifty comparisons yielded a changed result—just the sort of near 50 percent alternation we expect from coin tossing. Despite the seeming patterns in these data, the outcome of one toss gives no clue to the outcome of the next toss.

The "Bible code" craze of the late 1990s offers an example of what *Celestine Prophecy* author James Redfield called "seemingly 'Chance Coincidences'—strange occurrences that feel like they were meant to happen." If one turns the Hebrew text into a long string of letters minus spaces, computers can then find certain words turning up, formed of every nth letter going vertically, horizontally, or diagonally. For example, the letters spelling the name of Israel's assassinated prime minister, Yitzhak Rabin, were found close to "assassination." After the fact, however, one can find all sorts of words (unspecified in advance) seemingly encoded in all kinds of text. One NBA basketball fan, shortly before the Chicago Bulls won the 1998 title, used the "equidistant letter sequence" technique and found "Chicago" in *War and Peace.* Shall we say the "Tolstoy code" predicted the Bulls' sixth championship? Given enough random strings of letters tracked in enough directions, some words—some patterns—will become apparent.

Consider: Which of these patterns on a ten-by-ten grid appears to offer the most random placement of its fifty white and fifty black cells?

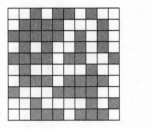 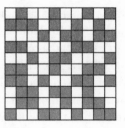

In a random pattern, the color of any cell would give us no clue to the color of the next one. It would be a toss-up. That's true of the pattern on the *left*. The right-hand pattern *looks* more random to most people, report Ruma Falk and Clifford Konold. But it's not, because it has a too-high (63 percent) rate of color change when moving either vertically or horizontally. The more complex and difficult to remember a pattern is, the more random people think it is. When attempting to generate random sequences, people overproduce alternations and underproduce the streaks and clusters that we see on the left.

A mathematician friend of mine once tried to create a brick wall inside her home using a table of random numbers to place the red, white, and black bricks. Alas, she had to discard the table, because she found herself with a big area with nothing but black bricks. The random placement just didn't look random.

Wartime Londoners experienced this tendency to see clusters in random patterns—and thus to think that the clusters were not really random. For example, seeing German bombs falling disproportionately in certain areas of the city prompted them to theorize that the working-class East Enders received more than their fair share because the Germans were trying to alienate the poor from the rich. After the war, a statistical analysis revealed merely a random bomb dispersion. The German V-1 buzz bombs and V-2 rocket bombs could find London but were just not accurate enough to spot particular areas.

More recently, Americans have suffered clusters of shark attacks and have found neighborhood clusters of cancer or leukemia. In one example—among thousands of clusters that have been reported to public health officials—a McFarland, California (population 6,400), woman, whose child developed cancer, found four other cases within a few blocks, and then doctors found six more cases. This led to lawsuits against the manufacturers of pesticides that were believed to have contaminated groundwater wells and to have caused the cancer. As miners stricken with black lung disease remind us, environments can be toxic. But to the disbelief of "stricken" communities, environmental causes have not been found to explain recent cancer clusters. California's chief environmental health investigator concluded that, given the many tens of thousands of cancers registered, some census tracts are bound to have random elevations. If yours does, he notes, "it almost certainly won't mean a thing."

My father once called from his Seattle retirement home, where about twenty-five people die each year. He was wondering about a curious phenomenon: "The deaths seem to come in bunches. Why is that?" How odd of God that folks should pass en masse.

The moral: More than we suppose, random sequences are streaky. And thanks to the nearly inevitable streaks in random sequences, we see order and pattern where there is none.

THE HOT HAND

Every basketball player, coach, and fan intuitively "knows" that players with the hot hand seldom miss and that those who are cold should hesitate to shoot. In their own words:

- "We see the guy with the hot hand, and Jeff had the hot hand," explained University of Kentucky coach Tubby Smith as his team set up Jeff Sheppard for three consecutive three-point shots that enabled Kentucky to advance to the 1998 NCAA championship game.
- "You never know who's going to be hot," explained North Carolina coach Sylvia Hatchell after her team defeated Alabama. "Today it was Juana, and I was telling our players to get her the ball. That's not good coaching—that's just common sense."
- "When a player's hot like that you wanna get him the ball and the kids did a good job of finding him," explained a local high school coach after his star's "simply unconscious" shooting.

- "You've got to find the guy with the hot hand, not the guy who hasn't hit a shot," explained our local sports columnist in criticizing Hope College's basketball coach after his point guard went 0-for-10 in an overtime loss to their archrival.
- Gym rats also routinely witness the hot hand phenomenon. Jay Parini, a Middlebury College English professor, sums up his noontime game strategy: "I try to work with my teammates, passing the ball to whoever has a hot hand that day."

These individuals speak for nearly all basketball junkies. When Thomas Gilovich, Robert Vallone, and Amos Tversky interviewed the Philadelphia 76ers, the players estimated that they were about 25 percent more likely to make a shot after they had just made one than after a miss. Nine of ten fans agreed that a player has a better chance of making a shot after just *making* two or three shots than after just missing two or three shots. Players therefore feed the one who's hot and coaches bench the one who's not.

But the facts reveal no hot hand phenomenon. When Gilovich and his collaborators studied detailed individual shooting records, from the 76ers, the Boston Celtics, the New Jersey Nets, the New York Knicks, and Cornell University's men's and women's teams, the hot hand phenomenon was nowhere to be found. Players were as likely to score after a miss as after a basket. If anything, there was a small tendency to *miss* after made shots. During one entire season, 76ers made 46 percent after making three in a row, 50 percent after making two, 51 percent after making one, 54 percent after missing one, 53 percent after missing two, and 56 percent after missing three in a row. (Given the opposite of a hot hand phenomenon, might we, in hindsight, theorize that after knocking down three baskets an emboldened player starts forcing shots? Or that the defense tightens?) The Gilovich group also analyzed two seasons of the Celtics' free throw statistics. After making a first free throw they made 75 percent on a second. After missing a first free throw they made 75 percent on a second. Celtics star Larry Bird made 88 percent of his free throws after making a free throw and 91 percent after missing. In the NBA's three-point shooting contests, psychologist Alan Reifman has likewise observed, players have been as likely to hit after a miss as after a hit.

Could it really be that nearly all players, coaches, and fans—after observing thousands of shot sequences—are deluded in believing that players are more likely to score after scoring and miss after missing? Yes, it really could be. And the reason is simple. They're not misperceiving streaks—basketball shooting *is* streaky—they are *misinterpreting* them. They're noticing the clusters, the streaks, that naturally appear in any random sequence and attributing them to a player's being "in a zone." They're like hospital workers who sometimes notice streaks of male or female births—like the twelve girls in a row born in Dansville, New York's hospital in August 1997—and attribute them to mysterious forces, such as moon phases during conception.* The streaks are real, the explanations are not.

Perhaps you can see the hot hand in one of the sequences of baskets made and missed below. Which of these samples of shots by 50 percent shooters (in these cases, 11 of 21 made) has outcomes most like what we would expect in a random sequence?

Player B, whose outcomes *look* more random to most people, actually has fewer streaks than expected. Chance shooting, like chance coin tossing, should produce a change in outcome about 50 percent of the time. But 70 percent of the time (14 out of 20) Player B's outcome

*Perhaps you also have noticed that boys or girls seem to run in some families. My next-door colleague comes from a family of eight boys and four girls, and these twelve siblings have produced twenty-eight boys and eight girls. Statistician Joseph Lee Rodgers was led to study this apparent phenomenon—which could, conceivably, have a biological basis—after his sister remarked that "Rodgers men produce boys." (Eight Rodgers men had produced twenty-one boys and three girls.) However, when Rodgers and Debby Doughty analyzed sex sequences in the children of 6,089 randomly sampled families, they found no clear evidence of sex bias. For example, among 132 four-child families that began with three children of the same sex, sixty-nine had a fourth child of that sex and a similar sixty-three had a child of the other sex. Since Rodgers' sister made her remark, the Rodgers men have had five more children, four of whom are girls.

changes on successive shots. Despite a 7-of-8 hot streak followed by a 1-of-6 cold streak, Player A is scoring more as we would expect from a 50 percent shooter; 10 times out of 20, Player A's next outcome changes.

Mathematicians have long argued about whether pi's digits form a true random sequence (new evidence suggests they may). Regardless, the sequence of even and odd numbers is, for our purposes, functionally random. Consider, then, the streaks that appear even in the digits of pi. Checking the first 1,254,543 digits of pi, I found the digit string of four of my five family members' birthdays. (If I go to the 131,564th decimal place, there begins my very own, 92042—a wink from the gods?*) Bruce Martin, a retired chemist having some retirement fun, notes that if we assign tails to the odd digits of 3.14159 . . . and heads to the even digits we get this sequence for the first one hundred decimal places:

THTTTHHTTTHTTTTHTHTHHHHHHHTTHTHTHTTTHHHHHTTTTHTTTTTTTTH
THHHTTHTHHTTHTHTHTHTHHHHHHHHHHHTTHHHHHTHHHTTHHTTTHHTT
Random sequences fluctuate, and these forty-nine tails and fifty-one heads are a tad streakier than usual, with fifty-seven repeating outcomes from one digit to the next. But that's all it takes to create dramatic streaks of eight consecutive tails and ten consecutive heads. If this were a basketball game, could you imagine the halftime commentary—including words of advice for coaches and players—after one player missed eight in a row and another made ten in a row? But for 50 percent shooters, or coin tossers, such streaks will happen. The Hope College player who went 0-for-10 in the big game was a 47 percent shooter.

To be sure, one can't prove that nonrandom streaks *never* occur. There may be days when particular players are ill or feeling on top of the world. But the cold facts about hot hands remain: in the sports

*To check for your birthday, visit www.facade.com/legacy/amiinpi. If you have a January to September birthday (taking five digits to express) you'll almost surely find it in the first million digits. Go to any pi digit and there's a 1 in 10 chance that it's the first digit of your birthday. There's a 1 in 100 chance that this and the next match your first two . . . and a 1 in 100,000 chance the five digits you'll find there will match your five (or a 1 in a million chance if you need six digits).

data examined, streaks happen about as often as we would expect. Most streaks therefore just don't need fancy explanations and shouldn't affect coaching to the extent they do.

Given these intuition-defying results, fans routinely protest: "Are you saying that basketball is just a game of chance—that skills, defense, emotion, and so forth don't matter—that people behave like tossed coins? Players *feel* the hot hand! Anyone can see it!"

I am saying nothing of the kind. All these things surely matter. Some players shoot better than others—Larry Bird's 90 percent free throw average testified to his skill—and all have better days and worse days for whatever reason. What the available data show, simply and clearly, is that what *doesn't* appear to predict the next shot outcome is the previous shot's outcome. In the absence of further data, which anyone is welcome to present, it would seem that the famed and influential hot hand myth is an illusion. Feeling "in a zone" appears more a result than a cause of baskets made.

Ah, but are there not some individual players who more than others get in a zone? Detroit Pistons fans will remember Vinnie "Microwave" Johnson, known as one of the NBA's premier streak shooters. During the 1987–88 season he took 20 percent of his team's next shots after missing the team's last shot, and 45 percent after making the team's last shot. Alas, although all this shooting after scoring increased his chances for baskets in bunches, he actually was no more likely to make a shot following a make than following a miss.

Still, basketball experts prefer to believe what their eyes seem to tell them—or, more precisely, what their intuition infers from what their eyes rightly tell them. When apprised of Gilovich's findings, Red Auerbach, the brains behind the onetime Celtic dynasty, replied, "Who is this guy? So he makes a study. I couldn't care less." After hearing CBS basketball commentator Billy Packer admonish college coaches to recognize the hot hand phenomenon, a friend of mine sent him my text synopsis of the apparent facts of life. Packer's reply: "There is and should be a pattern of who shoots, when he shoots, and how often he shoots, and that can and should vary by game to game situations. Please tell the stat man to get a life."*

---

*Credit Packer with consistency in his contempt for statistics. Three months

THE HOT BAT

Even if this stat man (and sports fan) has caused you to doubt the hot hand myth, you may be reassuring yourself that *teams* are streaky. During any season, a team will have times when its players are in a pitching or hitting slump, and then they'll snap out of it and go on a tear. In May 2001, baseball's perennial favorite losers, the Chicago Cubs, lost eight games in a row, and then promptly won the next thirteen.

Are team outcomes indeed streaky? Michigan State University psychologist Gordon Wood, another fan and stat man, wondered. So he collected the 1988 outcomes of all 160 or so games for each of the twenty-six major league baseball teams. Were teams indeed more at risk for another loss after a loss, and more victory prone when their confidence rose after a victory? Averaging across teams with data from more than 4,000 game sequences, what was the probability of a win after a loss? Fifty percent. And what was the probability of a win after a win? Fifty percent.

Wood did the same analysis for the eighty-two games played by each of twenty-five NBA teams during 1988–89 season. As we would expect, the league's top teams were more likely to win—whether playing after a win or a loss. But on average, how did teams fare after a win? They won almost exactly 50 percent. And after a loss? Again, 50 percent.

As shocking as these numbers are—no nonrandom streaks in team outcomes?—there surely are nonrandom hitting streaks by individual baseball players, yes? What's sure is that fans, players, managers, and announcers *think* there are. Listen to Cubs radio commentator Ron Santo:

- "Like anyone, when he gets hot, he stays hot—his home runs come in bunches" (referring to Sammy Sosa).

---

later he disputed TV ratings showing the NCAA women's tournament had outdrawn both a regular season men's game and the Bob Hope golf tournament: "The TV ratings are parallel to the SAT scores. They are both used by lazy people who don't have the time to talk about reality" ("Packer Irate," *USA Today*, April 4, 1995, p. 3C).

- After the Cubs pitcher threw a strike to Colorado's Todd Helton, with men on second and third: "Aw, they should just put him on. Helton has had eight hits in the last two days. He's red hot!"
- "Jeff Blauser has had three hits today. Do you think this might indicate he's going to get a hotter bat in the weeks to come, Ron?" "Yeah, I really think so. He's just waiting to break out."

Santo, if anyone, should know. While spending his adult lifetime playing and announcing baseball, he, like few others, has eyeballed the raw data. After viewing about 80 at-bats a game, 13,000 a year, more than a half million over his career, would his eyes deceive him? Are his intuitions about the hot bat not credible?

Several popular baseball myths have been tested and verified. Batters *do* average about 20 points higher (say, .280 rather than .260) when facing a pitcher of the opposite arm, 8 points higher when batting at home, and 123 points higher when ahead in the count rather than with two strikes. With a man on first and nobody out, the odds of scoring a single run *are* slightly increased (from .39 to .42) if the batter advances the runner with a sacrifice bunt (though the average net run production for the inning is reduced from .85 to .69 runs). And batters, like basketball players, *are* streaky. But more than we'd expect, given their season average? Should we expect that the last attempt, or the last few attempts, will predict the next outcome any better for Sammy Sosa than for Vinnie Johnson?

To find out, Indiana University statistician Christian Albright explored whether batting hot and cold streaks "occur more (or less) frequently than would be predicted by a probabilistic model of randomness." He pored over four seasons of major league player data, from 501 player seasons with more than 500 at-bats, noting the sequence of outs and hits (or, in a second analysis, of failures and successes, where a hit, walk, or sacrifice was defined as a success). Were batters more successful after a success the last time at bat? The last two times? The last three times? The last twenty times? A few players did exhibit more streakiness than expected during a given season, but this didn't carry over to other seasons, and it was offset by a few other players who exhibited more than expected stability. Overall, concluded Albright, "the behavior of all players examined, taken as a whole, does not differ significantly from what would be expected under a model of randomness." But don't expect Ron Santo to believe it.

Santo might take satisfaction, however, in another analysis, by sports statistician and consultant Scott Berry, who analyzed the distribution of home runs for eleven top home-run hitters during the great home-run-race season of 1998. As Santo sensed, Sammy Sosa's home runs *did* come more in bunches than expected for a random sequence. His cold start to the season was followed by his red hot June, when he hit a record twenty home runs. However, Sosa's streakiness was offset by Andres Galarraga's greater-than-expected consistency. For the other nine sluggers, the spread was in line with the statistics of randomness.

So, managers take note and players take heart: If your batting average or home-run production has slumped the last few games, it gives little or no clue to the odds of your getting a smash hit in the next at-bat. And remember, streaks will happen.

Enjoying some more retirement fun, Bruce Martin used pi's decimal digits to simulate random hitting streaks. To create a .300 hitter, he designated digits 0, 2, and 4 to hits and the other seven to outs. Sure enough, out of the first 100 decimal digits there are thirty hits and seventy outs. Dividing the 100 digits into successive groups of four creates twenty-five simulated games, including one three-hit game, four hitless games (three in succession during one short slump), and one thirteen-game hitting streak—a streak that arises from a mere random sequence of digits!

That does, however, leave unexplained what many regard as history's most improbable baseball achievement—Joe DiMaggio's 1941 fifty-six-game hitting streak. Given DiMaggio's 1941 .356 average and 3.9 at-bats per game (not counting walks and sacrifices), Iowa State University statistician Hal Stern calculated the odds of DiMaggio's having a 56-game streak in that 154-game season as 1 in 3,200. Broadening the question to "What is the probability that a single player of DiMaggio's ability would have a streak like that during his career of 1,736 games?" the odds improve to a still-unlikely 1 in 200. Stern also offers a still broader but unanswered question: "What is the probability that any player would have had a fifty-six-game hitting streak during the 100 years of recorded baseball history?" Or we could ask a still broader question: "What is the probability that somewhere in baseball's statistics we could find a highly improbable outcome such as the DiMaggio streak?" To paraphrase John Allen Paulos, "The most astonishingly incredible baseball probability imaginable would be the complete absence of all baseball improbabilities."

Although the unpredictability of outcomes makes sports both exciting and subject to superstition, be assured that basketball and baseball myths will survive this chapter. The hearty broth of streaky random sequences will continue to feed our interpretive minds. Thanks both to our preconceptions and the weird but natural clusters in random events, we will find patterns. We then will theorize *why* players exhibit streaks. "Some days a player is just in flow. The shooter is stroking it. A batter is in rhythm. The confidence is there." And as we noted previously, theories often survive the demolition of whatever evidence prompted them. It is easier to put an idea in someone's head than to get it out.

OTHER SPORTS INTUITIONS

Unpredictability, as we will see in chapters to come, is a soil in which illusory intuitions readily grow. In baseball, catching a fly ball is reasonably routine. Because it has a greater than 95 percent success rate, few superstitious behaviors accompany fielding. Batting is more fraught with uncertainties, and uncertainty nurtures peculiar hunches and habits. Batters therefore have a diverse repertoire of approaches to hitting, each with a peculiar sequence of warm-up swings, plate tappings, leg lifts, and bat wiggles.

Prime time power. Another common sports intuition is that points scored at the end of a game matter more. In the laboratory and in life, we tend to connect adjacent ("temporally contiguous") events. In a close game, we associate the last basket made with the game's outcome. In reality, it counts no more than a basket made at any other time. But cognitively the game's final moments seem more determinative of the outcome. Thus, most fans, coaches, players, and announcers (Billy Packer, included, I'm quite sure) concur that, at considerable cost, it's important to have one's best players available for the game's decisive moments. Use your best relief pitcher as the closer. Sit Shaquille O'Neal, if you must, to have him in at the end.

Social psychologists Dale Miller and Saku Gunasegaram have asked people to imagine that Jones and Cooper each flip a coin. If they land the same, each gets $1,000; if they land differently, each gets zero. Jones goes first and gets heads. Cooper goes second and gets tails. Who is to blame? Nearly everyone blames Cooper, intuiting that he'd feel more guilt. Likewise, Thomas Gilovich notes, if Shaq makes 10 of 20 free throws for the Lakers and teammate Kobe Bryant is 9 for 10—but his one miss is at the end of the game and the Lakers lose by one—Kobe, not Shaq, is considered to have lost the game.

I've asked coaches: If your star player picks up a fourth foul with ten minutes left, and you don't know how many more minutes of playing time he or she can contribute (because you don't want the player to play tentatively), would you rather maximize playing time or reduce playing minutes to ensure their availability for crunch time at the end? Would you rather have the star play six minutes (perhaps after a minute's rest) and foul out with three minutes to go, or play just three minutes—the *final* three minutes?

Because we humans intuitively impute causation to events in temporal contiguity, most coaches, with support from their fans, seem to presume that the final three minutes do more to determine the outcome than other three-minute game segments. "Have your prime time player available for prime time! How many times have you seen a game come down to the final basket?" (Never mind that some games come down to the final basket because the prime time players have been sitting on the bench.)

The Sports Illustrated *jinx*. Why is it that athletes whose peak performances get them on the cover of *Sports Illustrated* so often suffer a performance decline soon after? (The magazine in 2002 analyzed virtually all of its 2,456 covers and found 913 "jinxes"—demonstrable misfortunes or performance declines following a cover appearance.) And why do Nobel laureates often have diminished accomplishments after receiving the prize? Is it because the attention is distracting or unmotivating? Possibly. But a simpler phenomenon—"regression to the mean" (the average)—is more likely at work.

Think of it this way: Average results are always more typical, more to be expected, than are extreme results. (There are more cases near the middle of a bell curve than at the tails.) Thus, an extreme instance tends to be followed by one less extreme. After an unusual event, things tend to return to usual. Some examples: Students who score much lower or higher on an exam than they usually do are likely, when retested, to "regress" toward their average. ESP subjects who defy chance when first tested nearly always lose their "psychic powers" when retested. Last year's champion mutual fund will likely return to a more typical performance this year. This year's ten most accident-prone intersections in the United States (as announced by State Farm) will likely have fewer accidents next year (even without State Farm's benevolent improvements). And exceptional athletic performance by any individual is unlikely to be sustained.

Because chance variation looms large, sports offers many examples:

- The "sophomore slump": Nearly nine times out of ten, according to one analysis, American and National League rookies of the year have not performed as well in their second year.
- Of 58 Cy Young award-winning pitchers in another analysis, 52 had fewer victories and 50 had a higher earned-run averages the following year.
- Major league batters who have 30 home runs before the mid-season all-star game break virtually always have fewer than 30 after the break. Those who have more than 30 after the break virtually always had fewer than 30 before the break.
- Basketball players who make or miss all their shots in the first half of the game are likely to regress to their more usual performance level during the second half.

Sometimes we recognize that events are unlikely to continue at an unusually good or bad extreme. Experience has taught us that when everything is going great, something will go wrong, and that when life is dealing us terrible blows, we can usually look forward to things getting better. Often, though, we fail to recognize this regression effect. We puzzle at the *Sports Illustrated* jinx or wonder why rookies-of-the-year so often have a more ordinary second year—do they become overconfident or self-conscious? We forget that *exceptional performance tends to regress toward normality.*

The regression effect influences coaches in understandable but unfortunate ways. It restrains their praising players for good play and encourages their yelling at players after bad play. To see why, consider a clever experiment by Paul Schaffner that simulates the consequences of using praise and punishment. Schaffner invited Bowdoin College students to train an imaginary fourth-grade boy, "Harold," to come to school by 8:30 each morning. For each school day of a three-week period, a computer displayed Harold's arrival time, which was always between 8:20 and 8:40. The participants would then select a response to Harold, ranging from strong praise to strong reprimand. As you might expect, they usually praised Harold when he arrived before 8:30 and reprimanded him when he arrived after 8:30. Schaffner had programmed the computer to display a random sequence of arrival times. Thus, Harold's arrival time tended to improve (to regress toward 8:30) after being reprimanded. For example, if Harold arrived at 8:39, he was almost sure to be reprimanded, and his randomly selected next-day arrival time was likely to regress toward its average (to be earlier than 8:39). Thus, *even though their reprimands were having no effect,* most participants ended the experiment believing that their reprimands had been effective.

This experiment demonstrates what Amos Tversky and Daniel Kahneman have also noted: *Nature operates in such a way that we often feel punished for rewarding others and rewarded for punishing them.* Coaches who praise their team at halftime after an exceptional first half may notice that it seems to backfire—that performance becomes less exceptional during the second half. Those who yell at their players after an unusually bad first half may feel rewarded when the team's performance improves (returns to normal) during the second half. Ditto for the feedback they give to individual players who are having an exceptionally good or bad stretch of play.

Shortly after writing this, I opened my local sports page, which led with a story about how pitcher Jeff Weaver had sparked the Detroit Tigers to victory. "After a sloppy fifth inning [in which a] pair of throwing errors led to three unearned runs that put the Royals ahead

3–1," Weaver exploded in a tirade against his "sluggish teammates," following which there were no more errors and the Tigers went on to win. "I remember what I said," Weaver told reporters later, "but the only thing that is important to you is that it worked." Coaches, too, are subject to rewards and punishments. Fire a baseball manager in midseason after a team's exceptionally poor performance—a string of losses—and what we should expect is exactly what has been found: a rebound toward the team's more usual performance after the coaching change. Take two clubs with (for them) exceptionally bad previous months, switch the managers, and both teams will likely improve the next month.

In actuality, as every student of psychology knows, positive reinforcement for doing things right is usually more effective and has fewer negative side effects. It's just hard for coaches to see this when observing the results of their praise after the best moments and the results of their beratings after the worst.

INTUITIVE ATHLETIC GENIUS

We have noted how unexpected streakiness and unappreciated regression warps the intuitions of sports fans, coaches, players, and announcers. Is there something to be said for the *powers* of intuition in athletics? There is, indeed, for impressive examples of intuitive expertise are found among great athletes.

Consider the speed and sophistication of Venus Williams meeting an oncoming tennis ball, or of Mark McGwire's computations as he faced a Randy Johnson fastball. As the ball leaves Johnson's hand, McGwire detects the ball's speed, spin, and direction, and, within 0.15 seconds he calculates where and when it's going to cross by him. His brain begins directing his body to swing (or not), and where and when to rotate his shoulder, move his arms, swivel his hips, and shift his weight forward, all in synchrony and in hopes of intercepting the ball at precisely the right moment and with the desired force—and all less than half a second after exiting the pitcher's hand. As the well-struck ball rockets deep into center field, the fielder's brain now computes the ball's trajectory, enabling him to meet its return to earth precisely as it arrives. Intuition par excellence.

As Kobe Bryant shoots a leaning fall-away jump shot, his agile brain performs an incredible number of instant computations, adjusting for body position, movement, and distance. The Newtonian mechanics here are terribly complex. "Every shot represents the launching of a basketball on a parabolic arc," noted Carl Sagan, "a curve determined by the same gravitational physics that specifies the flight of a ballistic missile, or the earth orbiting the sun, or a spacecraft on its rendezvous with some distant world. To get the ball in the basket, you must loft it at exactly the right speed; a one percent error and gravity will make you look bad. Three-point shooters compensate for aerodynamic drag." As the ball swishes the net, Kobe grins and blows on his hot fingers, knowing that his intuitive mind has just aced a practical physics exam that would baffle an MIT graduate student.

Team sport athletes, like chess masters, also develop intuitive expertise at reading patterns in a developing play. Malcolm Gladwell explains how Wayne Gretzky liked to keep the game in front of him, enabling him to anticipate events. "When he sends a pass to what to the rest of us appears an empty space on the ice, and when a teammate magically appears in that space to collect the puck, he has in reality simply summoned up from his bank account of knowledge the fact that in a particular situation, someone is likely to be in a particular spot, and if he is not there now he will be there presently." (Recall Herbert Simon's surmise: "Intuition is nothing more and nothing less than recognition.")

Don't bother to ask Venus Williams, Mark McGwire, Kobe Bryant, or Wayne Gretzky how they do it. They couldn't articulate what they know. They just know. The coordinated sequence of muscular movements doesn't allow time for sequential conscious decisions. Indeed, stopping to think would disrupt their precise and graceful motions. When skilled athletes pay too much attention to the process of making a crucial golf putt or basketball free throw it disrupts their automatic rhythm. "Thinking is stinking," says a baseball axiom. Go with the flow. Even in the slower-paced game of golf, Tiger Woods reports that "I've learned to trust the subconscious. My instincts have never lied to me."

A quarterback reading the defense, a soccer midfielder recognizing where the swirl of players compels her to deliver the ball, and a point guard knowing how to anticipate his teammate's moves display similar intuitive genius. Although I am the least of players in my daily noontime pickup basketball games, even I, after thousands of games, am occasionally moved to release the ball with perfect timing to create that lovely gem—the backdoor layup—as the ball bounces through traffic to meet one's teammate sneaking around the wing, one step before he or she lays it softly in. There's no time to rationally plan all this (we don't call plays); one is just seized by the moment. As with midjump dish-off passes, it feels like "mere" intuition. Or should I say, intricate, graceful, sophisticated intuition.

Investment Intuition

Randomness is a difficult notion for people to accept. When events
come in clusters and streaks, people look for explanations and patterns.
They refuse to believe that such patterns—which frequently occur in
random data—could equally well be derived from tossing a coin.
So it is in the stock market as well.
—Burton G. Malkiel, A Random Walk Down Wall Street, *1989*

Once upon a time, economists viewed us *homo sapiens* as
homo economicus—as having preferences that rationally optimize our
self-interest. Undistracted by emotion and irrationalities, we were
presumed to create efficient marketplaces that accurately value
stocks and to coolly adjust our spending and savings in response to
economic fluctuations.

Sorry, say today's new behavioral economists, this assumed rationality does not reflect human reality. Emotions and group influences matter. Mr. Spock is a Vulcan, not a human.

Something more than rational self-interest obviously is at work
when, on a trip, we leave tips for unseen hotel maids and never-to-be-
seen-again servers. That's generosity, not irrationality. But irrationality is evident in these situations (inspired by behavioral economist
Richard Thaler and psychologists Daniel Kahneman and the late
Amos Tversky):

- Would you drive five miles to save $10? Many of us would drive
  five miles to the discount store that's selling the Walkman cas-

sette player we want for $25, rather than pay $35 for it at our neighborhood store. Yet we wouldn't drive five miles to buy a home entertainment system for $910 rather than $920.

- Would you pay $500 for a GPS navigation system for your car? Most of us wouldn't—unless, perhaps, we're buying a $20,000 car. Hey, what's an extra $500? Likewise, many hard-of-hearing people won't part with $5,000 for a pair of digital hearing aids (which would increase their quality of life) yet would hardly haggle over $5,000 in the price of their next house.
- How much of your next raise would you like diverted into a 401(k) retirement account? Likely, more—much more—if asked months before rather than after you start receiving the raise. Future sacrifice is sacrifice unfelt. (To increase the country's savings rate, Thaler shows, companies need only ask employees to allocate their raises well before they get them.)
- Would you rather work when making more per hour? Many New York cabdrivers work until they reach their day's income target. That means they work shorter hours on the most lucrative days and longer hours when customers are few.
- When is a raise not a raise? At the end of a year marked by 10 percent inflation, Sarah feels pleasure at her just-announced pay raise from $50,000 to $55,000. The next year, with inflation held to zero, her younger brother Sam, in a similar job, gets a mere $2,500 raise in his $50,000 salary, and feels disappointed.

ANOMALIES OF OUR ECONOMIC INTUITION

People, it's increasingly apparent, buy, sell, and invest not like computers but like, well, imperfect people. "People are not stupid," says another psychology-savvy behavioral economist, Robert Shiller, "but they have their limitations." When following our instincts we make decisions mostly swiftly, often smartly, but sometimes stupidly. Economic intuition sometimes defies economic logic. Consider five illustrative anomalies.

Loss aversion. You're about to buy that car, for which you need $20,000 (or was it $20,500?). You decide to sell some stock. Would you rather sell $20,000 of your GE shares, for which you paid $10,000, or $20,000 of your AT&T shares, for which you paid $30,000?

Terrance Odean's analysis of trading records for 10,000 accounts at a large discount brokerage shows that most people strongly prefer to "lock in" a profit rather than absorb a loss. Said differently, they prefer to sell the winner and hang on to the loser (or as Peter Lynch has said, to pull up the flowers and water the weeds). There's no logically right answer here—no investor knows the future value of either stock. But the preference is curious, given that, rationally, an investor's goal is to make money, not redeem past mistakes. Whether one has made or lost money to this point is irrelevant (if anything, tax considerations would favor selling the loser for a tax loss and avoiding the capital gains tax on the winner). Yet our aversion to loss deters us from locking in the loss, which becomes real and final—not just a paper loss—the moment we sell.

That's understandable psychologically if not logically, Kahneman and Tversky's studies show, because we derive more pain from losing than pleasure from gaining. We're therefore conservative when given a chance to lock in a win, but daring when given a chance to avoid loss. In experiments, people prefer a sure gain over flipping a coin for double or nothing. Yet they will readily flip a coin on a double or nothing chance to avert a loss. In fact, Kahneman and Tversky report, we feel the pain from a loss twice as keenly as we feel the pleasure from a similar-sized gain.

Our aversion to loss is readily apparent outside the laboratory as well:

- Hoping to wipe out losses, gamblers will bet on longer odds at the day's end.
- Given that only 60 cents or so of every insurance premium gets returned to insureds to cover losses (the rest funds the system), upstanding insurance agents must educate people to elect large deductibles and *not* to insure against small, affordable losses. In the long run, insurance companies profit from our aversion to loss. The same aversion motivates some people to buy service contracts that insure against appliance breakdowns, but for greater long-term costs.

- Your basketball team is behind by two points with time only for one last shot. Would you prefer a two-point or a three-point attempt? Many coaches, intuitively preferring to avoid loss, seek to put the game into overtime with a two-point shot. After all, an average three-point shot will produce a win only one-third of the time. But if that same team averages 50 percent of its two-point attempts, they have about a 50 percent chance of overtime—where, judging from the game to this point, the outcome is a toss-up. That yields only a 25 percent chance of a) an overtime followed by b) a victory.

The endowment effect. Would you trade lives with your next-door neighbor? Would you trade houses (or apartments)? Cars? Jobs? Noses? Unless you're depressed, you probably prefer the life and things you have to most alternatives. In economic terms, people often demand much more to give up something than they're willing to pay to acquire it. Economist Thaler has labeled this phenomenon the endowment effect.

In one study, the experimenters gave some people $2 and others a lottery ticket of equal value. Later, when they offered everyone a chance to trade, most preferred to keep whichever they had. In several other studies, researchers gave Cornell students coffee mugs and not long after asked them the lowest price they would sell it for. This sell price averaged more than three times what students not given the mugs said they would pay to buy one. Ownership creates inertia. Take home that home entertainment system on a money-back trial period, and you will likely never return it. As owners, we place a greater value on things simply because they're ours. Many music fans who wouldn't pay more than $30 for a particular concert ticket wouldn't sell one they own for less than $50.

The endowment effect is a corollary of loss aversion. We hate to lose what we have. Hoping to wipe out losses, and feeling the attachment that accompanies ownership, investors will therefore throw good money after bad. Loss aversion and the endowment effect together feed our hesitation to abandon failing projects in which "too much is invested to quit." In experiments, as in real life, people who have made a considerable investment in a failing project prefer to continue investing resources, even when they'd never invest if considering this as a new investment on its own merits and even when abandoning the effort is economically rational.

As investor for a family foundation, this is a phenomenon I know painfully well. Understanding the perils of our economic intuition helps. But understanding does not guarantee optimal rationality. Reflecting on his lifetime's research on why smart people make dumb decisions, Amos Tversky reflected that "all our problems fooled us, too." As powerful perceptual illusions fool those who study them, so compelling economic illusions can trip those who should know better.

The sunk cost effect. Put yourself in the participants' shoes in another of Kahneman and Tversky's experiments: Imagine that you have decided to see a play where admission is $20 per ticket. As you approach the theater you discover that you have lost a $20 bill. Would you still pay $20 for a ticket to the play?

Surely you would join the 88 percent of their participants who answered yes. Most others, however, when asked to imagine that they'd lost the $20 ticket, said they would *not* pay $20 for another ticket (because the play wasn't worth $40). Rationally, the $20 is a "sunk cost." It's gone, whether in the form of a ticket or a lost bill. So, looking to the future, the question is simply whether the play is still worth $20.

A similar sunk cost anomaly surfaced when Hal Arkes and Catherine Blumer invited Ohio University students to imagine buying a Michigan weekend ski trip ticket for $100, and later buying a ticket for an even more appealing Wisconsin skip trip ticket for just $50. On discovering that the two trips are the same weekend, Arkes and Blumer asked, "Which ski trip would you go on?" Most, not wanting to waste the larger sunk cost, said they'd go on the trip they would enjoy less.

Sunk costs also help explain the "too much invested to quit" phenomenon. The Ford Motor Company erred in bringing the Edsel to market in the late 1950s at a sunk cost of $250 million and then—not wanting the sunk cost to become a locked-in loss—compounded the error by continuing production for two and a half more years at an additional $200 million.

The Vietnam War continued well past the point where, if starting anew, the United States would never have begun it. With so much invested, in lives and money lost, it was hard to quit. Said Secretary of Defense Robert McNamara, "We could not simply walk away from an enterprise involving two administrations, five allied countries, and thirty-one thousand dead as if we were switching off a television channel."

Government spending on unworkable defense and public works projects has likewise continued because their termination would presumably waste monies already spent. Responding to critics who pointed out that the value of a completed Tennessee-Tombigbee Waterway Project would be less than the money needed to complete it, Senator Jeremiah Denton argued that "to terminate a project in which $1.1 billion has been invested represents an unconscionable mishandling of taxpayers' dollars."

The moral: The past is over. Learn from it. But when making decisions, remember that each day is indeed the first day of your future. Don't look back. "If we could, we'd send you a pill that erases the memory of every dollar you ever spent," say tongue-in-cheek Gary Belsky and Thomas Gilovich in *Why Smart People Make Big Money Mistakes*. "That's because once spent, it's gone. It has no relevance." Ergo, don't let sunk costs affect future decisions. Base decisions on the present, with an eye to the future.

Anchoring. Would you say the Mississippi River is more or less than 800 miles long? How long would you guess it is?

When estimating the river's length (which is 2,348 miles), arbitrary comparison numbers ("anchors") readily influence people's judgments. If I had first asked whether the river was more or less than 5,000 miles long, you would surely have said "less" but likely would have given a higher estimate than you just did.

Tversky and Kahneman later made the comparison number seem random, by spinning a wheel with numbers from one to a hundred. Still, people estimated about 25 percent of United Nations countries were African after the wheel was rigged to stop at ten, and 45 percent after the wheel stopped at sixty-five. (The correct answer at the time was 32 percent.) Given even these meaningless anchors, people calibrated their answers from that starting point.

The anchoring phenomenon colors our financial gut reactions as well. The Nasdaq's exuberant high-water mark, 5,132, forms a misleading comparison point for intuiting its realistic value today. Individual company stocks, too, can seem cheap if they're at half their previous high, and pricey if they've recently doubled. My aunt, who bought Microsoft when it went public in 1986 and has held it ever since, is glad she never judged it as overvalued relative to the anchor point of its first week's price (20 cents, adjusted for later splits).

Financial writer Belsky and social psychologist Gilovich recount Gregory Northcraft and Margaret Neale's clever 1987 experiment with experienced Tucson real estate agents. After touring a home and receiving a ten-page information packet indicating a $65,900 list price, agents offered an average appraisal of $67,811. Others went on the same tour and received the same information, except with an $83,900 listing. Their average appraisal: $75,190.

I can imagine real estate agents exploiting the anchoring effect by asking their clients, "Would you guess this house is listed at more or less than $250,000?" "Less, I'd hope." "How much would you guess?" "$230,000?" "No—only $219,000!"

Overconfidence. Overconfidence, as we noted in earlier chapters, routinely appears in our judgments of our past knowledge ("I knew it all along"), in our current knowledge (overestimating the accuracy of our factual judgments), and in predictions of our future behaviors, successes, and completion times (illusory optimism). Overconfidence also infuses economic intuition. Financial forecasts, for example, are consistently too optimistic:

- In 1984, *The Economist* asked four European former finance ministers, four chairs of multinational firms, four Oxford students, and four London garbage collectors to predict the next decade's inflation, growth rates, and sterling exchange rates. Adding up scores ten years later, the garbage haulers tied the company bosses for first place, and the finance ministers finished last.
- Ronald Reagan and his advisors were very confident (and very wrong) that economic growth stimulated by their massive tax cut would increase government revenues and decrease the deficit.

- Most start-up business plans are overly if not wildly optimistic about future success.
- Most industrial firms overestimate their future production.
- Wall Street analysts predicted that the companies in Standard & Poor's 500 index would average 21.9 percent earnings growth per year between 1982 and 1997. Despite the growing economy, reality (7.6 percent annual earnings growth) was barely one-third their estimates.
- Analysts' unrelenting optimism also appears in their buy and sell recommendations. Of the 8,000 analyst recommendations on S&P 500 stock companies at the end of 2000, only 29 recommended selling.

Overconfidence is greatest for the most unpredictable events. As we might expect, then, nowhere is overconfidence so abundant as in the stock market's recent hyperactivity. Each day about 2 billion shares exchange between buyers, who feel some confidence that a stock will rise, and sellers, who feel some confidence that it will not. Alas, as in Las Vegas, the only consistent winners in this game, which is near zero-sum on most days, are those who collect the trading costs and taxes. People who actively trade, notes Yale's endowment manager, David Swenson, "lose to the market by the amount it costs to play, in the form of management fees, trading commissions, and dealer spread. Wall Street's share of the pie defines the amount of performance drag experienced by the would-be market beaters."

Brad Barber and Terrance Odean, University of California–Davis researchers, analyzed trades by 66,465 discount broker accounts from 1991 to 1996. Those who, bullish on their prognostications, traded the most, earned 11.4 percent annually while the market returned 17.9 percent. Clearly, say Barber and Odean, emphasizing the perils of investment intuition, "investors trade too much and to their detriment."

In a follow-up study of data from 35,000 broker accounts, they found that "men are more overconfident than women." They traded 45 percent more often, earning results that underperformed the market by 2.65 percent (54 percent more than women's 1.72 percent underperformance). This confirms earlier findings that men rely less on brokers and anticipate higher returns than do women. In stock trading as in other realms, men make more self-serving attributions—by taking credit for their successes ("I had a feeling") and explaining away failures ("Were it not for the strike . . . the interest rate increase . . . the slowdown").

It doesn't take such fine-grained analysis to see psychological factors at work in what Federal Reserve Board chairman Alan Greenspan called the "irrational exuberance" of the late 1990s stock market bubble, and what some saw as the "irrational pessimism" after the bubble burst. Traders, like wolves, run in packs. "Momentum investing" creates self-fulfilling prophecies—times during which investors buy not because opportunities are undervalued but because prices are rising. "Everyone's Getting Rich in Tech: Here's How To Get Your Share," declared the cover of the May 1999 issue of *Money* magazine.

Before long, the same herd will frantically sell when prices are falling. In the short run, momentum investing can feed an upward spiral. As traders tell of their windfalls, others are enticed—who wants to miss out on the boom with cash that's gathering dust in a bond fund? Mutual funds that have bought the booming stocks attract investor dollars, which are then poured into more of the same stocks, driving their prices higher. Moreover, the media fan the exuberance with anecdotes and with theories of how a "new economy" justifies sky-high valuations. (Economist Burton Malkiel noted, just as the Nasdaq bubble began to deflate, that if Cisco Systems was to produce a 15 percent return to investors for the next twenty years its market capitalization would exceed the current gross domestic product.)

But as happened with Holland's seventeenth-century tulip mania, reality eventually reasserts itself. Stocks are ultimately worth only the value of the cash flow they earn for their investors. When prices begin falling, analysts change their tune. Speaking with the wisdom of hindsight, a chorus of voices then tells us that the market was "due for a correction." After the April 2000 week in which the Nasdaq fell 25 percent, one *New York Times* article quoted gloomy analysts:

> "By most measures, technology stocks have been in a bubble for years. . . . Friday's plunge was needed to wring excesses out of stock prices."

"Despite sharp declines, technology stocks are still overvalued, and many conservative investors will not be interested in buying them until they fall much lower."

"People are panicking and getting out at all costs. This thing could get a lot uglier."

"Investors who buy too soon may 'catch a falling knife.'"

When prices fell further, after the terrorist attacks of September 11, 2001, Malkiel warned that yesterday's irrational exuberance was in danger of becoming today's "unreasoned anxiety."

Noting how small bits of good news turn the chatter bullish and send stocks soaring, and how minor bad news does the opposite, reminds me of my own studies of "group polarization." Groups amplify their shared tendencies. In one study, we observed that when prejudiced high school students discussed racial issues, their attitudes became more prejudiced. When low-prejudice students discussed the same issues, they became more tolerant.

Group polarization can amplify a sought-after spiritual awareness and strengthen the mutual resolve of those in a self-help group. But it can also have dire consequences. In experiments, group decision making amplifies retaliatory responses to provocation. In the real world, terrorism arises among people who are drawn together out of a shared grievance and who become more and more extreme as they interact in isolation from moderating influences. In the marketplace, people who are lusting for gain or fearing loss feed off one another—amplifying their optimism, at one moment, and their pessimism, at another. The natural result is overreaction—irrational exuberance and irrational panic.

A RANDOM WALK DOWN WALL STREET?

Financial economists run a continuum. At one end are "efficient market" believers, who assume that the market knows all and responds swiftly and appropriately to information, and that stocks are at their true values. In one old joke, two hard-core efficient market theorists were walking toward their University of Chicago faculty club when a student pointed out a $100 bill on the ground. One of the professors replied that it couldn't be there because if it had been it would already have been taken. At the continuum's other end are behavioral finance theorists, who assume that emotions and herd behaviors drive the markets. There is wisdom, most economists agree, in both perspectives. The market's volatility indicates that emotions and herd behavior do play roles, and yet markets respond with amazing efficiency—within minutes—to relevant news.

"Economists disagree about many things," reports Cornell economist Robert Frank, "but one belief we share is that investors can almost never make financial headway by trading on the basis of numbers they hear about through the media." Within five minutes, earnings and dividend announcements get reflected in stock prices. "By the time any news reaches us, others will have long since acted upon it," notes Frank. Any scoop from CNBC, *The Economist*, the *Wall Street Journal*, or one's favorite financial newsletter has already been factored into the current price.

If we individual investors therefore can't hope, by active trading, to beat the market, can high-priced professionals working on our behalf do better? And is there a way to identify the top stock pickers? *Consumer Reports* and *Money* magazine offer us some ideas. They annually report on last year's, or even the last several years', top fund managers. The implication is that a fund that has enjoyed a recent streak of good performance will likely continue to outperform one that has been performing badly. But as Burton Malkiel has repeatedly documented, past performances of mutual funds do *not* predict their future performance. If on January 1 of each year since 1980 we had bought the previous year's top-performing funds, our hot funds would not have beaten the next year's market average. In fact, we would have done *worse* than the market average if we had put our money on the *Forbes* Honor Roll of funds each year—gaining us an annual return of 13.5 percent over nearly two decades since 1975 (compared with the market's overall 14.9 percent annual return). Of the top eighty-one Canadian funds during 1994, forty performed above average and forty-one below average during 1995.

What if we looked at longer time periods? Would a top money manager over a four-year period be more likely to excel again over the next four years? One study of 162 institutional money managers asked how the top quarter from 1991–94 fared in the ensuing four years. Surprisingly, slightly more than half performed below average from 1995 to 1998. Strong performers in one period were as likely as not to underperform in the next period.

Moreover, 86 percent of mutual funds, though managed by savvy, highly paid professionals, lagged the S&P 500 over a recent ten years. These fund managers are among the best of some 200,000 licensed professionals who make a living advising us how to invest our money. And they can't beat the market? A group of blindfolded people throwing darts at financial pages, if unencumbered by trading and administrative costs and the need to keep cash on hand, could hardly have done worse.

Think of it this way: any stock's price is roughly the midpoint between the weight of investors and brokers saying sell and those saying buy. Thus we can know that brokers who want us to pay them commissions for their stock picking advice are countered by other paid brokers giving opposite advice.

Although this sounds harsh and cynical, there is a balm in all this for maligned brokers. Another of the new behavioral economists, Matthew Rabin, notes how nature conspires to convince many investors that their analysts are worse than they really are. "The investor switches quickly from an analyst who initially performs poorly—and when he does so he has over-inferred that the analyst is bad. But he sticks with an analyst who initially performs well—until he discovers (as he will) that she is average. Because he corrects his overly positive inference but not his overly negative inference, his beliefs are biased downward." Impatient investors, who abandon one broker after another when performance sours, may also develop illusory intuitions about the value of switching—comparable to those of coaches who find their players' horrid performance improving (regressing to average) after yelling at them.

But are there not individual newsletters, or fund managers, who have had stellar records? John Templeton, Warren Buffet, and Peter Lynch have all, in their time, made billions of dollars for those who invested with them. If only our parents had remortgaged their house and put all their money on Buffet's Berkshire Hathaway in 1965. But

Templeton, Buffet, and Lynch are the outliers, and we can't be certain that even their approaches would work as well in the future. Given enough prognosticators, some are bound to put together several good years.

John Allen Paulos illustrates with the story of the cunning stock guru who each Friday evening for six consecutive weeks sent a thousand people a letter that correctly predicted whether the next week's market would rise or fall—and then signed up most of them as high-paying subscribers. His method was foolproof—certain to produce six out of six correct predictions for 1,000 prospects. His method was also simple. The first week he sent 64,000 letters, telling half that next week the market would rise and half that the market would fall. The second week he sent a follow-up letter to the 32,000 who received his correct "prediction," again telling half the market would rise and half the market would fall. After six weeks of this, he was guaranteed his final list of 1,000.

The universe of mutual funds is like those letters. Given 640 funds, we can expect, purely by chance, that ten will beat the average fund for six years consecutively. *Money* and *Consumer Reports* will document these winners for us. Stock brokers will sell them by showing us impressive charts depicting how these funds have *consistently* beaten the average, producing spectacular long-term results. If only we had invested in them! Fund companies approximate this by offering many funds with different strategies and then hyping their stars and hiding their duds. Individual investors often chase these recently successful mutual funds. The ironic result, note Belsky and Gilovich, is that from 1984 through 1995 the average stock mutual fund posted a yearly return of 12.3 percent while the average investor in a stock mutual fund earned 6.3 percent. (As the herd of fund hoppers leave their lagging investments and jump into those posting strong recent returns, the fund that has been growing by leaps and bounds often now regresses toward average.)

When funds have streaks of good months or years, it is tempting to think that their past portends their future. The *Wall Street Journal's* chosen stock pickers have outperformed dart throwers for some recent bull market years, but they've done so by picking volatile stocks that, given a bear market, would likely fall faster, notes Malkiel. The facts of life haven't changed, he says: "Stock prices are essentially unpredictable." In investing as in coin tossing, basketball, and base-ball, *streaks happen.* Random data are streaky, and the streakiness of the stock market is about what we should expect of what Malkiel famously calls a "random walk down Wall Street."

As awareness has grown that the emperor has no clothes—that e-traders, brokers, and mutual funds tend to underperform the mar-ket—an increasingly popular alternative has been simply to invest on cruise control, to buy the market through a virtually cost-free stock index fund. "Don't think of an index fund as average," says Jane Bryant Quinn. "Think of it as par. It's very hard to beat par." As John Templeton, now retired from mutual fund management, notes, "The unmanaged market indexes . . . don't pay commissions to buy and sell stock. . . . They don't pay salaries to security analysts or portfolio managers," and they defer most capital gains taxes until the index is sold. Besides, in an index fund all your money is in the market, none of it on the sideline in a cash reserve.

Of course, index funds are also subject to herd behavior. People flocking to them will drive up the prices of the stocks they must invest in. Indeed, if everyone bought only index funds the market would go haywire—with indexed stocks having inflated values and stocks out-side the indexes having no value. Already today, one in every ten mutual fund dollars is in index funds, which are weighted by a com-pany's market capitalization (which means that they must buy more of the largest companies, such as huge General Electric). Their need to buy big-cap stocks elevates these stocks' price. Not only do stocks drive the indexes, the indexes are beginning to drive the stocks. If a shrinking company drops off an index and is replaced by another, both their stock prices may shift by 10 percent with no fundamental change in their value. So, though index funds continue to serve inves-tors well, at minimal cost, it's not unthinkable that investors' faith in efficient markets could ironically drive the markets to inefficiency. And it's surely possible that the larger corporations favored by the index funds will have less stellar records in the decade ahead than in the decade past.

Do Malkiel and his economist colleagues have any advice other than to buy index or no-load funds when investing in stocks? They do. Recall that most people have an aversion to loss. Given choices, they will choose a sure gain and seek to avoid a sure loss. Because losses on stocks occur more often than losses on bonds, investors demand (and receive) a higher return for holding stock. Over time, those willing to suffer the up and down years of the stock market get compensated. In the long run, a willingness to take more risk brings more reward. From 1981 through 2000, stock returns averaged about 17 percent annually, bonds about 10 percent. But early twenty-first century investors realize that this was an especially bullish two decades. Taking a longer-term perspective that includes the Great Depression, consider the value, at the century's end, of a one dollar investment made in December 1925. In U.S. Treasury bills, the $1 would have grown to $16, in Treasury bonds to $40, and in large-company U.S. stocks (such as the S&P 500) to $2,846. Or take a *really* long perspective and fantasize that your ancestral grandparents had invested a mere $1 for your benefit in 1802. Although it would have cost them $14 in today's dollars, that dollar would now be worth about $10,000 if invested for the two centuries in Treasury bonds, and $10 million if invested in large-cap stocks.

Consider the long-term fortunes of two colleges. "Caution College" parks a just-received $1 million bequest in a bond fund that returns, historically, an average 7 percent. Fifty years later, the benefactors, gazing down from heaven, see that their fund is now worth $29 million. Meanwhile, its more optimistic neighbor, "Hopeful College," parks its $1 million bequest in a stock index fund that returns an average 11 percent. Fifty years later, its benefactors, gazing down from heaven, are all smiles. Their fund is now worth $184 million.* The fundraisers at Caution College are now working overtime seeking additional gifts to close the $155 million gap with its now much stronger neighbor college. Alas, Hopeful College is now out of their reach.

*I've assumed that each school's annual cash draw from their endowment is offset by donations.

This example also illustrates the counterintuitive mathematics of compounding. A twenty-two-year-old who puts $2,000 into an investment that earns 15 percent till age sixty-five, and who never saves another dime, can retire with an $800,000 nest egg. Someone who, for the decade starting in 1963, put $2,000 a year into stocks comprising the S&P 500 index on the *worst* (highest) day of every year would, by 1999, have accumulated $876,004. That's more money than someone who invested twice as much—$2,000 a year for twenty years starting in 1973—even if the second person invested annually on the *best* (lowest) day of every year! Wellington Mara understands the mathematics of patience. In 1925, when he was a nine-year-old, his dad bought the New York Giants for $500. In 2001, Mara sold half of his interest for $75 million.

Our fictional Hopeful College is not unlike the actual Princeton Theological Seminary, whose endowment was for many years managed by John Templeton. During his thirty-seven-year tenure as a trustee (which did not include the 1990s bull market years), the initial $3 million endowment was supplemented by $25 million in gifts but, more significantly, by investment growth—which multiplied the endowment to some $350 million (enabling the seminary today, with its $820 million endowment, to be one of the academically most excellent of theological schools).

A 2001 study by the CommonFund, which pools investments from more than 1,400 institutions, showed that Princeton Seminary is not alone in having understood the mathematics of risk and reward. Wealthy universities—with endowments of more than $1 billion—invested an average of 29 percent of their monies in "alternative investments" (more than half in venture capital and private equity) and only 20 percent in fixed income securities. Their average rate of return—16 percent over the 1990s—exceeded the 12 percent return of the more cautious schools with less than $100 million endowment, which placed only 6 percent of their monies in alternative investments and 28 percent in fixed income securities. (Remember that a 4 percent difference in return rate compounds to huge differences in results over long time periods.) In 2000, Yale University had only 9 percent of its endowment in bond funds and 14 percent in domestic stocks. Its private equity component—25 percent of its 2000 endowment—has returned an average of 34 percent annually since 1973, helping explode its endowment to $10 billion. With universities as with individuals, the rich tend to be (and can afford to be) venturesome, which over time accentuates the gap between rich and poor.

The risk of shifting most of one's endowment, pension fund, or personal investments into stocks and venture equity is that such investments are more likely to lose value with bad choices or bad times. The complementary risk, illustrated by Caution College, is lost opportunity cost, which means not having the resources needed to increase competitive excellence. Eyeing the future, Yale's endowment manager, David Swenson, reasons that accepting risks "rewards long-term investors with higher returns." Conservatively discounting the last quarter-century's boom, his office assumes that, over time, their bond investments will beat inflation by 1.5 percent, their U.S. stocks by 4.1 percent, and their carefully selected private equity funds by 9.8 percent.

Reducing perceived risk by aggregation. There is, fortunately, a way to enjoy greater long-term rewards with tolerable risk. Imagine someone invited you to bet your $100,000 life savings on a coin toss: heads you win $300,000, tails you lose it all. You'd probably say no thanks, and your aversion to the loss of your nest egg would be understandable. But what if we broke this up into ten smaller bets? What if ten people each offered you the same triple or nothing chance on a coin toss with $10,000 of your life savings at stake? Would you take the first offer? The second? . . . The tenth? When such risks are framed individually, Donald Redelmeier and Amos Tversky have found, people remain averse to risk. But not if *the same information* is framed in the aggregate, as in the table below.

Now it becomes apparent (see table) that by diversifying—by spreading the risk across ten venturesome bets—the odds for a positive return on the $100,000 are heavily stacked in one's favor, and most people will venture the program. They understand not to get too excited if they win $30,000 on the first bet, because they know they're going to lose a few. And they know not to be too distressed if they lose $10,000 on the first toss, because they know they'd have to be very unlucky not to come out ahead by the end.

The moral: The same gut instinct that urges caution when risks are

Number of wins	Probability (percentage)	Winnings (in dollars)
0	<1%	$0
1	1	30,000
2	4	60,000
3	12	90,000
4	21	120,000
5	25	150,000
6	21	180,000
7	12	210,000
8	4	240,000
9	1	270,000
10	<1	300,000

offered one at a time becomes venturesome when the identical risks are packaged as a group. By distributing risk—rational risks, not just desperate efforts to cover a loss—across many ventures, an institution or individual can enjoy higher rewards at tolerable aggregate risk levels.

INTUITIVE ENTREPRENEURS

This chapter's overarching message is that our financial intuition sometimes defies financial logic, and that awareness of certain anomalies in our financial intuition can help us make smarter decisions. But does our financial intuition not have powers as well as perils? Many successful executives say that they often make important decisions by "what my gut tells me," by "the seat of my pants," or "on a hunch." "It was this subconscious, visceral feeling. And it just felt right," recalled Chrysler's former president Bob Lutz in describing his vision for the Dodge Viper, which helped save his company during the 1990s.

Ralph Larsen, CEO of Johnson & Johnson, also uses his visceral sense when making big decisions. "When someone presents an acquisition proposal to me, the numbers always look terrific: the hurdle rates have been met; the return on investment is wonderful; the growth rate is just terrific. And I get all the reasons why this would be a good acquisition. But it's at that point—when I have a tremendous amount of quantitative information that's already been analyzed by very smart people—that I earn what I get paid. Because I will look at that information and I will know, intuitively, whether it's a good or bad deal."

Lutz and Larsen are harnessing their learned expertise. "Intuition and judgment are simply analyses frozen into habit," said Herbert Simon. Looking at this page, you are experiencing the results of sensory processes that you can't explain. So, too, Lutz, Larsen, and other savvy executives have learned rules and patterns they can't articulate. They are like basketball players with court sense. At Six Flags Entertainment, executive Rob Pittman saw more profits coming from selling merchandise and refreshments than from admission tickets. Later, at America Online, Pittman intuitively knew from experience to push AOL away from a business model based on hourly fees to one rooted in advertising and e-commerce revenues. For executives as for chess masters, intuition sometimes compresses years of experience into instant insight.

Sometimes. Other times experience fails to prepare even seasoned people for novel challenges and opportunities. The steamboat, the printing press, the telegraph, the incandescent lamp, and the typewriter were all met with skepticism. "Never did a single encouraging remark, a bright hope, a warm wish, cross my path," reminisced Robert Fulton of his efforts to launch the steamboat *Fulton's Folly*. John White's book *Rejection* is one story after another of the disdain that greeted the work of people ranging from Michelangelo and Beethoven to the American poet A. Wilber Stevens, who received back from his hoped-for publisher an envelope of ashes. Dr. Seuss was rejected by two dozen publishers, whose seasoned intuitions told them his work would never fly. Despite receiving fifteen rejections, including one from the editors at Doubleday—"There is no way to sell a book about an unknown Dutch painter"—Irving Stone's book about Van Gogh went on to sell 25 million copies. In a possibly apocryphal story, one of the seven publishers that rejected Beatrix Potter's *Tale of Peter Rabbit* said that the story "smelled like rotting carrots."

The fragility of entrepreneurial intuition was baldly demonstrated by an apparently frustrated writer named Chuck Ross. Using a pseudonym, Ross mailed a copy of Jerzy Kosinski's novel *Steps* to twenty-eight major publishers and literary agencies. All rejected it, including Random House, which had published the book a decade earlier and watched it win the National Book Award and sell more than 400,000 copies. The novel came closest to acceptance with Houghton Mifflin, publisher of three other Kosinski novels. "Several of us read your untitled novel here with admiration for writing and style. Jerzy Kosinski comes to mind as a point of comparison. . . . The drawback to the manuscript, as it stands, is that it doesn't add up to a satisfactory whole."

Recognizing the perils of intuition, many companies, including General Electric under Jack Welch, have turned to data-driven management systems, such as Six Sigma. To improve quality, companies define activities, set benchmarks, and measure performance. Gordon Food Service, a large midwestern food distributor, judges its suppliers not subjectively but quantitatively, with points earned for on-time, on-demand quality product. From month to month, the suppliers know what's expected and how they are measuring up.

When objective information is available, as in the worlds of quality control, finance, and investment, by all means attend to it. But not everything important is measurable. For some things, there are no decisive numbers. How does one measure Dr. Seuss's submitted manuscript? In such cases, our judgment must be guided by seasoned experience, by informed intuition, by the whispers of our accumulated, ineffable knowledge.

Clinical Intuition

The real purpose of [the] scientific method is to make sure Nature hasn't misled you into thinking you know something that you actually don't.
—Robert Pirsig, Zen and the Art of Motorcycle Maintenance, 1974

A parole board meets with a convicted rapist and ponders whether to release him. A worker on a crisis intervention line judges whether a caller is suicidal. A physician notes a patient's symptoms and surmises the likelihood of cancer. A school social worker ponders whether a child's overheard threat was a macho joke, a one-time outburst, or a sign of potential violence.

Each of these professionals must decide how to weigh their subjective judgments against relative objective evidence. Should they follow their intuition? Should they listen to their experience-based instincts, their hunches, their inner wisdom? Or should they rely more on research-based wisdom sometimes embedded in formulas, statistical analyses, and computerized predictions?

INTUITIVE VERSUS STATISTICAL PREDICTION

In the contest between heart and head, clinicians often listen to whispers from their experience and vote with their hearts. They prefer not to let cold calculations decide the futures of warm human beings. Feelings trump formulas.

Yet when researchers pit intuition against statistical prediction (as when pitting an interviewer's predictions of academic achievement against a formula based on grades and aptitude scores), the stunning truth is that the formula usually wins. Statistical predictions are, as you would expect, fallible. But when it comes to predicting the future, human intuition—even professional intuition—is even more fallible. Three decades after demonstrating the superiority of statistical prediction over intuition, University of Minnesota clinical researcher Paul Meehl, in a retrospective essay on what he called "my disturbing little book," found the evidence more convincing than ever:

> There is no controversy in social science which shows [so many] studies coming out so uniformly in the same direction as this one. . . . When you are pushing 90 investigations, predicting everything from the outcome of football games to the diagnosis of liver disease and when you can hardly come up with a half dozen studies showing even a weak tendency in favor of the clinician, it is time to draw a practical conclusion.

The evidence continues to accumulate. In 1998 a Canadian Solicitor General research team combined data from 64 samples of more than 25,000 mentally disordered criminal offenders. What best predicted risk of future offending? As in studies with other types of criminal offenders, it was the amount of past criminal activity (illustrating once again the maxim that the best predictor of future behavior is past behavior). And what was among the *least* accurate predictors of future criminality? A clinician's judgment.

A more recent review by a University of Minnesota research team combined data from 134 studies of clinical-intuitive versus statistical predictions of human behavior, or of psychological or medical prognoses. Clinical intuition surpassed "mechanical" (statistical) prediction in only 8 studies. In 63 studies, statistical prediction fared better. The rest were a draw.

Would clinicians fare differently when allowed to conduct a first-hand clinical interview rather than just a file to read? Yes, reported the research team: allowed interviews, the clinicians fared *worse.* Many of these studies don't engage the everyday judgments commonly made by mental health professionals. Moreover, the studies often lump judgments by experienced and inexperienced clinicians.

Nevertheless, "it is fair to say that the 'ball is in the clinicians' court,'" the researchers concluded. "Given the overall deficit in clinicians' accuracy relative to mechanical prediction, the burden falls on advocates of clinical prediction to show that clinical predictions are more [accurate or cost-effective]."

In some contexts, we do accept the superiority of statistical prediction. For life insurance executives, actuarial prediction is the name of the game. Or imagine that someone says, "I just have a feeling about today's presidential election. Something tells me X is going to win it." If you have the same feeling, but then learn that "the final Gallup Poll is just out, and Y is ahead," you probably know enough to switch your bet. Gallup Polls taken just before U.S. national elections over the past half-century have diverged from election results by an average of less than 2 percent. As a few drops of blood speak for the body, so a random sample speaks for a population.

But when it comes to judging individuals, intuitive confidence soars. In 1983, the U.S. Supreme Court ruled on a petition of murderer Thomas Barefoot. The petition challenged the reliability of psychiatric predictions of his dangerousness. Justice Harry Blackmun expressed skepticism of the clinical intuitions of two psychiatrists who testified for the prosecution. Although neither had examined Barefoot, one had testified with "reasonable medical certainty" that Barefoot would constitute a continuing threat to society. The other psychiatrist had concurred, noting that his professional skill was "particular to the field of psychiatry and not to the average layman" and that there was a "one hundred percent and absolute" chance that Barefoot would constitute a continuing threat to society. Their clinical judgment carried the day, and on October 30, 1984, Texas officials executed Thomas Barefoot. Such testimony is junk science, argues experimental psychologist Margaret Hagen in *Whores of the Court*. Hagen grants a place for expert testimony about such things as the accuracy of eyewitness recall. But "psychobabble" by self-important experts is to psychological science what astrology is to astronomy, she says.

The limits of clinical intuition have also surfaced in false memory experiments. In three different studies, psychiatrists, psychologists, social workers, attorneys, and judges have evaluated children's videotaped testimonies. Could they discern which children were reporting false memories formed during repeated suggestive questioning? The consistent finding: although often confident in their ability to winnow true from false memories, professionals actually did so at no better than chance levels. False memories feel and look like real memories.

What if we combined clinical intuition with statistical prediction? What if we gave professionals the statistical prediction of someone's future academic performance or risk of violence or suicide, and asked them to improve on the prediction? Alas, notes Carnegie-Mellon University psychologist Robyn Dawes, in the few studies where this has been done, prediction was better without the "improvements."

So what has been the effect of these studies on clinical practice? "The effect . . . can be summed up in a single word," says Dawes. "Zilch." Clinical researcher Paul Meehl, for example, was honored, elected to the American Psychological Association presidency at a very young age, elected to the National Academy of Sciences, and ignored.

Meehl himself attributed clinicians' continuing confidence in their intuitive predictions to a "mistaken conception of ethics":

If I try to forecast something important about a college student, or a criminal, or a depressed patient by inefficient rather than efficient means, meanwhile charging this person or the taxpayer 10 times as much money as I would need to achieve greater predictive accuracy, that is not a sound ethical practice. That it feels better, warmer, and cuddlier to me as predictor is a shabby excuse indeed. . . . It will not do to say "I don't care what the research shows, I am a *clinician,* so I rely on my clinical experience." Clinical experience may be invoked when it's all we have, when scientific evidence is insufficient (in quantity or quality) to tell us the answer. It is *not* a valid rebuttal when the research answer is negative. One who considers "My experience shows . . ." a valid reply to research studies is self-deceived, and must never have read the history of medicine, not to mention the psychology of superstitions. It is absurd, as well as arrogant, to pretend that acquiring a Ph.D. somehow immunized me from the errors of sampling, perception, recording, retention, retrieval, and inference to which the human mind is subject.

Given our capacity for social intuition (Chapter 2) and intuitive expertise (Chapter 3), *why* does professional intuition fare so poorly?

WHY CLINICAL INTUITION FALTERS

Consider what we as human judges must do to explain or predict behavior accurately. We must intuit correlations between different predictors and the criterion—academic achievement, violence, suicide, or whatever. Then we must appropriately weight each predictor. But as noted earlier, we're prone to err at such tasks. Expert intuition may allow us to excel at tasks ranging from chess to chicken sexing. But in grocery checkout lines—where the computations are comparatively simple—we need calculating machines.

In their pioneering experiments, Loren Chapman and Jean Chapman showed how illusory correlations can infect clinical interpretation. They invited professional clinicians to study some psychological test performances and some diagnoses. Clinicians who believed that suspicious people draw peculiar eyes on the Draw-a-Person test perceived what they expected to find. This was even so when they viewed cases in which suspicious people drew peculiar eyes *less* often than nonsuspicious people. Assume a relationship exists and we likely will notice confirming instances. To believe is to see.

Hindsight also boosts clinicians' sense that they could have predicted what they know to have happened. After the suicide of rock musician Kurt Cobain, Monday morning commentators thought they could see the depression leaking through his lyrics. David Rosenhan and seven associates provided a striking example of potential error in after-the-fact explanations. To test mental health workers' clinical insights, the study team members each made an appointment with a different mental hospital admissions office and complained of "hearing voices." Apart from giving false names and vocations, they reported their life histories and emotional states honestly and exhibited no further symptoms. Most got diagnosed with schizophrenia and remained hospitalized for two to three weeks. Hospital clinicians then searched for early incidents in the pseudo-patients' life histories and hospital behavior that "confirmed" and "explained" the diagnosis. Rosenhan tells of one pseudo-patient who truthfully explained to the interviewer that he "had a close relationship with his mother but was rather remote from his father during his early childhood. During adolescence and beyond, however, his father became a close friend, while his relationship with his mother cooled. His present relationship with his wife was characteristically close and warm. Apart from occasional angry exchanges, friction was minimal. The children had rarely been spanked."

The interviewer, "knowing" the person suffered from schizophrenia, explained the problem this way:

> This white 39-year-old male . . . manifests a long history of considerable ambivalence in close relationships, which begins in early childhood. A warm relationship with his mother cools during his adolescence. A distant relationship to his father is described as becoming very intense. Affective stability is absent. His attempts to control emotionality with his wife and children are punctuated by angry outbursts and, in the case of the children, spankings. And while he says that he has several good friends, one senses considerable ambivalence embedded in those relationships also.

Rosenhan later told some staff members (who had heard about his controversial experiment but doubted such mistakes could occur in their hospital) that during the next three months one or more pseudo-patients would seek admission to their hospital. After the three months, he invited the staff to use their clinical intuition to guess which of the 193 patients admitted during that time were really pseudo-patients. Of the 193 new patients, 41 were accused by at least one staff member of being pseudo-patients. Actually, there were none.

Once a clinician conjectures an explanation for a problem such as hearing voices, the explanation can take on a life of its own. In an early demonstration of belief perseverance, Stanford psychologist Lee Ross and his collaborators had people read some actual clinical case histories. Then they told some of them that a particular event, such as a suicide, later occurred and asked them to use the case history to explain it. Finally, they were told the truth—that the patient's later history was unknown. When the people then estimated the likelihood of this and other possible events, the event they had explained now seemed quite likely.

In another study, Ross led students to think that they had excellent clinical intuition. (He told them they had done well at distinguishing authentic from fictitious suicide notes.) After the students explained why they were so good at this, Ross and his co-workers let them know that he had fibbed. The positive feedback on their intuition was faked. Despite this revelation, the students retained their new belief in their clinical intuition, citing the reasons they had conjured up to explain their apparent success (their empathy, their insights from reading a novel about suicide, and so forth) and so maintained their new belief in their clinical intuition.

Clinical intuition is vulnerable to illusory correlations, hindsight biases, belief perseverance, and also to self-confirming diagnoses. In some clever experiments at the University of Minnesota, an epicenter of efforts to assess professional intuition and sharpen critical thinking, psychologist Mark Snyder and his colleagues gave interviewers some hypotheses to check out. To get a feel for their studies, imagine yourself meeting someone who has been told that you are an uninhibited, outgoing person. To see whether this is true, the person slips questions into the conversation, such as "Have you ever done anything crazy in front of other people?" As you answer such questions, will the person meet a different you than if probing for evidence that you're shy?

Snyder found that people indeed often test their hunches by looking for confirming information. If they are wondering whether someone is an extravert, they solicit instances of extraversion ("What would you do if you wanted to liven things up at a party?"). Testing for introversion, they are more likely to inquire, "What factors make it hard for you to really open up to people?" In response, those tested for extraversion seem more sociable, and those tested for introversion come off as shy.

Given a structured list of questions to choose from, even experienced psychotherapists prefer questions that trigger extraverted responses when testing for extraversion. Assuming they have definite preexisting ideas, the same is true when they make up their own questions. Strong beliefs generate their own confirmation.

To see whether he could get people to test a trait by seeking to *dis*confirm it, Snyder told interviewers in one experiment that "it is relevant and informative to find out ways in which the person . . . may not be like the stereotype." In another experiment, he offered $25 to the person who develops the set of questions that "tell the most about . . . the interviewee." Regardless, confirmation bias persisted: People resisted using "introverted" questions when testing for extraversion.

Snyder's experiments help us understand why the behaviors of psychotherapy clients so often seem to fit their therapists' theories. When Harold Renaud and Floyd Estess conducted life-history interviews of a hundred healthy, successful adult men, they were startled to discover that their subjects' childhood experiences were loaded with "traumatic events," tense relations with certain people, and parental miscues—the very factors often invoked to explain psychiatric problems. If someone is in a bad mood, such recollections get amplified. Ergo, when Freudian therapists go fishing for early childhood problems, they often find that their intuitions are confirmed. Robert Browning understood:

As is your sort of mind,
So is your sort of search:
You'll find
What you desire.

For clinicians the implications are easily stated (though less easily practiced): Monitor the predictive powers of your intuition. Beware the tendency to see associations you expect to see. Recognize the seductiveness of hindsight, which can lead you to feel overconfident (but sometimes also to judge yourself too harshly for not having foreseen and averted catastrophes). Recognize that theories, once formed, tend to persevere even if groundless. Guard against the tendency to ask questions that assume your ideas are correct; consider opposing ideas and test them, too. Remember Richard Feynman's cautionary words: "The first principle is that you must not fool yourself—and you are the easiest person to fool."

Better yet, harness the underappreciated power of statistical prediction. As college admissions officers use statistical predictors of college success, clinicians can use checklists such as the Violence Risk Appraisal Guide, which offers predictions of whether criminals being discharged from maximum-security hospitals will commit further violent acts. (In one study, 55 percent of those statistically predicted to be "high-risk" and 19 percent of "low-risk" offenders committed a new violent act.) Physicians now have similar statistical guides for predicting risk of breast and prostate cancer. All such guides are based on assembled objective data and do what our intuition cannot: systematically weight multiple factors. If I am a physician, what should I do if my own experience with prostate cancer patients indicates that PSA levels have not predicted mortality, though studies of thousands of other cases indicate otherwise? Well, I had better discount my own limited experience—or at least consider it as just a few more data points atop a mountain of other cases. If "medical intuitives" such as Caroline Myss —a former journalist who has demonstrated for an adoring *Oprah Winfrey Show* audience her supposed ability to "diagnose" people at a glance or after a brief conversation—can do better, they should welcome a chance to join the empirical competition.

Another research-based analysis enabled a guide for predicting school violence (the guide scores eighteen student characteristics, ranging from discipline record to displays of cruelty toward animals). Yet another predicts the likelihood of rearrest among sex offenders by adding up points from a simple list of predictors (never married? any victims who were strangers? age less than twenty-five? total number of prior sexual offenses? any violent offenses? total number of prior offenses?). The total score predicts risk of new offenses, which range from greater than 50 percent for the highest risk group to 10 percent for the lowest risk group. The moral: *actuarial science strengthens clinical judgment, or at least offers a second opinion.* Actuarial science also helps protect practitioners from malpractice suits, which might otherwise allege that the clinician made aberrant decisions without attending to relevant research.

Some fields don't hesitate to make smart use of actuarial prediction. For all the mockery that has been showered on them, weather forecasters have long been stars in the world of professional forecasting. Unlike clinicians, who may never learn whether their predictions of violence are fulfilled, forecasters receive repeated prompt feedback. With daily cycles of forecast and result, forecasters readily learn to gauge their shortcomings. Thus, even before the advent of modern computer forecasting they became adept at calibrating the accuracy of their forecasts. If they said there was a 25 percent chance of rain, the odds of rain indeed were about 25 percent. Now, aided by satellites and computer programs that incorporate models of the association between barometric pressure, wind speeds, temperatures, and a host of other variables, their predictions are better than ever. And when local meteorologists take the computer "guidance" and tweak it with their own professional expertise, predictive accuracy increases still further.

Credit card companies also make sophisticated use of computers to monitor human behavior and to detect activity that departs from a user's normal behavior. Three times in recent memory, Visa has called my home because of questionable activity on my daughter's or wife's card. In one case, there was an aberrant but valid overseas use. In the two other instances, the company's artificial intelligence instantly detected fraudulent activity, triggering a Visa representative to call us and the card to be deactivated within minutes. In all three cases, I was staggered by the speed and power of this fraud detection, which human judges could never rival.

THERAPEUTIC INTUITION

Amid the scathing critiques of clinical pretension, one does find glimmers of optimism. A Ball State University team led by Paul Spengler spent nearly six years tracking down more than a thousand studies of clinical decision making. In a sample of these studies that they examined, actuarial predictions had "only a slight edge" over clinical judgments on the sorts of judgments of risk and prognosis most commonly made by mental health professionals. Moreover, Spengler reports (and as we might expect from other research on learned expertise), clinicians become more accurate decision makers as they accumulate clinical experience.

Might accuracy also rise with clinicians' confidence? To find out,

Dale McNiel and his colleagues invited 78 psychiatrists to estimate the probability that 317 psychiatric inpatients would become violent in their first week of hospitalization. During that first week, 11 percent of the patients did behave violently, as reported by the nursing staff. When the psychiatrists' confidence was moderate or low, their predictions were no better than chance. But when the psychiatrists felt highly confident, 3 out of 4 patients they expected to behave violently did so, as did none of those expected to be nonviolent. So, when actuarial prediction isn't available or when useful information goes beyond the actuarial guidelines, wise clinicians draw on their reservoir of experience if it speaks loud and clear.

Judging the effectiveness of various therapies is, however, a delicate task. Not only do clinicians benefit less than weather forecasters from prompt and frequent feedback, they're prone, like all of us, to misinterpret natural "regression to one's average" effects. People enter therapy at their darkest hours and usually leave when they're less unhappy. Thus, most clients and their therapists will readily testify to any therapy's success. "Treatments" have varied widely—from bloodletting to rebirthing, from chains to herbal remedies, from submersion chambers to systematic desensitization—but all have this in common: their practitioners have viewed them as effective and enlightened. Clients enter emphasizing their woes, justify leaving by emphasizing their well-being, and stay in touch only if satisfied. To be sure, therapists are aware of failures, but these are mostly the failures of *other* therapists, whose clients are now seeking a new therapist for a persisting or recurring problem.

To discern whether any particular therapy represents more than either a placebo effect or a natural regression from the unusual to the more usual, we must experiment. Psychology's most powerful tool for sorting reality from wishful intuition is the control group. For every would-be patient assigned to a new therapy, another is randomly assigned to an alternative. What matters, then, is not my intuition or yours, but simply this: does it work? when put to the test, can its predictions be confirmed?

For several forms of psychotherapy, the results are somewhat encouraging. With or without therapy, troubled people tend to improve (to move from their worst times back toward normality). Nevertheless, as Mary Lee Smith and her colleagues exulted after conducting the first statistical digest of psychotherapy outcome studies, "psychotherapy benefits people of all ages as reliably as schooling educates them, medicine cures them, or business turns a profit." Follow-up synopses have mostly concurred: As one said, "Hundreds of studies have shown that psychotherapy works better than nothing." In one ambitious study, the National Institute of Mental Health compared three treatments for depression: cognitive therapy, interpersonal therapy, and a standard drug therapy. Twenty-eight experienced therapists at research sites in Norman, Oklahoma; Washington, D.C.; and Pittsburgh, Pennsylvania, were trained in one of the three methods and randomly assigned their share of the 239 people with depression who participated. Clients in all three groups improved more than did those in a control group who received merely an inert medication and supportive attention, encouragement, and advice. Among clients who completed a full sixteen-week treatment program, the depression had lifted for slightly more than half of those in each treatment group—but for only 29 percent of those in the control group (Elkin & others, 1989). This verdict echoes the results of the earlier studies: those not undergoing therapy often improve, but those undergoing therapy are more likely to improve.

But what about the newer and much publicized alternative therapies? For most therapies, there is insufficient evidence, mostly because proponents and devotees feel no need for controlled research. Intuitively, they seem effective. Satisfied clients testify to this. Millions of people—Princess Diana reportedly was among them—haven't felt a need for controlled experiments before seeking out spiritualists, hypnotherapists, "anger-release" therapists, reflexologists, aromatherapists, colonic irrigationists, and "mind-body" therapists. Some therapies, however, have commanded enough attention to demand scrutiny. Consider a quick synopsis of five counterintuitive therapies, three of which have been discounted, and two which have been found surprisingly effective.

Therapeutic touch. Across the world, tens of thousands of therapeutic touch practitioners (many of them nurses) have been moving their hands a few inches from a patient's body, purportedly "pushing energy fields into balance." Advocates say these manipulations help heal everything from headaches to burns to cancer. Skeptics say the evidence shows no healing power beyond the placebo effect. But can we confirm the theory? Can healers actually intuit the supposed energy field when someone's hand is (unseen by them) placed over one of their hands? Experiments to date indicate that they cannot. Thus it appears that therapeutic touch (actually non-touch) does not work, nor is there any credible theory that predicts why it might.

Eye movement desensitization and reprocessing (EMDR). Walking in a park one day, Francine Shapiro observed that anxious thoughts vanished as her eyes spontaneously darted about. Thence was born a new therapy, for which 22,000 mental health professionals have reportedly been trained. While clients imagine traumatic scenes, the therapist triggers eye movements by waving a finger in front of their eyes. Encouraged by some early reports of success with post-traumatic stress disorder clients, EMDR therapists have recently been applying the technique to anxiety disorders, pain, grief, schizophrenia, rage, and guilt. Alas, when others tested the therapy without the eye movements—with finger tapping, for example, or with eyes fixed straight ahead while the therapist's finger wagged—the therapeutic results were the same. The therapeutic effect, it seems, lies not in eye movements but in a combination of effective exposure therapy (from safely reliving the trauma) and a robust placebo effect.

Subliminal self-help tapes. Given that we process much information intuitively and outside conscious awareness, might commercial subliminal tapes with imperceptibly faint messages indeed "reprogram your unconscious mind for success and happiness"? Might procrastinators have their minds reprogrammed with unheard messages such as "I set my priorities. I get things done ahead of time!" To find out, Anthony Greenwald, a University of Washington researcher, ran sixteen experiments and found no therapeutic effect. In one, he gave a memory-boosting tape to some with memory problems and a self-esteem–boosting tape to some with self-esteem problems. For others, he played the merry prankster and switched the labels. Although neither tape had any effect on memory or self-esteem scores, those who *thought* they had heard a memory tape *believed* that their memories had improved. A similar result occurred for those who thought they had heard a self-esteem tape. Although the tapes were ineffective, the students perceived themselves receiving the benefits they expected.

Light exposure therapy. For some people, especially women and those living far from the equator, the wintertime blahs constitute a form of depression known as seasonal affective disorder (appropriately, SAD). To counteract these dark spirits, National Institute of Mental Health researchers in the early 1980s had a bright idea: give SAD sufferers a timed daily dose of intense light (via light boxes that can now be rented or purchased from health supply and lighting stores). After clinical experience confirmed that many SAD people became less sad after light exposure therapy, skeptics wondered: Is this another regression-to-the-mean or placebo effect? Experiments offered encouraging results. Some 50 to 60 percent of those given a daily half hour of light exposure found relief, as did fewer given evening exposure and fewer yet given a placebo treatment. Scientists have also identified a possible mechanism in the shifting of melatonin secretion to an earlier time. Thus the happy verdict: for many people, bright morning light does dim SAD symptoms.

Electroconvulsive therapy. When electroconvulsive therapy (ECT) was introduced in 1938, wide-awake patients were jolted into racking convulsions and rendered unconscious by 100 volts of electricity. Not surprisingly, ECT acquired a Frankensteinlike, barbaric image. Today's kinder, gentler ECT administers general anesthesia, a muscle relaxant, and brief shock, often to only one side of the brain. But does this weird treatment work? To my astonishment, ECT is now widely regarded as the most effective therapy for severe depression that resists psychotherapy and medication. After three such sessions each week for two to four weeks, 80 percent or more of people receiving ECT improve markedly, showing memory loss for the treatment period but no discernible brain damage. Despite uncertainties about *why* it works, committees of the National Institutes of Health and the American Psychiatric Association have given ECT their stamp of approval.

So, when put to the test, some crazy-sounding ideas find support, and scientific inquiry sometimes refutes the skeptics. Who would have guessed that bright light or an electrical buzz in the brain would prove therapeutic?

More often, however, scientific inquiry relegates crazy-sounding ideas to the mountain of forgotten claims of perpetual motion machines, out-of-body travels into centuries past, and miracle cancer cures. At the end of the day, soft-headed pseudo-remedies can have wrong-headed effects. A heart of gold is no substitute for a head of feathers. To sift true intuitions from false, sense from nonsense, requires a scientific attitude: being skeptical but not cynical, open but not gullible. By testing clinical intuition—discerning its wisdom and fallibility, and learning when to undergird it with actuarial science—a hard-headed process promises to pay kind-hearted dividends.

Interviewer Intuition

Science is the great antidote to the
poison of enthusiasm and superstition.
—*Adam Smith,* Wealth of Nations, *1776*

As any employment interviewer can verify, impressions form quickly. By the time a candidate has settled into the seat, animation, extraversion, warmth, and voice have already registered. These instant intuitions, as we noted in Chapter 2, can be revealing. A two-second silent video clip of a teacher in action is all it may take to intuit students' liking for this teacher at a semester's end.

In more recent social intuition research, University of Toledo psychologist Frank Bernieri and his colleagues spent six weeks training two people in job-interviewing skills. The two then spent fifteen to twenty minutes interviewing ninety-eight volunteers of varied ages and then completed a six-page evaluation of each. Later, one of Bernieri's undergraduate students, Tricia Prickett, decided to see just how quickly impressions form. She showed people fifteen-second clips of each applicant knocking on the door, coming in, shaking hands, and sitting down. Amazingly, the strangers were able to predict the interviewers' ratings for nine of eleven judged traits. "The strength of the correlations was extraordinary," said Bernieri. As the adage says, the handshake is everything.

Mere glimpses of someone's behavior can be revealing because of the potency of traits such as expressiveness. Some people are naturally expressive (and therefore talented at pantomime and charades); others are less expressive (and therefore better poker players). To evaluate people's voluntary control over their expressiveness, Bella DePaulo and her University of Virginia colleagues asked people, while stating opinions, to *act* as expressive or inhibited as possible. Remarkably, inexpressive people, even when feigning expressiveness, were less expressive than expressive people acting naturally. And expressive people, even when trying to seem inhibited, were less inhibited than inexpressive people acting naturally. In my daily noon-time basketball games, some people play silently, others comment, joke, congratulate, and tease. As the group's motor mouth, I have often vowed to be more subdued the next day. Never have I succeeded. It's hard to be someone you're not—or not to be the someone you are.

The irrepressibility of expressiveness explains why we can size up, in seconds, how outgoing someone is. Picture researchers Maurice Levesque and David Kenny seating groups of four University of Connecticut women around a table and asking each woman merely to state her name, year in school, hometown, and college residence. Judging from just these few seconds of verbal and nonverbal behavior, how well could you guess each woman's talkativeness? In their experiment, snap judgments proved reasonably accurate predictors of each woman's talkativeness during videotaped conversations. When we judge an expressive trait such as extraversion, even extremely thin slices of behavior can be revealing. At some tasks, intuition excels.

THE INTERVIEW ILLUSION

Given our proficiency at instantly reading traits such as expressiveness, it's understandable that we interviewers feel confident in our ability to predict long-term job performance from an unstructured get-acquainted interview. What's surprising—shocking, really—is how poor those predictions actually are. Whether predicting job productivity and success or achievement in graduate or professional school, interviews are weak predictors. From their review of eighty-five years of personnel selection research, Frank Schmidt and John

Hunter determined that for all but less skilled jobs, general mental ability was the best available predictor of on-the-job success. Informal interviews that yield a subjective overall evaluation are better than handwriting analysis (which is worthless). But informal interviews are less informative than aptitude tests, work samples, job knowledge tests, and peer ratings of past job performance. If there's a contest between what your gut tells you about someone and what test scores, work samples, and peer ratings tell you, go with the latter.

So commonly do interviewers overestimate their discernment that social psychologist Richard Nisbett has given the phenomenon a name: the interview illusion. "I have excellent interviewing skills, so I don't need reference checking as much as someone who doesn't have my ability to read people," is a comment sometimes heard by a friend who is an executive search consultant. "Maybe so," he replies, "but I doubt it. The interview is a fragile and imprecise investigative tool, as studies have documented."

The interview illusion in action. It's a lesson that I have learned from experience when people have been hired despite my misgivings (and have turned into splendid colleagues) or hired with my and others' urging (and have proved disappointing or even disastrous). If only we had made more phone calls, asked more questions, turned over more stones, and not just trusted our guts. Some oft-reported (though unverifiable) stories of other interview failures suggest that I may have much company:

"You'd better learn secretarial skills or else get married."
—Modeling agency, rejecting Marilyn Monroe in 1944

"You ought to go back to driving a truck."
—Concert manager, firing Elvis Presley in 1954

"Can't act. Can't sing. Slightly bald. Can dance a little."
—A film company's verdict on Fred Astaire's 1928 screen test

Interviewers for graduate and professional schools fare no better, says Robyn Dawes in his iconoclastic *House of Cards: Psychology and Psychotherapy Built on Myth.* Dawes reports that during the 1970s the University of Texas Medical School at Houston admitted 150 students annually based on interviewers' ratings of their 800 most qualified candidates. When the legislature suddenly required them to admit 50 more students, the school admitted the only ones still available—those to whom the interviewers had given low ratings. So what was the performance difference between the two groups? Nil. The top-rated 150 and lower 50 each had 82 percent of their group receive the M.D. and similar proportions receive honors. Even after the first year of residency, both groups were doing equally well. The unavoidable conclusion: some people just interview better than others.

My niece understands. She attended an elite college on a National Merit Scholarship, got all A's except for one A-, mastered the science curriculum sufficiently to make excellent scores on the Medical College Admissions Test, and along the way also majored in Spanish and spent a semester at a Spanish-speaking university—all in preparation for a career as a physician for underserved populations. Alas, her hometown University of Washington Medical School rejected her, based on an interview from which the learned interviewers discerned she wasn't informed and mature enough to excel in medical school. (Her downfall, she later learned, was not knowing the answers to a couple of science and current events questions and saying that she handled stress by praying and asking her mom and dad for advice and support.)

To explain the superiority of statistical prediction, Dawes invites us to consider an interviewer of a graduate school applicant:

> What makes us think that we can do a better job of selection by interviewing [students] for a half hour, than we can by adding together relevant variables, such as undergraduate GPA, GRE score, and perhaps ratings of letters of recommendation. The most reasonable explanation to me lies in our overevaluation of our cognitive capacity. And it is really cognitive conceit. Consider, for example, what goes into a GPA. Because for most graduate applicants, it is based on at least 3½ years of undergraduate study, it is a composite measure arising from a minimum of 28 courses and possibly, with the popularity of the quarter system, as many as 50. . . . Yet you and I, looking at a folder or interviewing someone for a half hour, are supposed to be able to form a better impression than one based on 3½ years of the cumulative evaluations of 20–40

different professors. . . . Finally, if we do wish to ignore GPA, it appears that the only reason for doing so is believing that the candidate is particularly brilliant even though his or her record may not show it. What better evidence for such brilliance can we have than a score on a carefully devised aptitude test? Do we really think we are better equipped to assess such aptitude than is the Educational Testing Service, whatever its faults?

Why the interview illusion? What prompts the interview illusion? Why in personnel and student selection is there so great a gap between professional intuition and actuality? It's as if T. S. Eliot had us interviewers in mind when he mused that "between the idea and the reality . . . falls the shadow."

The shadow falls, first, because interviews reveal the interviewee's present intentions, and present intentions are less revealing than habitual behaviors. Intentions matter. People can change. Still, the best predictor of the person we will be is the person we have been. Wherever we go, we take ourselves.

The shadow falls, second, because interviewers much more often follow the successful careers of those they've hired than the achievements of those they've rejected. Because most people succeed, this incomplete feedback enables them to confirm their self-perceived hiring ability. Rejected by the school that should have most eagerly welcomed her, my niece instead went to one of the world's leading medical schools, Johns Hopkins, where she sailed through, was recruited to stay for her residency, and went on to serve the poor in a community clinic on Chicago's South Side. But the folks at the University of Washington don't know this, so she never got counted in their tally of interview successes and failures.

The shadow falls, third, because of the enormous power of the fundamental attribution error—an intuitive bias that, when focused on others, leads us to underestimate the influence of their situation and to overestimate the influence of their inner dispositions. We presume that as they seem, in this situation, so they are. As I seem on the basketball court, so I am—on the court tomorrow, but not necessarily in a faculty meeting an hour later. Our underestimation of the power of the situation is one of social psychology's biggest lessons. We know that *we* act differently, depending on whether we're in church, hanging out with friends, or at a 7:00 a.m. job interview. Yet we tend to think, when meeting others, that what we see is what we'll get. But mountains of research on everything from chattiness to conscientiousness reveals that how we behave has, as Malcolm Gladwell puts it, "less to do with some immutable inner compass than with the particulars of our situation." An interview is a special situation that speaks for other situations no more than a voter speaks for an electorate. The interviewee who charms our socks off may later be often late for work.

Moreover, the interview setting and interviewer behavior will influence an interviewee's performance. I once assisted another department at my college by interviewing their two faculty candidates. One was interviewed by six of us at once, with each of us asking two or three questions. "What a stiff, awkward person he is," I came away thinking. I met the second candidate privately over coffee, and we immediately discovered that we had a close mutual friend. As we talked, I was impressed by how warm and engaging she was. Only later did I remember the fundamental attribution error and reassess my intuition. I had attributed his stiffness and her warmth to their dispositions; in fact, their behaviors no doubt resulted partly from my meeting them in different contexts.

The shadow falls, fourth, because interviewers' preconceptions and moods color their perceptions and interpretations of interviewees' responses. Gladwell tells of one interviewee who responded to his question about things he wasn't good at by saying, "There are a lot of things I don't know anything about, but I feel comfortable that given the right environment and the right encouragement I can do well at." "Great answer!" noted Gladwell, whose liking and high expectations for the candidate were being confirmed. Later he pondered how he might have reacted if he had decided early on that he didn't like this person. Would the same reply have confirmed the person's arrogance and bluster? First impressions can become self-fulfilling prophecies as we seek confirmation and hear what we expect.

In many cases, first impressions precede the interview. In real-life studies, the same applicants are judged more favorably by recruiters who know them to have been prescreened. First impressions may also be formed by knowing the person's age, gender, attractiveness, and race. In a classic experiment by Carl Word, Mark Zanna, and Joel Cooper, white male Princeton University students interviewed white and black job applicants. When the applicant was black, the interviewers sat farther away, ended the interview 25 percent sooner, and made 50 percent more speech errors than when the applicant was white. Imagine being interviewed by someone who sat at a distance, stammered, and ended your interview abruptly. Would it affect your performance?

To find out, the researchers, in a second experiment, had trained interviewers treat students as either the white or black applicants were treated in the first experiment. When videotapes of the student interviewees were later rated, those treated like the blacks seemed more nervous and less effective, and afterward reported that they *felt* more nervous and less effective. What we see in others we tend to provoke in them.

THE BIGGEST INTERVIEW: MATE SELECTION

"For most of us," observes Malcolm Gladwell, "hiring someone is essentially a romantic process, in which the job interview functions as a desexualized version of a date. We are looking for someone with whom we have a certain chemistry, even if the coupling that results ends in tears." Might we also turn this around and say that dating is essentially a sexualized version of a prolonged interview? For those seeking to recruit and screen a partner for life's journey, dating and courtship are the ultimate in-depth interview.

How well do most of us fare in this biggest of all interviews? As many people find themselves poorly matched with an employer, producing at least moderate turnover in most every occupation, so, too, compelling premarital interviews often are followed by marital turnover. Between the mid-1960s and 1980, the American divorce rate more than doubled; it has now settled at a point where nearly half of marriages end in divorce.* Even this familiar but dreary figure may

*The fact is not that nearly half of all *people* divorce, but that nearly half of all *marriages* end in divorce. Repeatedly married people (think Elizabeth Taylor and Mickey Rooney) inflate the divorce rate.

overestimate marital success. University of Texas marriage researcher Norval Glenn followed the course of marriages that began in the early 1970s. By the late 1980s, only a third of the starry-eyed newlyweds were still married *and* proclaiming their marriages "very happy."

From a 1988 national survey, the Gallup Organization offered a similarly dismal conclusion: Two out of three 35- to 54-year-olds had divorced, separated, or been close to separation. If this pattern continues, the report concluded, "our nation will soon reach the point where the dominant experience of adults will have been marital instability." And if marriage is often ill fated, cohabitations (which have displaced marriage for many) are even more unstable. In 1995, according to the National Center for Health Statistics, only 10 percent of 15- to 44-year-old women reported their first cohabitation still intact.

Think about it: marriage is probably the best predictor of personal happiness—40 percent of married adults say they are "very happy," versus only 23 percent of never-married adults and even smaller proportions of the divorced and separated. Marriage and stable co-parenting predict children's well-being. Marriage predicts economic thriving and minimal risk of child poverty. Marriage predicts health and longevity. Marriage matters. Yet we're increasingly *un*likely to marry and live happily ever after. As often as not, our initial passion and giddy euphoria mutates into a cold, loveless truce, or worse. Indeed, much as drug users always find a drug's kick diminishing with prolonged use, so lovers find that passion always cools. The intense absorption in the other inevitably fades, to be replaced, in successful relationships, by that steadier warmth that social psychologists call companionate love.

We can know all this is true, yet at the end of our own premarital screening, the interviewer illusion often rides again. Recall from Chapter 4 that most marriage license applicants assess *their* chance of divorce as zero percent. When in love, it's hard to imagine being otherwise. While enjoying the thrill of romance, we don't project ourselves into the stress of sleepless parenting, a messy house, and unpaid bills. "When two people are under the influence of the most violent, most insane, most delusive, and most transient of passions, they are required to swear that they will remain in that excited, abnormal, and exhausting condition continuously until death do them part," wrote George Bernard Shaw.

Ergo, if you ask me to predict the durability of a marriage, the first thing I'd want to know about is not your intuitive feeling about the relationship—how thrilled and excited and passionate you feel. If not blind, love is at least nearsighted. Given a contest between what your gut tells you and what the actuarial predictors tell you, I'd vote with actuarial predictors such as these:

- Are you marrying after age 20?
- Did you both grow up in stable, two-parent homes?
- Did you date for a long while before marrying?
- Are you well educated?
- Do you enjoy a stable income from a good job?
- Do you live in a small town or on a farm?
- Did you not cohabit or become pregnant before marriage?
- Do you participate together in a faith community?
- Do you share similar age, education, attitudes, and values?

None of these predictors, by itself, is critical. But if you answer no to nearly all these questions, marital breakdown is, sad to say, very likely. If you answer yes to nearly all, you can probably look forward to a long and happy marriage. How you feel today matters to some extent. (Feelings after unstructured interviews likewise have *some* predictive power.) But the marks of happy marriages matter more, as do the behavior styles of happy newlyweds, whose positive interactions (smiling, touching, complimenting, laughing) outnumber negative interactions (sarcasm, disapproval, insults) by at least 5 to 1.

The illusions of the big interview, the cooling of passionate love, and the growing importance of shared values are all evident in the experiences of those in India's arranged versus love-based marriages. Usha Gupta and Pushpa Singh asked fifty couples in Jaipur, India, to complete a love scale. They found that those who married for love reported diminishing feelings of love after being married more than five years. By contrast, those in arranged marriages—couples matched by those who knew them well—reported *more* love as time went on.

STRUCTURED INTERVIEWS

In employee selection as in mate selection, subjective feelings gleaned from unstructured interviews are only modestly helpful. An interview gives me a sense of someone's expressiveness, speaking voice, willingness to make eye contact, and warmth, at least during an interview with me. But this information reveals less about behavior toward others in different settings than I'm naturally inclined to suppose. Given the importance of happy matches, personnel researchers have sought to improve prediction by putting people in simulated work situations, scouring for information on past performance and relationships, administering tests, aggregating evaluations from multiple interviewers, and developing job-specific "structured interviews."

Structured interviews replace casual conversation aimed at global evaluation with a disciplined method of collecting focused information. Jobs are analyzed. Questions are scripted. Interviewers are trained. All applicants are treated similarly. And each is rated on established scales.

In the more common unstructured interview, someone might ask, "How organized are you?" or "How do you get along with people?" or "How do you handle stress?" Savvy interviewees know how to score high. "I handle stress by prioritizing and delegating, and making sure I leave time for sleep and exercise."

Structured interviews, by contrast, seek to itemize likely reactions to specific and varied situations. Like quizzes designed to show marriage compatibility—which engage couples in comparing their marriage-relevant likes, dislikes, habits, and values—structured interviews explore job-relevant behaviors. The preparation for a structured interview therefore begins by pinpointing attitudes, behaviors, knowledge, and skills that distinguish high performers in a particular job. The process then derives job-related situations and invites applicants to say how they would handle them. Interviewers may also ask candidates to provide specific examples of job-relevant behaviors in their prior employment. "Can you recall the last time a new idea of yours helped your organization? Where did you get this idea? How did you persuade the powers that be to do it? What effect did it have?" To reduce memory distortions, the interviewer takes notes and records ratings as the interview progresses. Irrelevant questions are avoided, and follow-up spontaneous questions—which open the door to bias—are minimized. Although the structured interview therefore feels less warm and fuzzy, the interviewer can explain its purpose and that "this conversation doesn't typify how we relate to each other within this company."

Management researcher Michael Campion and his colleagues report that "one of the most strongly supported conclusions" from employment interview research is this: "Structuring the interview enhances its reliability and validity and, hence, its usefulness for prediction and decision making." Another review of 150 findings revealed that structured interviews had double the predictive accuracy of seat-of-the-pants interviews. Campion notes that job-specific structured interviews also help ensure equal employment opportunity and "are easy to implement." So why not?

If, instead, says Malcolm Gladwell, "we let personability—some indefinable, prerational intuition, magnified by the Fundamental Attribution Error—bias the hiring process today, then all we will have done is replace the old-boy network, where you hired your nephew, with the new-boy network, where you hire whoever impressed you most when you shook his hand. Social progress, unless we're careful, can merely be the means by which we replace the obviously arbitrary with the not so obviously arbitrary."

Risk Intuition

It's as if we incarcerated every petty criminal with zeal,
while inviting mass murderers into our bedrooms.
—K. C. Cole, The Universe and the Teacup, *1999*

Time for one more chance to let your intuition point you to truth.

1. The terror of September 11, 2001, claimed two-thirds as many lives in one day as the Continental Army lost (4,435) in the entire Revolutionary War. In all of the 1990s, how many people were killed by other terrorist acts worldwide? How many in the year 2000? (Terrorism includes such acts as the bombing of the destroyer *Cole* in Yemen, bombings in Northern Ireland, and lethal acts in undeclared wars.)
2. In the United States, which more frequently causes death? What's your hunch?
   - All types of accidents, or strokes?
   - Motor vehicle accidents (car, truck, and bus combined), or cancer of the digestive system?
   - Homicide, or diabetes?
   - Commercial air crashes, or rail-crossing accidents?
3. Which country has more people?
   - Australia or Burma?
   - Iraq or Tanzania?
   - Mexico or Brazil?

4. In recorded history (since 1876), about how many people have died, worldwide, from unprovoked attacks by great white sharks?

PERCEIVED VERSUS ACTUAL RISK

How closely do your perceptions of what puts our lives at risk correspond to life's actual risks? Global terrorism, according to the U.S. State Department, claimed but 2,527 lives worldwide during the 1990s—423 in 2000 (of which 17 involved American citizens or businesses). In the United States alone, accidents kill nearly as many people per *week* as global terrorism did in the decade. And yet the Grim Reaper silently claims

- nearly twice as many lives by stroke as by accident,
- three times as many by digestive cancer as by vehicle accidents,
- four times as many by diabetes as by homicide, and
- several times more at train crossings than on planes (402 versus 83 fatalities in 1999).

Our perceptions of risk, studies show, are but modestly related to actual risk. We're informed enough to know that cancer takes more lives than botulism, and that homicide kills more than terrorism. Yet our fears of plane crashes, food additives, and toxins are skewed, the experts say. Some fears we exaggerate, others we underplay. While driving to the airport we may fret over the upcoming flight. Yet mile for mile, in the last half of the 1990s Americans were thirty-seven times more likely to die in a motor vehicle crash than on a commercial flight. When I fly to New York, the most dangerous part of my journey is the drive to the airport. Once on board, I should breathe a sigh of relief. With 1.0 fatalities per 5 million passengers on U.S. scheduled airlines, we were less likely to die on any flight than, when tossing coins, to flip twenty-two heads in a row.

"So what?" a postmodernist might say. What does this little flaw in our intuition matter? If truth is personally constructed, maybe *perceived* risk should guide our lives. Economic power brokers defending genetically modified foods, nuclear power, and pesticides all trot out numbers in hopes of defeating public fears. But the public knows better.

Actually, reply the defenders of objectivity, determining public policy by what group can best affect public perception gives a big edge to those *with* economic and social power. Lobbying then trumps scientific information. The world that George Orwell described in *Nineteen Eighty-Four* depended on the manipulation of public perception, as did Hitler's Nazi movement. Moreover, when subjectivity rules, we end up with the perils of intuition—spending to avoid minuscule risks while exposing ourselves to real threats. "If we frighten [people] about ant-sized dangers, they won't be prepared when an elephant comes along," notes John Stossel. Consider some examples:

- Even before September 11, 2001, many people refused to fly. Of those willing to risk flying, 44 percent in one Gallup survey reported feeling fearful. Some buy flight insurance. "Every time I get off a plane, I view it as a failed suicide attempt," says movie director Barry Sonnenfeld. Yet commercial air travel has become safer than ever. In one 1990s period, major U.S. airlines carried more than 1 billion passengers on 16 *million* consecutive flights without a single death. Even including September 11, the 1,118 airplane passenger fatalities worldwide in 2001 was 23 percent below the thirty-year average of 1,451. When a friend tells me of revising her will before flying to New York, I cannot resist saying, "Much better to have done so before you drove to Kansas." For even if she were to board a random jet every week, she would (if her experience matched the average) have to live more than 140,000 years before crashing to her death.

  The vivid horror of September 11, with its 266 fatalities on four hijacked planes, understandably produced a flood of flight cancellations and left airlines and travel agents flying into the red. Yet even in 2001 we were safer flying than driving (especially after September 11, thanks to heightened security, more reactive passengers, and the increased likelihood that any terrorists would now find other venues). Terrorists, perish the thought, could have taken down fifty more planes with sixty passengers in each and, if we'd kept on flying, we would still have finished 2001 safer in planes than in cars. Ironically, however, the September 11 terrorists continued to claim lives by scaring people onto more dangerous highways. "When we scare people about flying, more people drive to Grandma's house, and more are killed as a result," John Stossel has said. "This is statistical murder."

- In the mid-1980s, my family and I spent a year in Scotland, flying over on a painstakingly secured Air India 747 not long after Sikh terrorists blew apart a sister Air India 747 over the Atlantic. In the ensuing months, several plane hijackings and explosions in London were followed by the American bombing of Libya, in the aftermath of which the number of Americans visiting Europe dropped by about half. Ironically, even with such terrorist acts factored in, the would-be tourists faced much greater odds of being victimized by staying home and risking their own highways.

- In 2001, controversy erupted when some basketball teams from Catholic high schools on Chicago's North Side said they would not feel safe coming to play at Catholic schools on the South Side. Yet they felt sufficiently safe to play basketball, which produces (according to the *Consumer Product Safety Review*) more than 600,000 injuries per year.

- "A woman drives down the street with her child romping around in the front seat," writes John Allen Paulos. "When they arrive at the shopping mall, she grabs the child's hand so hard it hurts, because she's afraid he'll be kidnapped" (mindless of the rarity of stranger kidnapping relative to collisions). During a thunderstorm, a man calms his fear by smoking a cigarette. Another avoids the streets of a supposedly dangerous part of town while driving without a seat belt. Many auto passengers think that, in the event of a fenderbender, they could restrain a child in their lap, and many unbelted drivers think they could protect themselves by bracing themselves against the steering wheel; such mistaken intuitions have led to many an injured child and mouth full of loose teeth. Many public as well as personal decisions involve judgments of risk.

- After the Three Mile Island and Chernobyl disasters, people feared nuclear power more than its primary alternative— burning coal. After accounting for mining and power plant accidents, nuclear waste disposal, acid rain, air pollution, and global warming, which really poses the greater risks? Is physicist Richard Wilson right to have said that "the fear of Chernobyl has done more damage than Chernobyl itself"? Our common sense is ill-prepared to answer these terribly important questions.

- People also fear some diseases more than others. Many women, for example, fear breast cancer more than heart disease, although five times as many women die of heart disease. How prevalent are various deadly diseases, and how much should we spend to control or eradicate each?
- With movie images of crazed killers in mind, people will resist a neighborhood halfway house for recovering mental patients. Not in my backyard, they say. What, really, are the odds of being victimized by someone released from a mental hospital?

Such questions motivate us to ask: Why do our risk intuitions so often err? And how might we think smarter about risk?

WHAT INFLUENCES OUR INTUITIONS ABOUT RISK?

If people's probabilistic intuitions of any given risk are likely wrong, then we must wonder why. Four factors feed the disjuncture of perception and reality.

Biological predisposition. Human behavior was road-tested in the Stone Age. We are, therefore, biologically prepared to fear dangers faced by our ancestors. Those who feared spiders, snakes, closed spaces, heights, and storms more often survived to beget those who begat those who . . . begat us. Psychologists have found that it is easy to learn but hard to extinguish fears of such stimuli. In experiments, people much more readily develop conditioned fears of spiders than of flowers. Modern fears, too, may have evolutionary roots. Our biological past predisposes us to fear confinement and heights—and therefore flying, especially in small planes. Amusement parks thrill us by awakening our primal fears. An 80 mph roller coaster drop simulates a risk we're predisposed to fear. At the end of the ride, we know we've challenged the monster and won.

Moreover, consider what we tend *not* to learn to fear. World War II air raids produced remarkably few lasting phobias. As the blitz continued, British, Japanese, and German populations did not become increasingly panicked; rather, they grew indifferent to planes not in their immediate neighborhood. Evolution has not prepared us to learn to fear bombs dropping from the sky or concealed guns or leaded gasoline. Venomous snakes, lizards, and spiders, however, are another matter. Those we do fear—although the National Safety Council reports only twelve deaths per year in the United States from all three combined. Our brains, it seems, are wired to deter us from yesterday's risks.

The availability heuristic. "Most people reason dramatically, not quantitatively," said Oliver Wendell Holmes. Horrific television and magazine images of a DC-10 catapulting in a fireball across the Sioux City runway, or the Concorde exploding in flames in Paris, or of United Flight 175 slicing into the World Trade Center form indelible memories. And availability in memory provides our intuitive rule-of-thumb to the frequency with which things happen. Australia, Iraq, and Mexico are readily available in memory, and so may intuitively seem more populous than Burma, Tanzania, and Brazil. But in fact, the latter have 60 to 120 percent more people. Relative to their actual death rates, stories of air crash deaths are 6,900 times more likely to make page one of the *New York Times* than are cancer deaths. Something that kills unfamous people one at a time is not news; to make the front page or the network news, it needs to kill people in bunches.

Thousands of safe car trips (for those who've survived to read this) have extinguished our initial anxieties while driving. In less familiar realms, vivid, memorable images crash into our consciousness. Credit people with knowing and remembering what they've seen, notes risk researcher Baruch Fischhoff, "even if they don't realize how unrepresentative the observed evidence is." One can know the statistics on the infrequency of attacks by great white sharks—though did you guess close to the mere sixty-seven recorded unprovoked human fatalities worldwide since 1876? Yet after watching *Jaws* we may still feel skittish while enjoying the Atlantic surf. While working on this chapter I read a detailed account of eight-year-old Jessie Arbogast's loss of his arm to a shark while splashing fifteen feet from a Pensacola, Florida, beach. Will I be able to banish that shark image from my awareness while body surfing on a break from the ensuing week's meeting at a nearby beach hotel? Not likely. We may *know* our fears are irrational, but no matter. With images from horror movies stuck in our mind's recesses, the creaking house seems foreboding when we're alone at night. Even smokers (whose habit shortens their lives, on average, by about five years) may fret before flying (which, averaged across people, shortens life by one day).

Have some fun with a friend. Say, "Regis Philbin here, for $32,000. According to Consumer Product Safety Commission projections from data gathered in hospital emergency rooms, which of these products annually has the most associated injuries?"

a. Playground equipment
b. Home workshop power saws
c. Cooking ranges and ovens
d. Beds, mattresses, and pillows

"And—for $64,000—which of these elicits the most injuries?"

a. Scissors
b. Hammers
c. Chainsaws
d. Toilets

Although it is much easier to imagine injuries on playgrounds and with hot and sharp objects, the correct answers are (please read this sitting down): beds, mattresses, and pillows, and toilets.

Indeed, the fifth most injury-laden locale, after stairs, floors, basketball courts, and bicycles, is *beds*. One struggles to form images of the nearly 457,000 people (see table) injured while interacting with beds. "Doc, I threw my arm out fighting with my pillow." (Toilet injuries are said to overwhelmingly afflict men, but I won't even try to form that image.)

If, mindful of these weird facts, you think this means that you can relax when picking up a chainsaw but should dread climbing into bed or using the toilet, bear in mind the base rate of these activities. Recall from Chapter 6 the representativeness heuristic. Chainsawing is more representative of an injury-prone activity. Even if (I am making these numbers up) chainsaws are 5,000 times more dangerous than toilets—but we collectively spend 10,000 more hours on toilets—then toilet injuries will outnumber chainsaw injuries by 2 to 1.

Product	Estimated injuries, 1998
Beds, mattresses, pillows	456,559
Playground equipment	248,372
Home workshop power saws	91,771
Cooking ranges, ovens	44,824

Source: "NEISS Data Highlights—1998," Consumer Product Safety Review, Fall 1999.

Product	Estimated injuries, 1997
Toilets	44,335
Hammers	41,518
Scissors	30,290
Chainsaws	29,684

Source: U.S. Consumer Product Safety Commission's National Electronic Injury Surveillance System, reported in Statistical Abstract of the United States, 2000, table 213.

There is a bright side to the availability heuristic. Some years ago, Betty Ford and Happy Rockefeller developed breast cancer. Their well-publicized experiences sent millions of American women to their physicians for tests. If we experience some unfortunate event— an assault, a credit card theft, a breakdown of a particular make of car—we don't just add another data point to the mountain of human experience. We're changed by our own memorable experiences. Once burned, twice shy. Never again, we vow.

And there is a not-so-bright side. We overgeneralize from our memorable experiences. After our Northwest Airline flight arrives three hours late, without our bags, we may vow "I'm never taking another Northworst flight! They're totally unreliable!" But this was just one flight among many thousands. To assess the actual risks of flight problems, we need only check the Federal Aviation Administration tables of on-time arrival and lost baggage rates among the various airlines—tables that incorporate millions of experiences. But such numbers are mind-numbing. What sticks in our mind and colors our judgment is our own vivid experience.

Lack of control. Risks beyond our control strike more terror than those we determine. Skiing, by one estimate, poses 1,000 times the health and injury risk of food preservatives. Yet many gladly assume the risk of skiing but avoid preservatives. We may fear violent crime more than clogged arteries, planes more than cars, and genetically engineered foods more than biking—in each case partly because of our visceral reactions to things beyond our control. "We are loath to let others do unto us what we happily do to ourselves," noted risk analyst Chauncey Starr.

Some 150 studies comparing men's and women's risk-taking reveal that in fourteen of sixteen realms (including intellectual risk-taking, physical skills, smoking, and sex) men are the greater risk-takers. One evolutionary psychologist has speculated that bold males may have attracted more mates and thus enjoyed a reproductive advantage. But males' greater social power and sense of control may also be at work. As women have gained more power and control, the gender gap in risk-taking has shrunk.

Immediacy. We fear what we're biologically prepared to fear. We overestimate the likelihood of dreaded, publicized, and cognitively available events. We fear what we cannot control. And we fear what's on the near horizon. Teens are indifferent to the toxicity of smoking because they live more for the present than the distant future. Much of the plane's threat is telescoped into the moments of takeoff and landing, while the dangers of driving are diffused across many moments to come, each trivially dangerous. A nuclear accident would be now. Global warming is far off. (Our descendants may despise our generation, but we won't be around to know.)

THINKING SMARTER ABOUT RISK

For all these reasons, note Carnegie-Mellon psychologist George Loewenstein and his colleagues, "people's perceptions of the risks of hazardous technologies or activities are influenced by risk dimensions that have little to do with . . . possible outcomes and their probabilities." If, indeed, our intuitions of risk are out of touch with real outcomes and probabilities, and if our risk-related intuitions have consequences for our personal choices and public policies, how can we think and act more wisely?

Assessing costs and benefits. After a killer tornado ripped through Del City, Oklahoma, in 1998, President Clinton urged people to re-build with disaster shelters in their homes: "We know that lives can be saved under almost all conditions if there is at least one room properly encased and protected with concrete in a house." But given the $3,500 estimated average cost of such a room and the average person's 1 in 4.4 million annual chance of being killed by a tornado, is this the smartest expenditure for those wanting more security? Or would $45 for a bike helmet and $1,000 for anti-lock brakes do a lot more?

Was the Clinton administration smarter when it outraged safety advocates by not forcing General Motors to replace ill-designed fuel tanks on older-model pickup trucks? The decision saved General Motors an estimated $500 million, in exchange for which it contributed $51 million to traffic safety programs. "GM bought off the government for a pittance," said the safety advocates, "at the expense of thirty more people expected to die in fiery explosions." Actually, after additional time for litigation, there would only be enough of the old trucks left to claim six to nine more lives, said the Department of Transportation. Take that $500 million ($70 million per life) and apply it to screening children for preventable diseases or more vig-orous anti-smoking education programs and one will save many more lives (albeit lives that would have been extinguished not with a bang, but a whimper). By doing such cost-benefit analyses, say those who calculate risks, our government could simultaneously save us billions of dollars and thousands of lives.

Consider some other examples: Should building codes be sharply upgraded to mandate greater safety in new homes? Or would the resulting price increase require many middle- and lower-income fam-ilies to stay in older, unsafe structures longer—thus producing a net loss of health and life due to falls, fumes, and fires?

Should safety seats be required on airplanes for children under two, or should parents be able to hold them? Federal Aviation Administration regulations require that coffeepots and adults be strapped down, but not infants and toddlers. It sounds like a good idea. But an FAA-commissioned study determined that requiring safety seats (which means buying an extra ticket) would actually cost lives, by causing one-fifth of families to drive rather than fly. Airplane safety seats would save an estimated one small child per decade, while the extra driving would kill nine children.

We can quibble over the numbers and assumptions. Should we calculate total years of life gained by applying a regulation? (That favors regulations that protect children over equally effective and costly measures to protect senior citizens.) Should we protect people against risks they voluntarily undergo? How should we weight deaths relative to injuries? Should we aim for zero risk? Or should we prefer taking a risk of, say, insecticide poisoning from 15 in 10,000 to 5 in 10,000 rather than taking an equivalent threat from 5 in 10,000 to 0 in 10,000? (Most people are more bothered by the 0 to 5 difference between risk-free and small risk than by the 5 to 15 difference in degree of risk.) Such questions must be engaged. Still, say risk experts, cost-benefit calculations are worth considering as part of any new legislative or regulatory process. Knowledge is preferable to ignorance.

After the crash of TWA Flight 800, and again after September 11, polls showed that most people were willing to pay up to $50 more for a round-trip ticket if it increased airline safety. Take that money, or even the $5 or so added to every ticket for airport security, and one could save countless more lives in many other ways. Bread for the World president David Beckmann, formerly a World Bank economist, notes that "world hunger has been reduced over the past decades and that it's now feasible to make dramatic progress against hunger. According to one U.S. government estimate, the United States could do its share to cut world hunger in half by 2015 for about $1 billion a year—equivalent to about $4 per American per year. This assistance—and comparable contributions from the other industrialized countries—would fund agriculture, schools, basic health care, and other investments that help struggling families improve their lives."

But tell that to anxious and mildly claustrophobic passengers about to leave the security of planet Earth, with haunting images of terrorist explosions not so dimly in mind. If airport security does not significantly extend our lives, it at least extends our comfort, and that alone probably justifies it. (Besides, when we're in airports *we* are the ones being protected, not the hungry ones elsewhere. Spare me, let others die.) But the point remains: When considering ways to spend money to spare injuries and save lives, smart people will not be overly swayed by rare though dreaded catastrophes. To be wise is to be mindful of the realities of how and why humans suffer and die. The wise person's humanitarian plea will therefore be: "Show me the numbers." Big hearts and hard heads can come wrapped in the same skin.

Communicating risk. Imagine that cigarettes were harmless—except for an occasional innocent-looking one in every 50,000 packs that is filled with dynamite instead of tobacco. Not such a bad risk of having your head blown off. But with 250 million packs a day consumed worldwide, we could expect more than 5,000 gruesome deaths daily—surely enough to have cigarettes banned everywhere.*

Ironically, the lost lives from these dynamite-loaded cigarettes would be far less than from today's actual cigarettes. Each year throughout the world, tobacco kills some 3 million of its best customers. That's equivalent to 20 loaded jumbo jets daily. And the worst is yet to come. Given present trends, according to the World Health Organization, the death rate will grow to 10 million annually, meaning that half a billion (say that number slowly) people alive today will be killed by tobacco. A teen-to-the-grave smoker has a 50 percent chance of dying from the habit, and the death is often agonizing and premature (as Philip Morris acknowledged in 2001 when it responded to Czech Republic complaints about the health-care costs of tobacco by reassuring the Czechs that there was actually a net "health-care cost savings due to early mortality" and the resulting savings on pensions and elderly housing). Smoke a cigarette and nature will charge you twelve minutes—ironically, just about the length of time you spend smoking it.

*This analogy, which I have adapted with world-based numbers, was suggested by mathematician Sam Saunders and reported by K. C. Cole in *The Universe and the Teacup.*

The risks of smoking are hardly well-guarded secrets. The only smoker who hasn't realized that cigarettes are harmful, says Dave Barry, "is the type of smoker whose brain has been removed with a melon scoop." The "smoking can be harmful to your health" warning is on every pack. In the United States, 96 percent of people (though only 58 percent of tobacco farmers) believe that "smoking is harmful to people." In Canada, 97 percent of teens and adults agree that smoking is associated with lung cancer, and nearly as many acknowledge smoking's links with respiratory ailments and heart disease. But the statistics of smoking risks fail to persuade many teens. When asked to consider a sixteen-year-old smoker, four in ten adolescent smokers agree that "although smoking may eventually harm this person's health, the very next single cigarette he/she smokes will probably not cause any harm." (The next one and the next and the next don't matter, though, of course, the 300,000 smoked by a pack-a-day teen before age 60 do.) So how can the import of statistics be more effectively communicated?

The Canadian government has an idea. It is now using pictures of rotting teeth, cancerous lungs, and damaged brains and hearts to make smoking's consequences more vivid and cognitively available. New regulations require cigarette manufacturers to relinquish 50 percent of each cigarette pack to producing the grisly images, which Canadian research shows is sixty times more likely than text-only warnings to persuade smokers to quit. A picture is worth a thousand words.

But even the numbers can be more effectively communicated. What business writer David Dreman says of stock market psychology is true of much else: "The tendency to underestimate or altogether ignore past probabilities in making a decision is undoubtedly a most significant problem of intuitive predictions." To help people attend to probabilities, psychologist Kimihiko Yamagishi has framed information in various ways. People rate cancer as riskier when it is said to kill 1,286 out of 10,000 people rather than 12.86 out of 100. In fact, 1,286 out of 10,000 was rated as more threatening than 24.14 out of 100!

Other research confirms this anomaly in our intuitions about risk. Told about a violent patient whose risk of violence was 20 percent, only 21 percent of forensic psychologists and psychiatrists recom-

mended that the patient not be discharged. Twice as many—41 percent—recommended continued confinement if the risk was instead
said to be "20 out of 100." Tell people that some chemical exposure is
projected to kill 10 people in every 10 million and they will be more
frightened than if told the fatality risk is .000001. Given a chance to
win a prize by drawing a red jelly bean, many people prefer to draw
from an urn that has 7 red beans out of 100 rather than an urn with 1
red bean out of 10. In each such instance, people seem to focus on the
numerator and forget the denominator. With 7 out of 100, they see
seven chances to win! Alas, intuition gone awry defeats rationality.

If there are different ways of framing statistical information, we
can present it in more than one way and try to balance the biases,
advises the distinguished risk researcher Paul Slovic and his colleagues. One could, for example, say, "Of every 100 patients similar to
Mr. Jones, 20 are expected to be violent to others. In other words, Mr.
Jones is estimated to have a 20% likelihood of violence."

Framing accident statistics on a lifetime basis also makes more of
an impression. Drivers are more inclined toward seatbelt use if told
they have a 1 in 3 lifetime chance of serious injury than if told they
have a 1 in 100,000 chance of an accident on their next outing.

Numbers can also be communicated more vividly. If "statistics are
human beings with the tears dried off," note decision researcher
Melissa Finucane and her colleagues, then "put the tears back on."
"To sensitize legislators to the 38,000 annual gunshot fatalities in the
United States," create a photo of 38,000 victims' faces.

Risks as feelings. Having itemized our misguided intuition about
risk, let us, finally, reaffirm our general emotional intelligence.
Brain-damaged people who live without emotion, unable to intuitively adjust their behavior in response to others' feelings, are socially dysfunctional. Some unfeeling people are sociopaths. If conditioned to anticipate an electric shock, sociopathic individuals exhibit
a milder physiological response than do other people. They are cool—
and callous.

Emotional memories, supplemented by Pavlovian conditioning,
deter us from many real risks. Our brains, as noted in Chapter 2, come
with a built-in hotline from the eye to the amygdala, that pair of emotional control centers that enable our greased-lightning responses to

dangers before our intellect can interpret what's happening. This hard-wired alarm system, enhanced by a storehouse of emotional memories, helped our ancestors avoid predators and catastrophes.

Our emotional intuitions are often adaptive and even more often powerful. If an activity such as smoking or skiing gives us pleasure, we tend to downplay its risks and exaggerate its benefits (and just the reverse if we dislike such activities). Emotions are another heuristic that alter our intuitions, notes Slovic. Indeed, argue George Loewenstein and his colleagues, when emotional reactions to a situation diverge from cognitive assessments, "emotional reactions often drive behavior." Someone with a phobia of snakes or public speaking or flying may *know* that such fears are groundless. But feelings rule. As we also noted in Chapter 2, the primitive amygdala sends more neural projections up to the brain's cortex than it receives back. And that makes it easier for our feelings to hijack our thinking than for our thinking to rule our feelings. A movie's background music manipulates our emotions, which color our perceptions.

That being the case, cost-benefit analyses can help restrain misguided public fears. Before spending billions to save hundreds while millions would save thousands, let's consider the risks and the costs. Rather than being driven by terror and hysteria, let's step back and think.

Gamblers' Intuition

Suckers have no business with money anyway.
—*Canada Bill Jones, three-card monte dealer*

Americans annually walk into casinos, lottery agencies, video poker arcades, race tracks, and the like with more than $500 billion—up about thirtyfold from $17 billion in 1974—and walk out with some $450 billion. Gambling is rightly said to have replaced baseball as the American pastime. Seventy million people a year now attend major league baseball games, while 107 million visit casinos in just Las Vegas, Atlantic City, and Mississippi. The National Gambling Impact Study Commission, appointed by President Clinton and Congress, reported that the money spent on gambling—$54 billion, according to a 2000 General Accounting Office report—is more than Americans spend on recorded music, movie tickets, spectator sports, and theme parks combined. Las Vegas affords 100,000 hotel rooms, billion-dollar hotels, and tycoon profits, thanks to the $6 billion a year that visitors leave behind. But its influence is dwarfed by the legalization of gambling in forty-eight states, hundreds of Native American and riverboat casinos within easy reach of most, and tens of thousands of slot machines. Montana alone has a reported 17,400 video poker and keno machines in 1,700 bars and convenience stores.

Rather than restrain gambling, thirty-seven states now sponsor it, encouraging citizens to join in and depending on them to lose. States now spend more than $400 million a year trying to woo citizens into playing. "Saving for a rainy day takes too long," said one state ad. "You could win $50,000 instantly if you play the lottery." "You gotta be in it to win it," reminds another. "In Chicago's saddest, roughest ghetto," observes Chicago priest John Egan, "there's a billboard that shows a huge Lotto stub. Its single line of boldface copy: 'This might be your ticket out of here.' What the billboard does *not* say is that the odds are 12,913,583-to-1 against you."

Massachusetts mocked the value of education and hard work with an ad offering two options for how to "make millions." "Plan A: Start studying when you're about 7 years old, real hard. Then grow up and get a good job. From then on, get up at dawn every day. Flatter [your] boss. Crush competition ruthlessly. Climb over backs of co-workers. Be the last one to leave every night. Squirrel away every cent. Avoid having a nervous breakdown. Avoid having a premature heart attack. Get a face lift. Do this every day for 30 years, holidays and weekends included. By the time you're ready to retire you should have your money." But then there's Plan B: "Play the lottery."

Hoping to outdo Massachusetts in tastelessness, Connecticut has invited its citizens to "get even luckier than you did on prom night." While observing this exploitation of citizens, William Safire wondered, tongue-in-cheek, if states might want to go a step further: "Why let the profits from sex-for-sale go to predatory pimps when Washington could collect the procuring fee, with proceeds going to health care for the post-elderly?" We have state-run lotteries, why not state-run brothels?

With so much money at stake, it is little wonder that the gambling industry is now putting money in politicians' pockets, with 64 percent of soft money going to the GOP, reports public interest lobby Common Cause. In 1998, South Carolina's Republican governor, David Beasley, made getting rid of the "cancer" of 30,000 video poker machines—each averaging $22,000 in profits the previous year—a top issue in his run for a second term. He felt that too many families were losing homes and being put at risk for breaking up. The voters, however, got rid of Beasley. They chose his opponent, who was well funded by the gambling industry.

Gambling fever is not peculiarly American. A 1998 British Psychological Society report on Britain's National Lottery concluded that

"90 percent of the population is reckoned to have bought at least one Lottery ticket." In 2000, 60 percent of Britishers regularly bought lottery tickets.

What is the return on a gambled dollar? For state lotteries and for the British and Canadian lotteries, bettors receive back about 50 cents on every dollar. One of my statistician colleagues has noted that here in Michigan—where the state gives a 50-cent tax credit on every dollar (up to $400) given to charities such as colleges, and where the federal government credits us with another 15 percent or more if we itemize deductions—one gets 65 cents or more back on the donated dollar. Instead of buying a lotto ticket, just give that money to your local college and you are 15 cents or more richer.

In *What Are the Odds?* statistician and gambling expert Michael Orkin gives the return on various casino games. Roulette wheels, for example, have thirty-eight sections—eighteen red, eighteen black, and two white. If you bet on red and win, you get your dollar back plus another. The odds of nobody winning—the house's return—are 2:38, which is 5.3 cents per dollar bet. Those are much better odds than are offered by government lotteries. Quarter slot games in Las Vegas and Atlantic City mostly return 90 to 93 cents on the dollar. One form of craps, a dice game, offers even better odds—only a 1.4 percent skim by the house. But craps enables many more bets per hour. Indeed, enough people bet enough money, repeatedly, that casinos end up emptying far more money from people's pockets than do lotteries. Their profit margin isn't much, but the volume adds up.

WHO GAMBLES?

The millions of Americans who gamble each year fall along a continuum. At one end are the disciplined recreational gamblers who play the slots, the roulette wheels, and the craps tables knowing they will lose over time. They have a budget for exactly how much they will pay per day for the fun of playing. Some folks pay to ski, others to golf, others to ride roller coasters, and others to play at the MGM Grand. There may be physically and socially healthier recreations. (Standing alone in front of a video poker machine does not satisfy the human need to connect as does card playing with friends or a bingo night at the club—both of which have declined sharply as casinos have spread.) Still, families are not being bankrupted nor marriages crushed by such recreational "gaming" (the tame word for gambling).

At the continuum's other end are those whose search for phantom riches is fueled by inextinguishable illusions. *New York Times* writer Brett Pulley describes one Orange, New Jersey, convenience store where customers come looking for $4 "dream books" that advise one how to translate dreams or daily happenings into lottery numbers. If you dream about a cat, one advises, bet the number 114 (unless the cat is black, when you should bet 244). If you buy a hat, bet on 815 or 816. One thirty-six-year-old custodian with overdue bills was there each day for a month, betting $15 daily on 898. "I wish that 898 would come out," he said wistfully, because if it did, the $2,750 prize "would solve all my problems."

One needn't be so superstitious to be among the 15.4 million adults and adolescents estimated by a Harvard study to be plagued by problem or even pathological gambling. As access to casinos and lotteries has become increasingly easy, Gamblers Anonymous reports that local chapters in the United States grew from 650 in 1990 to 1,500 in 2001. Problem gamblers include the twenty-eight-year-old Bronx waiter who stood in the Powerball line to spend the $3,000 he had saved for aircraft trade school tuition. "If I win, I won't have to go to school. Heck, I can buy my own aircraft." Such hopeful people are among the estimated 10 percent of lottery players who account for half of all lottery purchases. A University of Illinois economist estimates that 52 percent of casino revenues come from problem or pathological gamblers. One Gamblers Anonymous member, Joyce, started playing New York's Pick 6 Lotto, lured by ads offering a dream for a dollar. Four years later she had won $30 and owed between $40,000 and $60,000. "It was more like a dollar and a nightmare," she later reflected.

And who are these "best" customers? They are, says Common Cause director and former Massachusetts attorney general Scott Harshbarger, "those who can least afford to throw their money away." In Massachusetts, reported the *Boston Globe,* the poor Chelsea area has one lottery agent for every 363 residents; upscale Wellesley has one for every 3,063 residents. In New Jersey, people living in the one hundred lowest-income zip code areas in 1998 each spent $53 on instant-win lottery scratch tickets per $10,000 income—more than four times the $12 per $10,000 spending rate of people in the one hundred wealthiest zip codes. On the popular Pick 4 game, the poor neighborhoods had six times the spending rate. Likewise, neighborhoods with the least educated people spent at five times the rate of the most educated neighborhoods. I imagine New Jersey officials, gazing out across the Hudson River at the Statue of Liberty, plotting a new state lottery ad campaign: "Bring me your tired, your poor, your huddled masses."

Iowa's Tourism Task Force has said that "gambling creates wealth." Actually, it *redistributes* wealth. As a way to make money it is the "antithesis of love," noted Archbishop William Temple, because gambling attempts "to make a profit out of the inevitable loss and possible suffering of others." Indeed, state lotteries play Robin Hood in reverse, by taking from economically marginal people and giving the revenues as reduced taxes for the wealthy. In states where lotteries support education (a bait-and-switch ploy that merely diverts tax revenues to other priorities), poor bettors are subsidizing the state university tuition of the middle class. State lotteries are a tax on the poor. As such, they are the only tax "that conservatives support," says William Safire, and "the only regressive tax embraced by liberals."

WHY DO PEOPLE GAMBLE?

We have, then, at least two groups of gamblers—the disciplined recreational gamers, who have no illusions of long-run winning), and the problem gamblers, whose flawed intuitions go before many a fall. But in both cases, gambling obviously sucks money from the gambler. A $1 lottery ticket has but a 50-cent "expected value" (because states pay out in prizes only half what people bet). So why do so many people hold false hopes? Why will people stand three hours in a Powerball queue after driving two hours from a neighboring state? Why do some customers become so convinced that their slot machine is about to pay off that they refuse to leave it for bathroom breaks (creating problems for the cleanup crew: urine in plastic coin cups and on the floor for those not wearing adult diapers).

The thrill of the play is surely part of the answer. Greed is another motivator. But given that intelligent greed would never pay $1 for something worth 50 cents, we must look deeper. Why is greed deluded? What cognitive viruses infect gamblers' intuitions?

The misperception of probabilities. Lotteries are not only a tax on the poor, but "a tax on the mathematically challenged," observes DePaul University mathematician Roger Jones. We find it hard to intuitively comprehend very long odds. Try explaining 10,000-to-1 odds to a high school sophomore basketball player who neglects schoolwork while fantasizing about making it to the NBA.

Psychologists have explored the "subjective overestimation" of improbable events. Bettors "overestimate the chances of low probability but highly favorable outcomes," notes Iowa State University statistician Hal Stern. His analysis of bets placed on 38,047 horses in 3,785 Hong Kong horse races in one study, and similar analyses by other researchers, reveal that the public tends to underestimate the probability that a big favorite will win and to overestimate the success of longshots. "Individuals have a poor intuition for probability," Stern surmises.

But longshots do happen. When Illinois retired electrician Frank Capaci threw five dollars into a multistate Powerball lottery in 1998, each of his five tickets faced 80.1 million-to-one odds. Among the 138.5 million tickets purchased—making it likely that one or two people would win—he was the single lucky winner of $195 million (actually, about $70 million when taken as a lump sum, after taxes). Two months later, thirteen Ohio assembly line workers each kicked in $10 to buy 130 tickets and became the sole winners—among nearly 211 million tickets purchased—of a $295.7 multistate Powerball lottery. Nine months later in Boston, Maria Grasso, a Chilean immigrant who worked days as a babysitter and nights helping handicapped children, bought three tickets for the six-state Big Game. One of them was the lone winner among 83 million tickets sold for that drawing, netting her a $197 million payoff (again, taken as a $70 million lump sum, after taxes).

Three tickets won, and made big news. Hardly noticed were the billion-plus losing tickets purchased in all the drawings leading up to these three lottery jackpots. (Each was won, as we might have expected, by the sorts of people attracted to lotteries—those who feel the most need for the money but who also can least afford gambling debts.) Fantasies of winning enticed Joe, a forty-two-year-old New York truck driver, to put down $30 to $50 a week playing the Lotto. Although he hadn't won a dime in four years—after forking over $10,000 in hopes of a jackpot—he persists. "Well, hey, you never know."

Indeed, you never know. Think of the thousands of hopeful people whom Publishers Clearing House (the sweepstakes outfit) reports call to warn the prize patrol that "their house is hard to get to or that they'll be at Uncle Jack's." It's true—you never do know—but with only a 1-in-100 million chance of winning the $10 million grand prize, they can probably comfortably visit Uncle Jack. We understand chances like 1 in 100 or 1 in 1,000. But the difference between 1 in 10,000 and 1 in 80 million or 100 million gets fuzzy. If you've got only a 1-in-10,000 chance of a prize, the odds may seem impossibly slim. But don't give up hope—even 1 in 10,000 gives you 80,000 times the chance of winning as does that Powerball ticket.

Lightning has to strike somewhere (although lightning is many times more likely to strike you than is a Powerball win). Strange things do happen. For Maria Grasso, winning was an incredibly lucky accident. In 1999, the passengers of a Serbian train and three weeks later of a Kosovo bus had similarly freakish *un*lucky accidents. Both vehicles were crossing bridges at the precise moments that NATO bombs hit them. The coincidences were incredible. But drop enough ammunition (or buy enough tickets), and we can expect someone to die (or win).

If, despite the odds, you're going to bet in Powerball lotteries, there is one smart thing you can do. Do as the three solo winners above did, and pick numbers not likely to be chosen by others who would split the prize with you. Given that any combination of five random numbers from 1 to 49 is as likely as any other, don't space your numbers the way most people imagine a random series might look (say, 3, 17, 25, 32, and 46). The Ohio "lucky 13's" solo winning ticket had four numbers between 39 and 49. In 2001, retired San Jose, California, supermarket clerk Carmen Castellano became the sole winner of a $141 million SuperLotto jackpot with choices of 3, 22, 43, 44, 45 (and mega number 8).

Psychologist Eileen Hill has discerned a similar phenomenon in Britain's National Lottery, in which people choose six numbers from 1 to 49. Lottery weeks with no jackpot winners have usually been weeks with nonrandom looking little streaks, such as 2, 5, 21, 22, 25, 32. Weeks with multiple winners have usually been streakless weeks, with spaced-out numbers—just what many people expect from random data. The ninth lottery draw, with winning numbers 7, 17, 23, 32, 38, and 42 produced 133 winners who had to divide the prize. The irony is that most people who try to generate random-seeming sequences miss the bunches and streaks so often found in random data. And when they do generate sequences, they often lack creative flair. The sequence 1, 2, 3, 4, 5, 6 is as likely as any other. But nearly 30,000 players among the 128 million tickets purchased for the sixty-third weekly draw chose it. Although there is no better way to pick a random sequence than to let the machine do it for you, many people seem to think they can do better.

Another common nonrandom preference is for numbers that represent birthdays. To explore this preference, Dartmouth researcher Laurie Snell examined 102,006 numbers chosen by 17,001 people in a 1996 Powerball lottery with picks from 1 to 45. As the figure shows, the smaller numbers associated with birthdays (and lucky numbers) were indeed more likely. Seven was the most popular pick; less than one-third as many picked the least popular number, 37. The inaugural drawing of the British Lottery did have a preponderance of low numbers—five of the six were under 31 (out of 49)—and produced five times the expected number of winners, including seven who had to share the jackpot. So, to avoid sharing the jackpot, don't favor the popular numbers.

Psychologists Thomas Holtgraves and James Skeel exposed people's perceptions of randomness in their bets placed in Indiana's Pick 3 Lottery. You can play, too: Pick any three-digit number from 0 to 999.

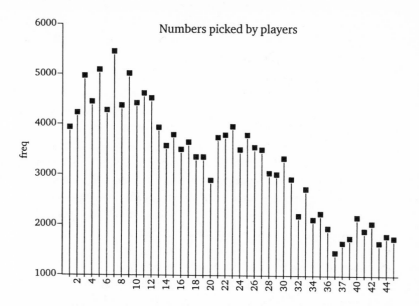

Numbers picked by players

Did your number have a repeated digit (as in 737)? Probably not. Only 14 percent of 2.24 million number strings chosen in July 1991 had a repeated digit. Although repeated digits actually occur in 28 percent of the available numbers, such numbers *look* less random (and people prefer to bet random-looking series). In actual random sequences, as we noted in Chapter 7, seeming patterns and streaks (such as repeating digits) occur more often than people expect.

One can also capitalize on others' flawed intuitions by betting on numbers that have recently won. In one analysis of bets placed over twelve weeks in Maryland's Pick 3 lottery, it took the full three months for winning numbers to fully recover their popularity. Another analysis, with data from 1,785 daily drawings for New Jersey's Pick 3 lottery, revealed that 25 percent fewer people than usual bet on a number that won the previous week. This urge to "bet on numbers that are due" and avoid recent winning numbers—the "gambler's fallacy"— makes a nifty class demonstration. I flip a coin, but before each flip I invite the students to write down their prediction—heads or tails. I announce the outcomes as heads, tails, tails, tails, tails. Then, just before the sixth toss, I say, "Since it's 50–50 whether it will be heads or tails, half of you will have predicted each, right?" However, a show of hands reveals the overwhelming majority has picked heads—as if the paucity of heads to this point has some bearing on the next outcome.

The gambler's fallacy feeds a gambler's intuitions. "My luck has to change." "Soon the odds will switch in my favor." It's true that exceptionally bad luck is likely to be followed by less extremely bad luck (because randomly variable outcomes always tend to regress from the unusual to the more normal). If you've lost four times in a row on the roulette wheel, notes Thomas Gilovich, there's a 95 percent chance that you will do better in the next four spins. But this is not due to an automatic self-correcting process: your chances of winning would be the same if you had *won* on the previous four. Coins, dice, roulette wheels, and lottery balls have no memory!

Statistician Ruma Falk offers a delightful parallel. Pause to consider: Do men have more sisters than women do?

Most introductory probability students at Jerusalem's Hebrew University presumed they do. Falk notes that "intuitively, it may seem that, because 'on the average' families have an equal number of sons and daughters," the average family would tend to have a sister to balance the brother. But this is akin to the gambler's fallacy. The first child's gender doesn't influence the gender of a family's other children. At conception, the egg and the sperm don't know the gender of children previously conceived. In two-child families, there are four equally likely arrangements of offspring: boy, boy; boy, girl; girl, boy; and girl, girl. Notice that half the offspring in these families have a sibling of the same sex, half have a sibling of the opposite sex. The same is true if we extend the analysis to larger families. The answer to Ruma Falk's question, then, is no: men have the same number of sisters as women do.

The illusion of control. Flawed misperceptions of probability are not the only virus infecting gamblers' intuitions. Harvard psychologist Ellen Langer demonstrated an "illusion of control" with experiments on gambling. Compared to those given an assigned lottery number, people who chose their own number demanded four times as much money when asked about selling their ticket. When playing a game of chance against an awkward and nervous person, they bet significantly more than when playing against a dapper, confident opponent. When rolling the dice for themselves they feel more confident than when the croupier rolls for them. Given an opportunity to practice, their confidence increases. In such ways, more than fifty experiments have consistently found people acting as if they can predict or control chance events.

Observations of real-life gamblers confirm these experimental findings. Dice players may throw softly for low numbers and hard for high numbers. To improve luck they may blow on the dice, concentrate on the desired number, switch to the left hand, or walk around their chair three times. The gambling industry thrives on gamblers' illusions. Gamblers attribute wins to their skill and foresight. Losses become "near misses" or "flukes"—perhaps (for the sports gambler) a bad call by the referee or a freakish bounce of the ball. Mindful of such illusory intuitions, Samuel Johnson, the eighteenth-century English wit, viewed lotteries as a "tax on fools."

Memorable winners. From casinos to state lotteries, losers are invisible, winners are in the limelight. Casinos signal even small wins with bells and lights—or quarters clanging into buckets—making them vividly memorable while keeping losses soundlessly obscure. Our own wins are also more salient and memorable (like the memorable times we've caught fish rather than the times we got skunked). This helps explain the 1999 finding by the National Opinion Research Center that America's gamblers perceive themselves as having won about $4 billion more than they lost in casinos, when in fact they left with $20 billion less than they came with.

Big lottery winners—Frank Capaci, Maria Grasso, and the Lucky 13—are front-page, prime-time news. Such vivid examples also become readily available in our memories, and as we have seen, "cognitive availability" is the mind's rule-of-thumb for intuiting the actual frequency of events. After Frank Capaci won the $195 million lottery ($104 million after taxes), a woman in Kansas complained to Ann Landers that her lottery-playing husband said, "See, lightning DOES strike. That could have been ME." "Yes, Jim," she told him, "it could have been you, but it wasn't."

CORRECTING GAMBLERS' INTUITIONS

In other chapters on specific intuition domains, we have found defects in our intuition but also strengths. Athletes display flawed intuitions yet exhibit intuitive brilliance during performance. Stock pickers exhibit illusory confidence yet skilled business managers often exhibit the acquired intuitions that accompany learned expertise. Gamblers, however, would be better advised, when feeling a hunch, to say, "Intuition, get thee behind me!"

If the gambling industry cultivates illusory intuitions as it peddles false hopes, how might public information efforts sharpen awareness of statistical realities? Might vivid product warnings help, similar to those accompanying prescription drugs and cigarettes? Here are some ways to communicate what long odds really mean:

- If you toss a coin twenty-six times, your odds of getting twenty-six heads in a row are greater than the chance that your Powerball ticket will win you the jackpot.
- To have a reasonable chance of winning the Massachusetts lottery by purchasing a lottery ticket each week, you would need to persist for 1.6 million years.
- If you drive ten miles to buy a Powerball ticket, you are sixteen times more likely to die en route in a car crash than to win.
- If you are an average British citizen who buys a ticket in Britain's National Lottery on Monday, you are 2,500 times more likely to die before the Saturday draw than to win the jackpot. Viewers of the Lottery's weekly draw are three times more likely to die during the twenty-minute program than to win.

The National Gambling Impact Study Commission offered other corrective suggestions, such as ceasing convenience store gambling operations, restricting political contributions, restraining lotteries targeting the poor, controlling deceptive advertising, and raising the gambling age limit to twenty-one. The commission also recommended removing ATMs and credit machines from gambling areas and posting warnings about the risks and odds of gambling.

Perhaps public education in school math programs could contribute to greater understanding of the long-term costs, benefits, and odds that accompany various forms of risk-taking. Betting on the unpredictable stock market and betting in casinos and lotteries are both gambling. They both give a certain thrill, risk a possible loss, offer a possible gain. The difference is that, over the past seventy-five years, money gambled on publicly traded stocks has returned more than 11 percent annually on average, while casino and lottery gambles have collectively lost as much. So if one enjoys the thrill of risk and the hope of riches, why not gamble one's money where the deck is stacked in one's favor? If Joe, the truck driver who was betting $40 a week on the lottery, had instead bet $40 a week on a stock market index fund—or even on a diverse mix of twenty self-chosen stocks that he bought and held—he would be a much richer man today. If, as a twenty-five-year-old, he had begun putting $40 a week into a stock retirement fund that averaged an annual 11 percent return, he would upon retirement at age sixty-five have accumulated a certain jackpot: $1.51 million.

Gambling to lose rather than gambling to win reflects people's illusory intuitions, not economic masochism. Given such powerfully flawed intuitions about gambling, there surely is a need for new forms of risk awareness information and education.

Psychic Intuition

At the heart of science is an essential tension between two seemingly contradictory attitudes—an openness to new ideas, no matter how bizarre or counterintuitive they may be, and the most ruthless skeptical scrutiny of all ideas, old and new.
—Carl Sagan, *"The Fine Art of Baloney Detection," 1987*

Apart from curiosity about women's supposedly superior intuition, no idea about intuition seems to evoke more fascination than that of a presumed sixth sense—a weird and wonderful human capacity for reading minds, thinking about someone just before they phone, intuiting what's happening elsewhere, communicating with the dead.

Several years ago, a colleague posted my text discussion of extrasensory perception on our department website. With no effort to promote the site, it became the first-listed "extrasensory perception" site at the search engine Google, generating thousands of visits a year and many interesting letters from people telling me stories of psychic intuition or asking questions. One of these people—let's call her Kendra—wondered if people could take "this gift of intuition and develop it into ESP. Or could the idea of ESP be something that was only exaggerated from intuition?" Kendra believes that she has revealing dreams and an unusual gift of discernment. "Is it possible," she asks, "for someone like myself to develop my intuition further, and how would I go about doing it?"

Medium-to-the-masses James Van Praagh would encourage Kendra: "Everyone is born with a sense of intuition. There are some that are born with a higher degree of sensitivity. But every single person, if they choose to and discipline themselves, can become aware of spirit."

Kendra has much company in her assumption that psychic intuition is for real. In a May 2001 Gallup survey, 50 percent of Americans declared their belief in extrasensory perception. Only 27 percent said they don't believe; the rest were unsure. More specifically, "telepathy, or communication between minds without using the traditional five senses" was believed by 36 percent and disbelieved by 35 percent. "Clairvoyance, or the power of the mind to know the past and predict the future"* found 32 percent believing and 45 percent disbelieving.

The media kindle our fascination with reports of psychic wonders: of police psychics solving cases, of John Edward communicating with the dead, of "unsolved mysteries." Fictional television and movies (*The X-Files, The Sixth Sense, The Blair Witch Project*) create vivid and available images of strange things that *might* be true. The dial-a-psychic industry topped $1 billion a year recently, much of that revenue from low-income people. Even in the laboratory, parapsychologists have in times past been enchanted by people who seemed capable of discerning the contents of sealed envelopes, influencing the roll of a die, or drawing a picture of what someone else was viewing at an unknown remote location.

Contemporary psychological science, as we saw in Chapters 1 to 3, is revealing our previously unappreciated intuitive powers. We know more than we know. We have a rational, conscious mind, and we have a backstage mind, what psychologist Guy Claxton calls an "undermind." Thinking, memory, and attitudes all engage dual processing—deliberate, controlled, aware processing, but also automatic, uncontrolled, out-of-sight processing. Might these unseen intuitive powers enable people—perhaps a special few people who, as Kendra suggests, have developed their intuitive gifts—to read minds, see through walls, or foresee the future?

*Actually, parapsychologists—those who study paranormal (beyond the normal) occurrences—label the ability to predict the future as "precognition."

Research psychologists and other scientists—including 96 percent of National Academy of Science members surveyed—doubt it. If ESP exists, what shall we make of the vast evidence that we are creatures whose minds are tied to our physical brains and whose perceptions are built of sensations? What form of energy would enable mind-to-mind communication yet be undetectable by physicists? Well, respond the believers, sometimes new evidence does overturn our scientific preconceptions. When subjected to such scrutiny, crazy-sounding ideas sometimes find support. During the 1700s, scientists scoffed at the notion that meteorites had extraterrestrial origins. When two Yale scientists dared to deviate from conventional opinion after a meteor fell in Weston, Connecticut, Thomas Jefferson reportedly jeered, "It is easier to believe that two Yankee Professors would lie, than that stones would fall from heaven." Sometimes scientific inquiry refutes skeptics.

More often, science relegates crazy-sounding ideas to the mountain of forgotten claims of perpetual-motion machines, miracle cancer cures, and out-of-body travels into centuries past. Winnowing reality from fantasy is enabled by a scientific attitude of open-minded skepticism, of putting claims to the test. If, when tested, someone's claim of psychic intuition produces the predicted result, so much the better for it. If not, so much the worse for it.

CLAIMS OF PSYCHIC DISCERNMENT

Can psychics discern the future? Between 1978 and 1985, the "leading psychics" identified by the *National Enquirer* offered 486 predictions of the future. Two came true. During the 1990s, tabloid psychics were all wrong in predicting surprising events (Madonna did not become a gospel singer, Bill Cosby was not appointed ambassador to South Africa, Queen Elizabeth did not abdicate her throne to enter a convent). And they missed all the actual surprising big events, such as the O. J. Simpson case, Saddam Hussein's assault on Kuwait, Timothy McVeigh's Oklahoma City bombing, and the horror of September 11, 2001. Sadly, the psychic whom Princess Diana consulted shortly before her death failed to see the danger that lay ahead.

Police psychics. Psychic intuitions offered to police departments have also, on analysis, fared no better than guesses made by ordinary folks. Psychics working with police have scored some hits, but only after generating dozens or even hundreds of predictions. As an old Spanish proverb says, "A person who talks a lot is sometimes right." And when that person is, there's a story to sell. It also helps to be a little vague, because ambiguous intuitions can later be interpreted ("retrofitted") to match events. Looking back, knowing that President Kennedy was assassinated, one can interpret Jeanne Dixon's intuition as a precise forecast of the later event. Nostradamus, a sixteenth-century French psychic, explained in an unguarded moment that his ambiguous prophecies "could not possibly be understood until they were interpreted after the event and by it."

Most major police departments are now wise to this. When Jane Ayers Sweat and Mark Durm asked the police departments of America's fifty largest cities whether they ever used psychics, 65 percent said they never had. Of those that had, not one had found them helpful. Reflecting on the flood of psychic tips concerning the whereabouts of Chandra Levy, Washington, D.C., police chief Terrance Gainer said, "They haven't proven very useful. You got 100 different psychics and they've got 100 different places." Indeed, over the years, notes psychologist Robert Baker, dogs have located more missing persons, dead bodies, and drug stashes than psychics ever have or ever will.

The art of the scam. There's no telling how many of these self-proclaimed psychics are sincere, though self-deluded, and how many are practicing the art of the scam. There is a rich history of fortune-takers posing as fortune-tellers, of mediums feigning contact with the dead while actually bilking the living, of business psychics making a profit by advising how to make a profit.

One ex-con, James Hydrick, managed to attract a lucrative following of customers for his psychic seminars by demonstrating, on ABC television and in other public venues, his psychokinetic "mind over matter" ability.* These powers apparently enabled Hydrick to flip the pages of a telephone book while merely staring at it. Unlike most

---

*This psychic claim is illustrated by the wry comment, "Will all those who believe in psychokinesis please raise my hand?"

celebrated psychics, such as Uri Geller, Hydrick strangely agreed to be tested by magician-skeptic James Randi, who has a longstanding offer (now $1 million on deposit with Goldman Sachs) available to the first human "who proves a genuine psychic power under proper observing conditions." Having determined, by sensitive microphones, that Hydrick was blowing on the pages, Randi simply sprinkled Styrofoam particles around an open phone book and invited Hydrick to turn the pages without blowing the particles, or to turn the pages while wearing a germ mask that would allow breathing but not blowing. Alas, the pages suddenly refused to turn, and the panel of judges (which included a parapsychologist) agreed that Randi's money was still unclaimed. Later, Hydrick acknowledged his scam, adding, "My whole idea behind this in the first place was to see how dumb America was. How dumb the world is."

Public fascination has recently shifted to John Edward, James Van Praagh, Sylvia Browne, and other mediums who claim they can make a "really, really long-distance call"—contact with the dead. In 2001, Gallup reported that 28 percent of Americans—up from 18 percent in 1990—reported believing "that people can hear from or communicate mentally with someone who has died"; another 26 percent are not sure. Edward, born John MaGee, Jr., is a charismatic former ballroom-dance instructor who has seen his gig soar from New York radio stations to nationwide seminars to a popular Sci Fi Channel program (*Crossing Over*) that got moved from late night to primetime and then to daytime syndication. "Alternatively funny, sarcastic and compassionate, he comes off as sensitive yet strong, a sort of all-in-one priest, father and husband figure for the show's predominantly female audience," reports the *New York Times*. "He's telling me to acknowledge the wedding, do you understand this?" Edward asks an audience member to whom he relays information from her recently deceased father. In response, the woman crumbles, breaking into sobs.

On the edited-for-entertainment broadcast, the television audience sees this impressive hit, but not, the *Times* reports, the twenty minutes Edward spent during the same taping shooting blanks. The televised hits, say skeptics, are accomplished, first, by a "throw-it-all-against-the-wall-and-see-what-sticks" routine. Searching the crowd, Edward says, "They are telling me to acknowledge an M connection;

two people's names begin with M in the family. They're telling me that somebody had the Parkinson's, or somebody had some sort of neurological disease as well. I'm in this area over here"—he points to a row in the audience. "Do you understand this? Yes? No? Hello?" When a couple of people nod, he focuses on one of them and continues to spew statements ("Somebody in your family is a very heavy smoker") and questions ("Does *Dr. Zhivago* have any meaning to you?"). Much of the information is ambiguous enough to allow the target to impute meaning: Edward gets "a J or a G" sound for a name and sees "blackness in the chest."

Skeptics also see Edward applying classic "cold reading" techniques long practiced by mediums, palm readers, and crystal-ball gazers. Cold readers "read" our clothing, physical features, nonverbal gestures, and reactions to what they are saying. Psychologist Ray Hyman, who once read palms to supplement his income from magic and mental shows, understands the art of cold reading. Imagine yourself as the character reader who was visited by a young woman in her late twenties or early thirties. Hyman described the woman as "wearing expensive jewelry, a wedding band, and a black dress of cheap material. The observant reader noted that she was wearing shoes which were advertised for people with foot trouble." Do these clues suggest anything?

Drawing on these observations, Hyman reports, the reader proceeded to amaze his client. He assumed that the woman had come to see him, as did most of his female customers, because of a love or financial problem. The black dress and the wedding band led him to reason that her husband had died recently. The expensive jewelry suggested that she had been financially comfortable during the marriage, but the cheap dress suggested that her husband's death had left her impoverished. The therapeutic shoes signified that she was now on her feet more than she had been used to, implying that she had been working to support herself since her husband's death. Any reader of Sherlock Holmes stories is familiar with this art of cold reading.

If you are not as shrewd as this character reader (who correctly guessed that the woman was wondering whether she should remarry in hope of ending her economic hardship), Hyman says it hardly matters. If people seek you out for a reading, start with safe sympathy: "I sense you're having some problems lately. You seem unsure what to do. I get the feeling another person is involved." Then tell them what they want to hear. Memorize some universally true statements from astrology and fortune-telling manuals and use them liberally. Tell people it is their responsibility to cooperate by relating your message to their specific experiences. Later they will recall that you predicted the specifics. Phrase statements as questions, and when you detect a positive response, assert the statement strongly. Be a good listener, and later, in different words, reveal to people what they earlier revealed to you. If you dupe them, they will come.*

The technique works so well that, while seeing others accept his cold readings as psychic intuitions, Hyman himself became a firm believer in palmistry—until one day a respected professional mentalist suggested an interesting experiment. The mentalist proposed that Hyman deliberately give readings opposite to what the lines indicated. "I tried this out with a few clients," Hyman reported. "To my surprise and horror my readings were just as successful as ever. The medium was the message. Ever since then I have been interested in the powerful forces that convince us, [palm] reader and client alike, that something is so when it really isn't."

Prophetic dreams. A 2001 UCLA conference on dreaming began with dream researcher Kelly Bulkeley posing such questions as, "In light of post-modernity, are dreams a nonrational way of knowing? What is the value of dreams and dreaming?" While psychologists and physiologists study and debate the psychological and biological functions of dreaming, others wonder about the prophetic value of dreams. If the intuitions of self-proclaimed psychics and mediums lack credibility, is there more to glean from the spontaneous visions of everyday people? Do dreams foretell the future or convey hidden truth, as about half of university students believe? Or do they only seem to do so because we are more likely to recall or reconstruct

*For more secrets to how psychics set up cold readings and produce amazingly specific information about their clients, see Ian Rowland's *The Full Facts of Cold Reading* (available from www.ian-rowland.com).

dreams that seem to have come true? Dreams are vague and hard to remember. Perhaps, then, we later modify our memories of dreams to match the car crash, surprise gift, or unexpected visit that we know has occurred. Happenings do shape recollections.

Nearly seventy years ago, Harvard psychologists Henry Murray and D. R. Wheeler tested the prophetic power of dreams. After aviator Charles Lindbergh's baby son was kidnapped and murdered but before the body was discovered, the researchers invited the public to report their dreams about the child. Of the 1,300 dream reports submitted, how many accurately envisioned the child dead? Five percent. And how many also correctly anticipated the body's location—buried among trees? Only 4 of the 1,300. Although this number was surely no better than chance, to those four dreamers the accuracy of their *apparent* precognitions must have seemed uncanny.

EXPERIMENTING WITH PSYCHIC INTUITION

The scientific search for psychic phenomena is replete, notes Ray Hyman, "with examples of psychical researchers claiming they finally proved the existence of the paranormal. In each instance, subsequent generations of parapsychologists have had to discard as badly flawed what had seemed to the previous generation to be irrefutable proof of psi, or psychic phenomena." Writing in the *Journal of the American Society for Psychical Research,* parapsychologist Rhea White acknowledges that "the image of parapsychology that comes to my mind, based on nearly 44 years in the field, is that of a small airplane [that] has been perpetually taxiing down the runway of the Empirical Science Airport since 1882 . . . its movement punctuated occasionally by lifting a few feet off the ground only to bump back down on the tarmac once again."

Indeed, after thousands of experiments, no reproducible ESP phenomenon has ever been discovered, nor has any researcher produced any individual who can convincingly demonstrate psychic ability. A National Research Council investigation of ESP similarly concluded that the "best available evidence does not support the contention that these phenomena exist." In 1995, a CIA-commissioned report evaluated ten years of military testing of psychic spies, in which $20 million had been invested. The result? The program produced nothing and the psychic spy program was scrapped.

The scientific attitude—test it to see if it works—has led both believers and skeptics to agree that what parapsychology needs to give it credibility is a reproducible phenomenon and a theory to explain it. In seeking such a phenomenon, how might we test ESP claims in a controlled experiment? An experiment differs from a staged demonstration. On stage, the "psychic," like a magician, controls what the audience sees and hears. The perceived effects can be staggering. In the laboratory, the experimenter controls what the psychic sees and hears. Time and again, skeptics note, so-called psychics have exploited unquestioning audiences with amazing performances in which they *appeared* to communicate with the spirits of the dead, read minds, or levitate objects—only to have it revealed that their acts were nothing more than the illusions of stage magicians. "A psychic," psychologist-magician Daryl Bem has said, "is an actor playing the role of a psychic."

In the United Kingdom and the United States, hopes are periodically raised that the science of parapsychology has at last discovered a phenomenon. I recall pioneering parapsychologist J. B. Rhine describing his intriguing results during a long-ago visit to my campus. Alas, someone else comes along, tightens the control against cheating or subtle communication, and the effect disappears. Occasionally someone performs beyond chance until the "decline effect" sets in (as it does with gamblers and stock pickers who temporarily occupy the upper tail of the distribution). "This drop in scores," reports John Beloff, a former president of the Parapsychological Association, "is perhaps the most reliable and consistent aspect of parapsychology."

Still, the search for psi continues. Hertfordshire University psychologist Richard Wiseman created a "mind machine" to see whether people can influence or predict a coin toss. Using a touch-sensitive screen, visitors to festivals around the country were given four attempts to call heads or tails. Using a random-number generator, a computer then decided the outcome. When the experiment concluded in January 2000, nearly 28,000 people had predicted 110,972 tosses—of which 49.8 percent were correct.

The latest round of excitement was triggered by findings published by Daryl Bem and parapsychologist Charles Honorton using the *ganzfeld* procedure. The procedure would place you in a reclining chair, play hissing white noise through headphones, and shine diffuse red light through Ping-Pong ball halves strapped over your eyes. This reduction of external distractions ostensibly would put you in an ideal state to receive thoughts from someone else, which you might hear as small voices from within.

Building on earlier studies using this procedure, Bem and Honorton isolated the "sender" and "receiver" in separate, shielded chambers and had the sender concentrate for half an hour on one of four randomly selected visual images. The receivers were then asked which of four images best matched the images they experienced during the session. In eleven studies, the receivers beat chance (25 percent correct) by a bigger than usual margin (32 percent).

Psychology-based critical inquiry always asks two questions: What do you mean? And how do you know (what's your evidence)? Parapsychologists say the ganzfeld tests of ESP offer clear answers to both questions. Skeptic Hyman granted that the methodology surpasses that of previous ESP experiments, but he questioned certain procedural details that may have introduced bias. Intrigued, other researchers set to work replicating these experiments. Would this be the first reliable ESP phenomenon? Or one more dashed hope?

Alas, Julie Milton and Richard Wiseman's statistical digest of thirty follow-up ganzfeld experiments found no effect. "We conclude that the ganzfeld technique does not at present offer a replicable method for producing ESP in the laboratory," they reported. But—hold the phone—one very recent study does find an effect.

Stay tuned, and remember: The scientific attitude blends curious skepticism with open-minded humility. It demands that extraordinary claims be supported by clear and reliable evidence. (If at 5 feet 7 and age fifty-nine I claim to be able to dunk a basketball, the burden of proof would be on me to show that I can do it, not on you to prove that I couldn't.) Given such evidence, science is open to nature's occasional surprises.

WHAT IF PSYCHIC INTUITION EXISTED?

Michael Shermer's *Skeptic* magazine poses a playful question: If powerful psychic intuition existed, what else would be true? Imagining answers to these questions could enliven a party, or a class. If people really could foresee the future . . .

- We would have no surprise parties.
- Psychic Friends Network owner Michael Lasky would not need to have spent $500,000 to purchase Eddie Murray's 500th home-run baseball. He could have dialed his own line, then gone to the right seat to catch it himself.
- More than one out of the 138.5 million tickets purchased for that 1998 multistate Powerball lottery would have won.
- Psychics would be richer than Warren Buffet.
- Casinos would go broke. (Jesting aside, even a little precognition would enable more lottery, stock market, and casino winners.)

If people really could read minds . . .

- There would be no need for a football huddle.
- We wouldn't pay for Caller ID.
- Hands of "rocks, paper, scissors" would end in a draw.
- Teens would often be in trouble with their parents.

If people really could view happenings at remote places . . .

- Hide and seek would be a short, dull game.
- You could leave your poker cards face up.
- Search and rescue teams would become rescue teams.

WHY DO PEOPLE BELIEVE?

If H. L. Mencken was right to suppose that believing "passionately in the palpably not true . . . is the chief occupation of mankind," then we must wonder why. If people, for example, believe in nonexistent psychic intuitions, the question naturally arises, why do so many people believe so fervently, and why are so many others inclined to believe?

Illusory cognitions: misperceptions, misinterpretations, and selective recall. The first reason is cognitive. Whether or not genuine psychic intuition exists, the perils of intuition would surely lead many to believe. Nature's recipe for convincing us of phenomena that may not exist consists of our human tendencies to invent false explanations for what we have done and why; to have difficulty assessing our mind's workings; to be overconfident of our intuitions; to notice, interpret, and recall events that confirm our expectations; to be overly persuaded by unrepresentative experiences and anecdotes; and to misperceive the probabilities of random coincidence.

By this account, notes former parapsychologist Susan Blackmore, the "paranormal illusion" is simply "misinterpreting perfectly normal events." Like perceptual illusions, paranormal intuitions are the price we pay for our brains' built-in tendency to look for connections and seek explanations for unlikely events. It is, she says, no more stupid to have apparently psychic experiences than it is to have visual illusions.

The power of coincidence. "Things that happen by chance are effects in search of causes," observes K. C. Cole. If we can't find or even imagine a natural cause for an unsolved mystery, we may presume a paranormal one. Moments after a friend from long ago crosses our mind, the friend calls. Too weird, too improbable to have any explanation other than telepathy? But *some* weird coincidences are inevitable (see box). When they happen, they capture our attention and remain available in memory. All the nonevents—the premonitions not followed by a phone call or an accident—pass unnoticed and unremembered.

I delight in my own experiences of weird coincidences:

- Checking out a photocopy counter from the Hope College library desk, I confused the clerk when giving my six-digit department charge number—which just happened at that moment to be identical to the counter's six-digit number on which the last user had finished.
- Shortly after my daughter, Laura Myers, bought two pairs of shoes, we were astounded to discover that the two brand names on the boxes were "Laura" and "Myers."
- My wife, Carol, called for help in verifying Mark Twain's quote that "the man who does not read good books has no advantage

over the man who cannot read them." In my fifty-nine years this was my first encounter with that quote. My second was about ninety minutes later, in a *Washington Post*.com article.

Everyone has these experiences. My colleague, Don, writes of browsing in a bookstore one day when, while looking through *The Dictionary of the Kazars*, he haphazardly opened to a page and his eye fell on the sentence, "He was exiled from Dubrovnic." "At that very moment," a man nearby showed his companion a magazine picture, exclaiming, "Look! This is a picture of Dubrovnic." "Time and chance happen to [us] all," noted the sage author of Ecclesiastes.

And then there are those remarkable coincidences that, with added digging, have been embellished into really fun stories, such as the familiar Lincoln-Kennedy coincidences (both with seven letters in their last names, elected one hundred years apart, assassinated on a Friday while beside their wives, one in Ford's theater, the other in a Ford Motor Co. car, and so forth). My favorite such coincidence, however, is this lesser-known fact: in Psalm 46 of the King James Bible, published in the year that Shakespeare turned 46, the 46th word is "shake" and the 46th word from the end is "spear." (What's most remarkable is that someone should have noted this!) Social scientist Anatol Rapoport and his sons played further and discovered that Shakespeare's presumed birth date, April 23 (1564) was originally the second month in the Julian calendar, making his birthday 2/23. And $2 \times 23 = 46$. Moreover, Shakespeare's thirty-four plays (collapsing the parts of *Henry IV* and *Henry VI* into two plays) goes into 1564 exactly (you guessed it) 46 times.

Enough. What shall we make of these weird coincidences? Was James Redfield right to suppose, in *The Celestine Prophecy,* that we should attend closely to "strange occurrences that feel like they were meant to happen"? Is he right to suppose that "they are actually synchronistic events, and following them will start you on your path to spiritual truth"? Without wanting to rob us of our delight in these serendipities, much less of our spirituality, statisticians agree: they tell us absolutely nothing of spiritual significance. "In reality," says mathematician John Allen Paulos, "the most astonishingly incredible coincidence imaginable would be the complete absence of all coincidences."

STRANGE BUT TRUE: WEIRD COINCIDENCES

With a large enough sample, any outrageous thing is likely to happen.
—Statisticians Persi Diaconis and Frederick Mosteller, 1989

- Patricia Kern of Colorado was born March 13, 1941, and named Patricia Ann Campbell. Patricia DiBiasi of Oregon also was born March 13, 1941, and named Patricia Ann Campbell. Both had fathers named Robert, worked as book-keepers, and had children ages twenty-one and nineteen. Both studied cosmetology, enjoyed oil painting as a hobby, and married military men within eleven days of each other. They are not genetically related.

- Twins Lorraine and Levinia Christmas, driving to deliver Christmas presents to each other near Flitcham, England, collided.

- Philip Dodgson is a clinical psychologist at Sussex, England's South Downs health center who does psycho-therapy with clergy and members of religious orders. One day he surfed the web to see if there were any other Philip Dodgsons out there. He found one in Ontario, and out of curiosity he wrote to ask him his occupation. Surprise! The second Philip Dodgson was also a clinical psychologist who was working at, believe it or not, Southdown Center—a residential psychotherapy center for clergy and members of religious orders.

- Utah's Ernie and Lynn Carey gained three new grand-children when three of their daughters gave birth—on the same day, March 11, 1998.

- Three of the first five presidents of the United States (Adams, Jefferson, and Monroe) died on the same date—which was none other than the Fourth of July. A more recent death coincidence—or might these have been lives lived to a goal?— was Charles Schulz dying unexpectedly of a heart attack on the day that people began reading his last published Peanuts comic strip.

- In Aalesund, Norway, Kristin Nalvik Loendahl, nine, suffered bumps and bruises when she rode her bike through a stop sign and was knocked into the air by an oncoming car. The driver of the car stopped to help the girl, but she had disappeared. Several hours later he learned why: she had landed in the bed of a truck passing at that instant heading in the opposite direction.

- "We print winning numbers in advance!" headlined Oregon's *Columbian* on July 3, 2000. State lottery officials were dismayed and incredulous when the newspaper announced their 6-8-5-5 winning Pick 4 numbers for June 28 in advance.

The explanation: The *Columbian*'s computers had crashed, and in the scramble to re-create a news page, a copyeditor accidentally included Virginia's Pick 4 numbers in a lottery news item; those numbers were the exact numbers that Oregon was about to draw.

When Evelyn Marie Adams won the New Jersey lottery *twice*, newspapers reported the odds of her feat as 1 in 17 trillion—the odds that a given person buying a single ticket for two New Jersey lotteries would win both. But statisticians Stephen Samuels and George McCabe report that, given the millions of people who buy U.S. state lottery tickets, it was "practically a sure thing" that someday, somewhere, someone would hit a state jackpot twice.

The moral: That a particular specified event or coincidence will occur is very unlikely; that *some* astonishing *un*specified events will occur is certain (which is why remarkable coincidences are noted in hindsight, not predicted with foresight).

The media. Others' reported experiences also influence our beliefs. "Psychic Foresaw Tornado" is a much more likely headline than "Remote Viewing Test Fails." Supposed psychic intuition is news; its nonoccurrence is not. Most publishers of books about paranormal phenomena turn down proposed books that debunk the paranormal. As positive stories accumulate, they begin to persuade. The mere repetition of statements, experiments show, creates an illusion of truth. A feeling of recognition evokes a feeling of truth. This media bias adds to the cognitive availability of alleged paranormal events.

Motivation. In addition to the cognitive processes, the weird coincidences, and the vivid accounts, there is also a motivational force.

Many people have an unsatisfied hunger for wonderment, an itch to experience the magical. In Britain and the United States, the founders of parapsychology were mostly people who, having lost their religious faith, began searching for a scientific basis for believing in the meaning of life and of existence beyond death. In the upheaval after the collapse of autocratic rule in Russia there came an "avalanche of the mystical, occult and pseudoscientific." In Russia as elsewhere, "extrasensorial" healers and seers fascinate the awestruck public. "Many people," declared a statement by thirty-two leading Russian scientists, "believe in clairvoyance, astrology, and other superstitions to compensate for the psychological discomforts of our time."

New Age thought looks for evidence of the divine within us. Do we not have even a small bit of God-like omniscience (reading minds, foretelling the future)? Of omnipresence (viewing remote locations)? Of omnipotence (levitating objects or influencing dice)? Alas, say the scientific researchers, we are finite creatures. We possess, it seems, dignity but not deity.

For those yearning for mystery, Sherlock Holmes offers an alternative. "The most commonplace crime is often the most mysterious," Holmes observed in *A Study in Scarlet*. "Life is infinitely stranger than anything which the mind of man could invent." To feel awe and reverence for life, we need not look to mind-boggling mysteries such as the eternity of time, the infinity of space, or the improbability of our own existence. We need look no further than our own perceptual system and its capacity for organizing formless nerve impulses into colorful sights, vivid sounds, and evocative smells.

Think about it: As you look at someone, particles of light energy are being absorbed by your eyes' receptor cells, converted into neural signals that activate neighboring cells, which down the line transmit a million electrochemical messages per moment up to your brain. There, separate parts of your brain process information about color, form, motion, and depth, and then—in some still mysterious way—this information converges to form a consciously perceived image, which is instantly compared with previously stored images and recognized as, say, your grandmother. The whole process is as complex as taking a house apart, splinter by splinter, transporting it to a different location, and then, through the efforts of millions of specialized workers, putting it back together. Voilà! The material brain gives rise to consciousness. That all of this happens instantly, effortlessly, and continuously is better than cool: it is truly bewildering. We can empathize with Job: "I have uttered what I did not understand, things too wonderful for me."

SCIENCE AND SPIRITUALITY

Reduced to a sentence, this book's message is that psychological science reveals some astounding powers and notable perils of unchecked intuition, and that creative yet critical thinkers will appreciate both. Having over and again displayed and celebrated the insights of psychological science, I should also acknowledge its limits. Science illuminates why we think, feel, and act as we do. But it cannot answer the ultimate questions posed by Leo Tolstoy: "Why should I live? Why should I do anything? Is there in life any purpose which the inevitable death that awaits me does not undo and destroy?" Searching for meaning, for significance, for inspiration, many people therefore turn from science to seek spiritual truth and insight.

The growing scientific appreciation of nonrational, intuitive forms of knowing lends credence to spirituality. There's a lot of activity beneath the ocean's surface, and beneath our conscious, rational mind. Perhaps there is untapped wisdom down there as well. This much we know for sure: our rational, scientific understanding of nature is incomplete. As the Concorde would have bewildered Columbus, so the science-to-be of A.D. 2500 would likely bewilder us. Hamlet's surmise rings true: "There are more things in heaven and earth, Horatio, than are dreamt of in your philosophy." Hamlet is echoed in the more recent words of the population geneticist J. B. S. Haldane: "The universe is not only queerer than we suppose, but queerer than we can suppose." And in the much older words of Isaiah: "For as the heavens are higher than the earth, so are my ways higher than your ways and my thoughts than your thoughts." We have learned much, and we have much yet to learn.

After discarding spirituality's psychic bathwater, does there remain a baby? Can one challenge the sort of spiritual intuitions that give spirituality a bad reputation without expressing a condescending cynicism toward all forms of spirituality? "Is there a way to express how the 'wind of the Spirit' can blow in the life of someone who is mindful of the powers and perils of intuition?" asked a friend after reading most of the preceding manuscript chapters. "Is there a warm, gentle, spontaneous approach that keeps intuition's perils in mind but doesn't automatically feel the need to 'explain away' rationally what very well might be a prompting of the Spirit?"

"Faith seeking understanding," was St. Anselm's eleventh-century motto. Today, understanding seeks faith. In St. Anselm's world, faith was a given, and Anselm yearned for a more informed, intelligent depth of understanding. Today, scientific understanding is a given. What we seek are answers to Tolstoy's questions about our identity, purpose, and ultimate destiny and to our wonderings about why anything exists rather than nothing. What explains this fine-tuned universe? Against astronomical odds, what made it—like Baby Bear's porridge—"just right" for producing enduring matter, living organisms, human consciousness? How did it come to be, in the words of Harvard-Smithsonian astrophysicist Owen Gingerich, "so extraordinarily right, that it seemed the universe had been expressly designed to produce intelligent, sentient beings"? Is there a benevolent super intelligence underneath it? A divine mind behind its rational beauty? A divine purpose behind its fine tuning? If so, does that supreme reality have significance for us? Science does not pretend to answer such questions. In his own way, Albert Einstein seemed to appreciate both the rigors and rationality of science and the wonder of existence. There are two ways to live, he reportedly said. "One is as though nothing is a miracle. The other is as though everything is a miracle."

Science can, however, help winnow some forms of genuine spirituality from pseudo spirituality. When people make testable claims of spiritual realities—of reincarnation, of near-death experiences, of the powers of prayer—science can put them to the test. If people wonder whether an active religious faith correlates with health, happiness, coping, morality, and compassion, well, we have data. Putting spiritual claims to scientific test may sound like letting the scientific fox into the spiritual chicken coop. But there is actually a religious mandate for science, even science applied to spirituality and religion.

Biblical monotheism—the idea, someone has said, that 1) there is a God, and 2) it's not you—mandates humility. Humility before nature and skepticism of human authority were religious ideas that fed the beginnings of modern science. Pascal, Bacon, Newton, and Galileo were wary of human intuition, and they viewed themselves in God's service as they explored the creation.

Sociologist Peter Berger writes that "a colleague of mine, Adam Seligman, a sociologist and an observant Jew, has coined the attractive term 'epistemological modesty' to describe this religious posture. It is a mellow synthesis of skepticism and faith that, in principle, can be found in any religious tradition." Epistemological modesty—faith-based skepticism—can help us critically analyze both New Age spiritual claims and ideas about self-empowering prayer. Faith-based skepticism can build as well as destroy. It can help point us toward an alternative to both fanaticism and materialism—toward what University of California at Davis psychologist Robert Emmons sees as the growing evidence of a fruitful "spiritual intelligence"—an adaptive spirituality that facilitates "everyday problem-solving and goal attainment."

Emmons identifies five components of his proposed spiritual intelligence:

- *"The capacity for transcendence."* Highly spiritual persons perceive a reality that transcends the material and physical.
- *"The ability to sanctify everyday experience."* Spiritually intelligent persons have an ability to invest everyday activities, events, and relationships with a sense of the sacred or divine. They consider its implications for their understanding of self, others, nature, and life. For the spiritually intelligent person, work is seen as a calling, parenting as a sacred responsibility, marriage as having spiritual significance. I write this chapter in St. Andrews, Scotland, a short walk from the opening scene of *Chariots of Fire*. The film portrays Eric Liddell's reflection on the spiritual significance of running: "When I run, I feel His pleasure."
- *"The ability to experience heightened states of consciousness."* While engaged in meditation and certain forms of mystical

prayer, spiritually intelligent persons experience spiritual ecstasy. They are receptive to mystical experience.

- *"The ability to utilize spiritual resources to solve problems."* Spiritual transformations often lead people to reprioritize goals. If spiritual intelligence is indeed a form of intelligence, it will also lead people to cope more effectively with problems and to lead more effective lives, with higher levels of well-being.
- *"The capacity to engage in virtuous behavior."* Spiritually intelligent people have an enhanced ability to show forgiveness, express gratitude, feel humility, display compassion. (This last component, Emmons now concedes, might also be considered a result of spiritual intelligence rather than as one of its cognitive elements.)

There is growing evidence that, with notable exceptions, faith is indeed associated with increased health, happiness, coping, character, generosity, and volunteerism. This supports Emmons' concept of spiritual intelligence, but it cannot tell us whether spirituality pursues an illusion or a deep truth. Is "God" merely a word we use to cover our ignorance? Is spirituality an opiate of the people? Or is it human ignorance to presume God's absence from the fabric of the universe?

If we are honest with ourselves, we cannot *know* which is right. In the dark of the night, the theists and atheists will each have moments when they wonder if the other side might be right. Perhaps all spiritual intuitions are illusions. Or perhaps those missing a spiritual dimension are, like those in Edwin Abbott's fictional two-dimensional world, flatlanders whose myopia misses another dimension of existence. If we could prove the nature of ultimate reality we would not need faith to place our bet on God's existence.

Lacking proof or certainty, should we straddle the fence with perfect indecision? Sometimes, said Albert Camus, life beckons us to make a 100 percent commitment to something about which we are 51 percent sure. Credit religion's critics for reminding us of instances of faith providing justification for greed, war, bigotry, and terrorism. It is understandable that the successes of scientific explanation combined with the superstition and inhumanity sometimes practiced in religion's name might push some people off the fence toward skepticism.

And credit people of faith, including those who practice faith-based skepticism, for venturing a leap of faith—mindful that they might be wrong, yet choosing to bet their lives on a humble spirituality, on an alternative to purposeless scientism, gullible spiritualism, and dogmatic fundamentalism. What united Dietrich Bonhoeffer, Martin Luther King, Jr., and Mother Teresa was a spirituality that helped make sense of the universe, gave meaning to life, opened them to the transcendent, connected them in supportive communities, provided a foundation for morality and selfless compassion, and offered hope in the face of adversity and death.

We're all surely wrong to some extent. We glimpse ultimate reality only dimly, both skeptics and faithful agree. Perhaps, though, we can draw wisdom from both skepticism and spirituality. Perhaps we can anchor our lives in a rationality and humility that restrains spiritual intuition with critical analysis, and in a spirituality that nurtures purpose, love, and joy.

Epilogue

In C. S. Lewis' *Chronicles of Narnia,* Bree, a proud talking horse, is exposed by the great lion Aslan while blustering a false proclamation. "Aslan," said a shaken Bree, "I'm afraid I must be rather a fool." "Happy the horse who knows that while he is still young," Aslan gently replied. "Or the human either."

In exposing our capacity for foolishness, this book runs the danger of being too humbling. Perhaps at times you have felt an urge to exclaim with Hamlet's mother, "Speak no more: Thou turn'st mine eyes into my very soul; and there I see such black and grained spots." Indeed, those of us who uncover the perils of intuition risk playing the part of Gregers Werle in Henrik Ibsen's play *The Wild Duck*— demolishing people's illusions but leaving them without hope or meaning.

Yet the new cognitive science underlying this book is fundamentally constructive. It aims not to destroy but to fortify our rationality, to sharpen our thinking, to deepen our wisdom. Scientists who expose flaws in our intuition and seek remedies are like a physician who says, "You're doing pretty well. Your heart's fine. Your lungs are clear. But your vision could use some correction."

Awareness that our intuition could benefit from some correction, in realms from sports to business to spirituality, makes clear the need for disciplined training of the mind. Intuition works well in some realms, but it needs restraints and checks in others. As Norman Cousins has argued, transforming schooling into mere vocational education misses the "biggest truth of all about learning: that its purpose is to unlock the human mind and to develop it into an organ capable of thought— conceptual thought, analytical thought, sequential thought." College students do think smarter when effectively introduced to principles of research methods and statistical reasoning. The Project on Redefining the Meaning and Purpose of Baccalaureate Degrees explains why college education should therefore prioritize developing clear and critical thinking ability:

> If anything is paid attention to in our colleges and universities, thinking must be it. Unfortunately, thinking can be lazy. It can be sloppy. . . . It can be fooled, misled, bullied. . . . Students possess great untrained and untapped capacities for logical thinking, critical analysis, and inquiry, but these are capacities that are not spontaneous: They grow out of wide instruction, experience, encouragement, correction, and constant use.

Democracy, too, is nurtured by awareness of our imperfections and resulting need for checks, balances, and open competition among ideas. "Fallibility implies that perfection is unattainable," notes George Soros, "and that we must content ourselves with the next best thing: an imperfect society that is always open to improvement. That is my definition of an open society."

In exposing the magnitude, efficiency, and adaptiveness of intuition, I have sought also to celebrate the powers of intuition. Intuition is huge. More than we realize, thinking occurs off-screen, with the results occasionally displayed on-screen. Intuition is adaptive. It enables us to drive on automatic and it feeds our expertise, our creativity, our love, and our spirituality. And intuition is a wonder. The wind blows where it chooses, unseen—an apt image for both intuition's mystery and its unbidden insights and inspirations.

Like most writers, I have time and again felt that mystery even while writing this science-based book, which is partly the result of a planned accumulation of information and partly the result of ideas, images, and words that spontaneously pop into awareness. At such times I feel delight and joy, and sometimes more like a scribe than an author, as if I were merely recording what something or someone pours onto my mental screen. It's akin to the feeling I sometimes get near the end of a long jog—that I am merely riding along on a pair of legs that are ferrying me home. The wind blows where it will.

Neurological evidence supports my sense that consciousness may be the outcropping of wonders beneath the surface. Consciousness has been shown to lag the brain events that evoke it. When we lift a finger at will, our brain waves jump about 0.3 seconds ahead of our conscious perception of the decision. The idea is not even in our awareness before our brain knows it. My sense of wonder at my own experience is perhaps akin to the Psalmist's:

> The word is not even on my tongue,
> Yahweh, before you know all about it . . .
> Such knowledge is beyond my understanding,
> a height to which my mind cannot attain. . . .
> For all these mysteries I thank you:
> for the wonder of myself, for the wonder of your works.

Notes

INTRODUCTION

1 Richard Feynman: E. Hutchings (ed.), *"Surely You're Joking, Mr. Feynman!"* (New York: Norton, 1997).

1 Daniel Kahneman in B. Mellers, R. Hertwig, and D. Kahneman, "Do Frequency Representations Eliminate Conjunction Effects? An Exercise in Adversarial Collaboration," *Psychological Science* 12 (2001): 269–275.

2 Prince Charles, Reith Lecture, http://news.bbc.co.uk/hi/english/static/events/reith_2000/lecture6.stm

2 Edgar D. Mitchell, from an undated solicitation letter for the Institute of Noetic Sciences.

2 Intuition Cruise: Magazine ad, "The Inner Voyage," the "ultimate conscious vacation," presented by *New Age Journal* and Inner Voyages.

2 "Let intuition be your guide": Deborah Duenes, *New Woman*, May 1998, pp. 113–115, 134, 141.

3 Belleruth Naparstek, "Extrasensory Etiquette," *Utne Reader*, November 1998, pp. 86–89.

4 David Milner, "Sight Unseen," Presentation to the Royal Society of Edinburgh "Human Nature" conference, August 2000.

5 Donald Hoffman, *Visual Intelligence: How We Create What We See* (New York: Norton, 1998), p. xiii.

5 George A. Miller, *Psychology: The Science of Mental Life* (New York: Harper & Row, 1962).

6–7 Row houses illusion: From Al Seckel, *The Art of Optical Illusions* (London: Carlton, 2000).

8 Lloyd Humphreys, "Acquisition and Extinction of Verbal Expectations in a Situation Analogous to Conditioning," *Journal of Experimental Psychology* 25 (1939): 141–158.

8 800 trillion: My thanks to Thomas Gilovich for this example from *How We Know What Isn't So: The Fallibility of Human Reason in Everyday Life* (New York: Free Press, 1991).

9 A. M. Mecca, N. J. Smelser, and J. Vasconcellos (eds.), *The Social Importance of Self-Esteem* (Berkeley: University of California Press, 1989).

9 The dark side of high self-esteem: See Roy F. Baumeister, "Violent Pride:

Do People Turn Violent Because of Self-Hate, or Self-Love?" *Scientific American,* April 2001, pp. 96–101.

9 Parental influence: This well-established result of behavior genetics studies is widely reported, perhaps most powerfully by Judith Rich Harris in *The Nurture Assumption* (New York: Free Press, 1998).

10 Repression: I discuss the evidence in my *Psychology,* 6th ed. (New York: Worth, 2001).

10 Crystals, tapes, therapeutic touch: I also discuss these studies in my *Psychology,* 6th edition. Christopher French of Goldsmith's College, London, presented research on quartz versus fake crystals to the British Psychological Society Annual Conference, 2001.

10 Texas official: Quoted by Molly Ivins from "a very, very high-ranking Texas public official" (unnamed, but when George Bush was governor): "I know there's no evidence that shows the death penalty has a deterrent effect, but I just feel in my gut it must be true" (syndicated column in *Holland [Mich.] Sentinel,* November 27, 1999).

10 Diana quoted by Roger Cohen, "Collision Course: How Diana's Life Ended," *New York Times,* September 6, 1997 (www.nytimes.com).

CHAPTER I. THINKING WITHOUT AWARENESS

15 John A. Bargh and Tanya L. Chartrand, "The Unbearable Automaticity of Being," *American Psychologist* 54 (1999): 462–479.

16 Cornell students: Ulric Neisser, "The Limits of Cognition," in P. Jusczyk and R. Klein (eds.), *The Nature of Thought* (Hillsdale, N.J.: Erlbaum, 1980).

16 James Reason and Klara Mycielska, *Absent-Minded? The Psychology of Mental Lapses and Everyday Errors* (Englewood Cliffs, N.J.: Prentice-Hall, 1982), p. 38.

17 Alfred North Whitehead, *An Introduction to Mathematics* (London: Williams & Norgate, 1911).

18 Bull's-eye gaze: R. L. Fantz, "The Origin of Form Perception," *Scientific American,* May 1961, pp. 66–72.

18 Eight to twelve inches: D. Maurer and C. Maurer, *The World of the Newborn* (New York: Basic Books, 1988).

18 Nursing baby: A. MacFarlane, "What a Baby Knows," *Human Nature,* February 1978, pp. 74–81.

18 Mother's voice: M. Mills and E. Melhuish, "Recognition of Mother's Voice in Early Infancy," *Nature* 252 (1974): 123–124.

18 Intuitive physics: R. Baillargeon, "Infants' Understanding of the Physical World," in M. Sabourin, F. I. M. Craik, and M. Roberts (eds.), *Advances*

in *Psychological Science, vol. 2: Biological and Cognitive Aspects* (Hove, England: Psychology Press, 1998).

18 Karen Wynn, "Psychological Foundations of Number: Numerical Competence in Human Infants," *Trends in Cognitive Science* 2 (1998): 296–303.

19 Michael Gazzaniga, "The Split Brain in Man," *Scientific American,* August 1967, pp. 24–29.

20 Priming right/left brains: M. J. Beeman and C. Chiarello, "Complementary Right- and Left-Hemisphere Language Comprehension," *Current Directions in Psychological Science* 7 (1998): 2–8.

20 Roger Sperry, "Problems Outstanding in the Evolution of Brain Function," James Arthur Lecture, American Museum of Natural History, 1964, New York. Cited by R. Ornstein, *The Psychology of Consciousness,* 2nd ed. (New York: Harcourt Brace Jovanovich, 1977). See also R. W. Sperry, "Some Effects of Disconnecting the Cerebral Hemispheres," *Science* 217 (1982): 1223–1226.

20 Michael Gazzaniga, "Organization of the Human Brain," *Science* 245 (1988): 947–952.

21 Oliver Sacks, *The Man Who Mistook His Wife for a Hat* (New York: Summit, 1985).

22 Implicit memory: See Daniel Schacter, "Understanding Implicit Memory: A Cognitive Neuroscience Approach," *American Psychologist* 47 (1992): 559–569, and *Searching for Memory: The Brain, the Mind, and the Past* (New York: Basic Books, 1996); and Larry R. Squire, *Memory and Brain* (New York: Oxford University Press, 1987).

23 Daniel M. Wegner and Laura Smart, "Deep Cognitive Activation: A New Approach to the Unconscious," *Journal of Consulting and Clinical Psychology* 65 (1997): 984–985.

23 C. S. Lewis, *Four Loves* (1948).

23–24 See L. Sechrest, T. R. Stickle, and M. Stewart, "The Role of Assessment in Clinical Psychology," in A. Bellack, M. Hersen (series eds.), and C. R. Reynolds (vol. ed.), *Comprehensive Clinical Psychology,* vol. 4: *Assessment* (New York: Pergamon, 1998). "Not empirically supported": Scott O. Lilienfeld, James M. Wood, and Howard N. Garb, "The Scientific Status of Projective Techniques," *Psychological Science in the Public Interest* 1 (2001), 27–66, and "What's Wrong with This Picture?" *Scientific American,* May 2001, pp. 81–87.

24 Robyn Dawes, *House of Cards: Psychology and Psychotherapy Built on Myth* (New York: Free Press, 1994).

25 William R. Wilson, "Feeling More Than We Can Know: Exposure Effects

Without Learning," *Journal of Personality and Social Psychology* 37 (1979): 811–821.

26 "Making names famous": Larry L. Jacoby, Vera Woloshyn, and Colleen Kelley, "Becoming Famous Without Being Recognized: Unconscious Influences of Memory Produced by Dividing Attention," *Journal of Experimental Psychology: General* 118 (1989): 115–125.

26 Bernard J. Baars and Katharine A. McGovern, "Consciousness," in V. Ramachandran (ed.), *Encyclopedia of Human Behavior* (Orlando, Fla.: Academic Press, 1994).

26 Aging words and walking: John A. Bargh, Mark Chen, and Lara Burrows, "Automaticity and Social Behavior: Direct Effects of Trait Construct and Stereotype Activation," *Journal of Personality and Social Psychology* 43 (1996): 437–449.

27 Subliminal experiments: For an easy-to-read review and bibliography of these experiments, see Nicholas Epley, Kenneth Savitsky, and Robert A. Kachelski, "What Every Skeptic Should Know About Subliminal Persuasion," *Skeptical Inquirer,* September–October 1999, pp. 40–45, 58. See also R. F. Bornstein and T. S. Pittman (eds.), *Perception Without Awareness: Cognitive, Clinical, and Social Perspectives* (New York: Guilford, 1992), and P. M. Merikle, D. Smilek, and J. D. Eastwood, "Perception Without Awareness: Perspectives from Cognitive Psychology," *Cognition* 79 (2001): 115–134.

27 Moshe Bar and Irving Biederman, "Subliminal Visual Priming," *Psychological Science* 9 (1998): 464–469.

27 Subliminal kittens: J. A. Krosnick, A. L. Betz, L. J. Jussim, and A. R. Lynn, "Subliminal Conditioning of Attitudes," *Personality and Social Psychology Bulletin* 18 (1992): 152–162.

27 Smiling/scowling face: S. T. Murphy and Robert B. Zajonc, "Affect, Cognition, and Awareness: Affective Priming with Optimal and Suboptimal Stimulus Exposures," *Journal of Personality and Social Psychology* 64 (1993): 723–739.

27 Adviser's face: M. W. Baldwin, S. E. Carell, and D. F. Lopez, "Priming Relationship Schemas: My Advisor and the Pope Are Watching Me from the Back of My Mind," *Journal of Experimental Social Psychology* 26 (1991): 435–454.

28 Spiders and shocks: E. S. Katkin, S. Wiens, and A. Ohman, "Nonconscious Fear Conditioning, Visceral Perception, and the Development of Gut Feelings," *Psychological Science* 12 (2001): 366–370.

28 Anthony Greenwald, "Subliminal Semantic Activation and Subliminal Snake Oil," paper presented to the American Psychological Association

convention, Washington, D.C. For a sample of this research, see A. G. Greenwald, E. R. Spangenberg, A. R. Pratkanis, and J. Eskenazi, "Double-Blind Tests of Subliminal Self-Help Audiotapes," *Psychological Science* 2 (1991): 119–122.

29 John A. Bargh, "The Automaticity of Everyday Life," in R. S. Wyer, Jr. (ed.), *Advances in Social Cognition,* vol. 10 (Mahwah, N.J.: Erlbaum, 1997). For a state-of-the-art handbook of research on the two ways of knowing, see S. Chaiken and Y. Trope (eds.), *Dual-Process Theories in Social Psychology* (New York: Guilford, 1999).

30 Seymour Epstein, "Integration of the Cognitive and the Psychodynamic Unconscious," *American Psychologist* 49 (1994): 709–724.

30 Questionnaire: Rosemary Pacini and Seymour Epstein, "The Relation of Rational and Experiential Information Processing Styles to Personality, Basic Beliefs, and the Ratio-Bias Problem," *Journal of Personality and Social Psychology* 76 (1999): 972–987.

CHAPTER 2. SOCIAL INTUITION

31 Jackie Larsen: Pieced together from personal correspondence and from Vicki Biggs, "Murder Suspect Captured in Grand Marais," *Cook County (Minn.) News-Herald,* April 13, 2001.

32 Nalini Ambady and Robert Rosenthal, "Thin Slices of Expressive Behavior as Predictors of Interpersonal Consequences: A Meta-Analysis," *Psychological Bulletin* 111 (1992): 256–274; "Half a Minute: Predicting Teacher Evaluations from Thin Slices of Nonverbal Behavior and Physical Attractiveness," *Journal of Personality and Social Psychology* 64 (1993): 431–441. See also J. A. Hall and F. Bernieri (eds.), *Interpersonal Sensitivity: Theory and Measurement* (Mahwah, N.J.: Erlbaum, 2001).

32–33 Various experiments: Leslie A. Zebrowitz and Mary Ann Collins, "Accurate Social Perception at Zero Acquaintance: The Affordances of a Gibsonian Approach," *Personality and Social Psychology Review* 1 (1997): 204–223.

33 John Bargh quoted by Beth Azar, "Split-Second Evaluations Shape Our Moods, Actions," *Monitor* (American Psychological Association), September 1998, p. 13.

33 Chinese and Americans: Linda Albright, Thomas E. Malloy, Qi Dong, David A. Kenny, Xiaoyi Fang, Lynn Winquist, and Da Yu, "Cross-Cultural Consensus in Personality Judgments," *Journal of Personality and Social Psychology* 72 (1997): 558–569.

33 Timothy Wilson with Samuel Lindsey and Tonya Y. Schooler, "A Model of Dual Attitudes," *Psychological Review* 107 (2000): 101–126.

34 Nine experiments: T. D. Wilson, D. S. Dunn, D. Kraft, and D. J. Lisle, "Introspection, Attitude Change, and Attitude-Behavior Consistency: The Disruptive Effects of Explaining Why We Feel the Way We Do," in L. Berkowitz (ed.), *Advances in Experimental Social Psychology,* vol. 22 (San Diego, Calif.: Academic Press, 1989).

34 Theodore Roethke, *The Collected Poems of Theodore Roethke* (Garden City, N.Y.: Anchor, 1975).

34 Poster study: T. D. Wilson, D. J. Lisle, J. W. Schooler, S. D. Hodges, D. J. Klaaren, and S. J. LaFleur, "Introspecting About Reasons Can Reduce Post-Choice Satisfaction," *Personality and Social Psychology Bulletin* 19 (1993): 331–339.

34 Timothy D. Wilson and Jonathan W. Schooler, "Thinking Too Much: Introspection Can Reduce the Quality of Preferences and Decisions," *Journal of Personality and Social Psychology* 60 (1991): 181–192.

35 Nancy Cantor and John F. Kihlstrom, *Personality and Social Intelligence* (Englewood Cliffs, N.J.: Prentice-Hall, 1987).

35 Seymour Epstein and Petra Meier, "Constructive Thinking: A Broad Coping Variable with Specific Components," *Journal of Personality and Social Psychology* 57 (1989): 332–350.

35 Carroll Izard with Sarah Fine, David Schultz, Allison Mostow, Brian Ackerman, and Eric Youngstrom, "Emotion Knowledge as a Predictor of Social Behavior and Academic Competence in Children at Risk," *Psychological Science* 12 (2001): 18–23.

36 John D. Mayer, David R. Caruso, and Peter Salovey, "Emotional Intelligence Meets Traditional Standards for an Intelligence," *Intelligence* 27 (2000): 267–298.

37 Joseph LeDoux and Jorge Armony, "Can Neurobiology Tell Us Anything About Human Feelings?" in D. Dahneman, E. Diener, and N. Schwartz (eds.), *Well-Being: The Foundations of Hedonic Psychology* (New York: Sage, 1999).

38 Frontal lobe damage: Antoine Bechara, Hanna Damasio, Daniel Tranel, and Antonio R. Damasio, "Deciding Advantageously Before Knowing the Advantageous Strategy," *Science* 275 (1997): 1293–1297.

38 An ounce of intuition: Bruce Bower, "Hunches Pack Decisive Punches," *Science News,* March 22, 1997, p. 183.

38 Michael Domjan, "Behavior Systems and the Demise of Equipotentiality: Historical Antecedents and Evidence from Sexual Conditioning," in M. E. Bouton and M. S. Fanselow (eds.), *Learning, Motivation, and Cognition: The Functional Behaviorism of Robert C. Bolles* (Washington, D.C.: American Psychological Association, 1997).

39 Matthew Birnie: O. Craig and J. Shields, "For Pity's Sake," *Sunday Times* (London), July 14, 1996, sec. 3, pages 1–2.

39 Abused children: S. Pollak, D. Cicchetti, and R. Klorman, "Stress, Memory, and Emotion: Developmental Considerations from the Study of Child Maltreatment," *Developmental Psychopathology* 10 (1998): 811–828.

39 Disgust: P. Rozin, L. Millman, and C. Nemeroff, "Operation of the Laws of Sympathetic Magic in Disgust and Other Domains," *Journal of Personality and Social Psychology* 50 (1986): 703–712.

39 Childlike faces: D. S. McArthur and L. Z. McArthur, "Perceiving Character in Faces: The Impact of Age-Related Craniofacial Changes on Social Perception," *Psychological Bulletin* 100 (1986): 3–18.

39 Mere exposure: Research on this phenomenon, initially explored by Robert Zajonc, has been reviewed by Robert F. Bornstein, "Exposure and Affect: Overview and Meta-Analysis of Research, 1968–1987," *Psychological Bulletin* 106 (1989): 265–289, and "Source Amnesia, Misattribution, and the Power of Unconscious Perceptions and Memories," *Psychoanalytic Psychology* 16 (1999): 155–178.

39 Richard L. Moreland and Scott R. Beach, "Exposure Effects in the Classroom: The Development of Affinity Among Students," *Journal of Experimental Social Psychology* 28 (1992): 255–276.

40 Taiwanese mail carrier: N. Steinberg, "Astonishing Love Stories" (from an earlier United Press International report), *Games,* February 1993, p. 47.

40 Robert B. Zajonc, "Emotions," in D. Gilbert, S. T. Fiske, and G. Lindzey (eds.), *Handbook of Social Psychology,* 4th ed. (New York: McGraw-Hill, 1998).

40 Spontaneous trait inference: Leonard S. Newman and James S. Uleman review this research in "Spontaneous Trait Inference," in J. S. Uleman and J. A. Bargh (eds.), *Unintended Thought* (New York: Guilford, 1989).

40 Hannah: John M. Darley and Paget H. Gross, "A Hypothesis-Confirming Bias in Labelling Effects," *Journal of Personality and Social Psychology* 44 (1983): 20–33.

40 Lynda Mae, Donal E. Carlston, and John J. Skowronski, "Spontaneous Trait Transference to Familiar Communicators: Is a Little Knowledge a Dangerous Thing?" *Journal of Personality and Social Psychology* 77 (1999): 233–246.

41 Jonathan Haidt, "The Emotional Dog and Its Rational Tail: A Social Intuitionist Approach to Moral Judgment," *Psychological Review* 108 (2001): 814–834.

41 Snow shoveling story: Jonathan Haidt, "The Positive Emotion of Eleva-

tion," *Prevention and Treatment* 3 (2000): article 3 (journals.apa.org/prevention/volume3).

41 "Moral reasoning" struts: Jonathan Haidt, "The Moral Emotions," in R. J. Davidson, K. Scherer, and H. H. Goldsmith (eds.), *Handbook of Affective Sciences* (Oxford: Oxford University Press, in press).

42 Joshua Greene with R. B. Sommerville, L. E. Nystrom, J. M. Darley, and J. D. Cohen, "An fMRI Investigation of Emotional Engagement in Moral Judgment," *Science* 293 (2001): 2105–2108.

42 Natural mimicry: F. J. Bernieri, J. M. Davis, and R. Rosenthal, "Interactional Synchrony and Rapport: Measuring Synchrony in Displays Devoid of Sound and Facial Affect," *Personality and Social Psychology Bulletin* 20 (1994): 303–311, and E. Hatfield, J. T. Cacioppo, and R. Rapson, "The Logic of Emotion: Emotional Contagion," in M. S. Clark (ed.), *Review of Personality and Social Psychology* (Newbury Park, Calif.: Sage, 1992).

42 Mood linkage: P. Totterdell, S. Kellett, R. B. Briner, and K. Teuchmann, "Evidence of Mood Linkage in Work Groups," *Journal of Personality and Social Psychology* 74 (1998): 1504–1515.

42 Desmond Tutu, *No Future Without Forgiveness* (New York: Image/Doubleday, 1999), p. 286.

42 Subtle muscle movements: Ulf Dimberg, Monika Thunberg, and Kurt Elmehed, "Unconscious Facial Reactions to Emotional Facial Expressions," *Psychological Science* 11 (2000): 86–89.

42 Tanya L. Chartrand and John A. Bargh, "The Chameleon Effect: The Perception-Behavior Link and Social Interaction," *Journal of Personality and Social Psychology* 76 (1999): 893–910. See also Roland Neumann and Fritz Strack, "'Mood Contagion': The Automatic Transfer of Mood Between Persons," *Journal of Personality and Social Psychology* 79 (2000): 211–223.

43 Intuiting types: Data provided by Mary McCauley of the Center for Applications of Psychology Type and reported by William Ickes, Carol Marangoni, and Stella Garcia, "Studying Empathic Accuracy in a Clinically Relevant Context," in W. Ickes (ed.), *Empathic Accuracy* (New York: Guilford, 1997).

43 Ickes, *Empathic Accuracy*.

44 Clever experiment: J. D. Milojkovic and Lee Ross, "Telling Truths from Lies: Miscalibration of Confidence and Base-Rate Utilization," paper presented to the American Psychological Association convention, 1991.

44 Paul Ekman and Maureen O'Sullivan, "Who Can Catch a Liar?" *American Psychologist* 46 (1991): 913–920.

44 Paul Ekman, Maureen O'Sullivan, and Mark G. Frank, "A Few Can Catch a Liar," *Psychological Science* 10 (1999): 263–266.

44 Why people miss lies: Paul Ekman, "Lying and Deception," in N. L. Stein, P. A. Ornstein, B. Tversky, and C. Brainerd, *Memory for Everyday and Emotional Events* (Mahwah, N.J.: Erlbaum, 1997), and "Why Don't We Catch Liars?" *Social Research* 64 (1996): 802–817.

45 Aphasia patients: N. L. Etcoff, P. Ekman, J. J. Magee, and M. G. Frank, "Lie Detection and Language Comprehension," *Nature* 405 (2000): 139.

46 Gender and empathy: N. Eisenberg and R. Lennon, "Sex Differences in Empathy and Related Capacities," *Psychological Bulletin* 94 (1983): 100–131.

46 Friendships with women: L. B. Rubin, *Just Friends: The Role of Friendship in Our Lives* (New York: Harper & Row, 1985), and L. A. Sapadin, "Friendship and Gender: Perspectives of Professional Men and Women," *Journal of Social and Personal Relationships* 5 (1988): 387–403.

46 Judith A. Hall, *Nonverbal Sex Differences: Communication Accuracy and Expressive Style* (Baltimore: Johns Hopkins University Press, 1984).

46 Children reading faces: Erin B. McClure, "A Meta-Analytic Review of Sex Differences in Facial Expression Processing and Their Development in Infants, Children, and Adolescents," *Psychological Bulletin* 126 (2000): 424–453.

46 Women and lie detection: Bella M. DePaulo, "Spotting Lies: Can Humans Learn To Do Better?" *Current Directions in Psychological Science* 3 (1994): 83–86.

47 Photo experiments: M. L. Barnes and R. J. Sternberg, "Social Intelligence and Decoding of Nonverbal Cues," *Intelligence* 13 (1989): 263–287; R. J. Sternberg and C. Smith, "Social Intelligence and Decoding Skills in Nonverbal Communication," *Social Cognition* 2 (1985): 168–192.

47 Women's emotional responsiveness: M. Grossman and W. Wood, "Sex Differences in Intensity of Emotional Experience: A Social Role Interpretation," *Journal of Personality and Social Psychology* 65 (1993): 1010–1022.

47 Gender and expression: E. J. Coats and R. S. Feldman, "Gender Differences in Nonverbal Correlates of Social Status," *Personality and Social Psychology Bulletin* 22 (1996): 1014–1022.

47 Women's ways of knowing: M. F. Belenky, B. M. Clinchy, N. R. Goldberger, and J. M. Tarule, *Women's Ways of Knowing: The Development of Self, Voice, and Mind* (New York: Basic Books, 1986).

47 *Skeptical Inquirer* list: Deborah Frisch, "Skeptical of Skepticism," *Skeptical Inquirer,* May–June 2000, pp. 59–60.

47 110 male and 4 female: This total included authors of books, editors of books, and authors of forewords; it did not include authors whose gender could not be discerned from the name.

47 Penney Peirce, "The Silent Mind," www.intuitionmagazine.com.

48 Subordinates' intuition: Sara E. Snodgrass, "Women's Intuition: The Effect of Subordinate Role on Interpersonal Sensitivity," *Journal of Personality and Social Psychology* 49 (1985): 146–155, and "Further Effects of Role Versus Gender on Interpersonal Sensitivity," *Journal of Personality and Social Psychology* 62 (1992): 154–158.

48 Judith A. Hall, *Nonverbal Sex Differences: Communication Accuracy and Expressive Style* (Baltimore: Johns Hopkins University Press, 1984), pp. 152–153.

48 Tiffany Graham and William Ickes, "When Women's Intuition Isn't Greater Than Men's," in Ickes, *Empathic Accuracy,* emphasis in original.

48 Evelyn Fox Keller: As reported by Sasha Nemecek, "The Furor Over Feminist Science," *Scientific American,* January 1997, pp. 99–100.

48 Belenky et al., *Women's Ways of Knowing.*

49 Rosemary Pacini and Seymour Epstein, "The Relation of Rational and Experiential Information Processing Styles to Personality, Basic Beliefs, and the Ratio-Bias Phenomenon," *Journal of Personality and Social Psychology* 76 (1999): 972–987.

49 Myers-Briggs: "Construction and Properties of the MBTI," national sample reported in I. B. Myers, M. H. McCaulley, N. L. Quenk, and A. L. Hammer, *MBTI Manual: A Guide to the Development and Use of the Myers-Briggs Type Indicator,* 3rd ed. (Palo Alto, Calif.: Consulting Psychologists Press, 1998). A. L. Hammer and W. D. Mitchell, "The Distribution of MBTI Types in the U.S. by Gender and Ethnic Group," *Journal of Psychological Type* 37 (1996): 2–15, report a different sample in which 68 percent of males scored as thinking types and 61 percent of women as feeling types.

50 Care for preschoolers/parents: A. H. Eagly and M. Crowley, "Gender and Helping Behavior: A Meta-Analytic Review of the Social Psychological Literature," *Psychological Bulletin* 100 (1986): 283–308.

50 Gifts, cards, letters, and calls: Needham surveys reported in R. Putnam, *Bowling Alone* (New York: Simon and Schuster, 2000).

50 Photos: S. M. Clancy and S. J. Dollinger, "Photographic Depictions of the Self: Gender and Age Differences in Social Connectedness," *Sex Roles* 29 (1993): 477–495.

CHAPTER 3. INTUITIVE EXPERTISE AND CREATIVITY

52 Detecting complex patterns: Pawel Lewicki, "Conclusions of the Research on Nonconscious Information Processing (A Quick "Non-Technical" Summary)." www.personal.utulsa.edu/pawel-lewicki/simple.html

52 Recognizing a shape: Pawel Lewicki, Thomas Hill, and Maria Czyzewska, "Nonconscious Acquisition of Information," *American Psychologist* 47 (1992): 796–801. A synopsis and citations of Lewicki's other research can be found here.

54 Warsaw student experiment: Pawel Lewicki, "Nonconscious Biasing Effects of Single Instances on Subsequent Judgments," *Journal of Personality and Social Psychology* 48 (1985): 563–574.

54 Ron "Suki" King: Dave Hamill, "Checkers King Crowned," *Games,* October 1998, p. 6.

54 William G. Chase and Herbert A. Simon, "Perception in Chess," *Cognitive Psychology* 4 (1973): 55–81. Also, Herbert A. Simon and William G. Chase, "Skill in Chess," *American Scientist* 6 (1973): 394–403.

54 50,000 chess patterns: Jean Bedard and Michelene T. H. Chi, "Expertise," *Current Directions in Psychological Science* 1 (1992): 135–139.

54 Hubert L. Dreyfus and Stuart E. Dreyfus, *Mind Over Machine: The Power of Human Intuition and Expertise in the Era of the Computer* (New York: Free Press, 1986), p. 33.

55 Chicken sexers: Dreyfus and Dreyfus, *Mind Over Machine,* pp. 196–197, and Gazza's Poultry Page, "Chicken Sexing" www3.turboweb.net.au/garrys/poultry/chickensexing.html.

55 Carolyn Yewchuk, "Savant Syndrome: Intuitive Excellence Amidst General Deficit," *Developmental Disabilities Bulletin* 27 (1999): 58–76.

56 Herbert A. Simon, "What Is an 'Explanation' of Behavior?" *Psychological Science* 3 (1992): 150–161.

56 Medical students: G. Bordage and R. Zacks, "The Structure of Medical Knowledge in the Memories of Medical Students and General Practitioners: Categories and Prototypes," *Medical Education* 18 (1984): 406–416.

56 Cardiologists: V. L. Patel, D. A. Evans, and G. J. Groen, "Biomedical Knowledge and Clinical Reasoning," in D. Evans and V. Patel (eds.), *Cognitive Science in Medicine: Biomedical Modeling* (Cambridge, Mass.: MIT Press, 1989).

56 Selecting interns: E. J. Johnson, "Expertise and Decision Under Uncertainty: Performance and Process," in M. T. H. Chi, R. Glaser, and M. J. Farr (eds.), *The Nature of Expertise* (Hillsdale, N.J.: Erlbaum, 1988).

56 Kasparov analogy: Thanks to Gordon W. Gribble, Letter, *Science News,* August 20, 1996.

56 Robert J. Sternberg, "Theory of Successful Intelligence," *Review of General Psychology* 3 (1999): 292–316.

57 Michael Polanyi, *The Tacit Dimension* (London: Routledge & Kegan Paul, 1966).

57 Tacit knowledge and success: R. K. Wagner and R. J. Sternberg, "Practical Intelligence in Real-World Pursuits: The Role of Tacit Knowledge," *Journal of Personality and Social Psychology* 49 (1985): 436–458; R. J. Sternberg and R. K. Wagner, "The g-ocentric View of Intelligence and Job Performance Is Wrong," *Current Directions in Psychological Science* 2 (1993): 1–5; R. J. Sternberg, R. K. Wagner, W. M. Williams, and J. A. Horvath, "Testing Common Sense," *American Psychologist* 50 (1995): 912–927; R. J. Sternberg and J. A. Horvath (eds.), *Tacit Knowledge in Professional Practice: Researcher and Practitioner Perspectives* (Mahwah, N.J.: Erlbaum, 1999).

57 Dreyfus and Dreyfus, *Mind Over Machine.*

57 *Pad/bad/dad:* I adapted this example from Malcolm Gladwell's report of psychologist Richard Ivry's research in "The Physical Genius: What Do Wayne Gretzky, Yo-Yo Ma, and a Brain Surgeon Have in Common?" *New Yorker,* August 2, 1999 (from www.gladwell.com).

59 Thousands of hours of practice: K. A. Ericsson, "Attaining Excellence Through Deliberate Practice: Insights from the Study of Expert Performance," in M. Ferrari (ed.), *The Pursuit of Excellence in Education* (Hillsdale, N.J.: Erlbaum, 2001).

59 Fermat and Andrew J. Wiles: I draw my account from Simon Singh and Kenneth A. Riber, "Fermat's Last Stand," *Scientific American,* November 1997, pp. 68–73, and from Simon Singh, *Fermat's Enigma* (New York: Walker, 1997).

59 "Indescribably beautiful": Quoted by Singh, *Fermat's Enigma,* p. 275.

59 Robert J. Sternberg and Todd I. Lubart, "An Investment Theory of Creativity and Its Development," *Human Development* 34 (1991): 1–31; "Buy Low and Sell High: An Investment Approach to Creativity," *Psychological Science* 1 (1992): 1–5; *Defying the Crowd: Cultivating Creativity in a Culture of Conformity* (New York: Free Press, 1995).

60 Teresa M. Amabile and Beth A. Hennessey, "The Motivation for Creativity in Children," in A. K. Boggiano and T. S. Pittman (eds.), *Achievement and Motivation: A Social-Developmental Perspective* (New York: Cambridge University Press, 1992). See also T. M. Amabile, *The Social Psychology of Creativity* (New York: Springer-Verlag, 1983).

60 "Obsessed by this problem": Quoted Singh and Riber, "Fermat's Last Stand," pp. 68–73.

60 Dean Keith Simonton, "The Social Context of Career Success and Course for 2,026 Scientists and Inventors," *Personality and Social Psychology Bulletin* 18 (1992): 452–463.

61 "Subconscious appears": Quoted by Singh, *Fermat's Enigma*, p. 208.

61 John Maynard Keynes, "Newton the Man," in J. R. Newman (ed.), *The World of Mathematics*, vol. 1 (New York: Simon & Schuster, 1956).

61 Einstein: Quoted by Michael Balter, "What Makes the Mind Dance and Count," *Science* 292 (2001): 1636–1637.

61 Nobel laureates: F. Marton, P. Fensham, and S. Chaiklin, "A Nobel's Eye View of Scientific Intuition," *International Journal of Science Education* 16 (1994): 457–473. Cited by G. Claxton, "Investigating Human Intuition: Knowing Without Knowing Why," *Psychologist* 11 (1998): 217–220.

61 Bach: Quoted by Ellen J. Langer, *Mindfulness* (Reading, Mass.: Addison-Wesley, 1990).

"Painting is stronger": Marie-Laure Bernadac and Paule DuBouchet, *Picasso—Master of the New Idea* (New York: Abrams, 1993), p. 125.

"Someone who works": Dore Ashton (ed.), *Picasso on Art* (New York: Da Capo, 1972), p. 9.

Larry Gelbart: Ann Oldenburg, "In a Word, He's Funny," *USA Today*, March 25, 1998, p. D2.

62 Anne Lamott: *Bird by Bird: Some Instructions on Writing and Life* (New York: Anchor Books/Random House, 1994), pp. 112–113.

62 Robert S. Siegler, "Unconscious Insights," *Current Directions in Psychological Science* 9 (2000): 79–83; R. S. Siegler and E. Stern, "A Microgenetic Analysis of Conscious and Unconscious Strategy Discoveries," *Journal of Experimental Psychology: General* 127 (1998): 377–397.

63 Henri Poincaré quoted in Langer, *Mindfulness*, p. 116.

CHAPTER 4. INTUITIONS ABOUT OUR PAST AND FUTURE

68 Martie G. Haselton and David M. Buss, "Error Management Theory: A New Perspective on Biases in Cross-Sex Mind Reading," *Journal of Personality and Social Psychology* 78 (2000): 81–91.

68 Ralph N. Haber, "How We Remember What We See," *Scientific American*, May 1970, pp. 104–112.

68 Memory survey: P. A. Lamal, "College Students' Common Beliefs About Psychology," *Teaching of Psychology* 6 (1979): 155–158.

69 Daniel Offer with Marjorie Kaiz, Kenneth I. Howard, and Emily S. Ben-

nett, "The Altering of Reported Experiences," *Journal of the American Academy of Child and Adolescent Psychiatry* 39 (2000): 735–742.

69 University of Michigan study: G. B. Markus, "Stability and Change in Political Attitudes: Observe, Recall, and 'Explain,'" *Political Behavior* 8 (1986): 21–44.

69 George E. Vaillant, *Adaptation to Life* (Boston: Little, Brown, 1977), p. 197.

70 Cathy McFarland and Michael Ross, "The Relation Between Current Impressions and Memories of Self and Dating Partners," unpublished manuscript, University of Waterloo, 1985.

70 Diane Holmberg and John G. Holmes, "Reconstruction of Relationship Memories: A Mental Models Approach," in N. Schwarz and S. Sudman (eds.), *Autobiographical Memory and the Validity of Retrospective Reports* (New York: Springer-Verlag, 1994).

70 *Parade* medical columnist: Isadore Rosenfeld, "PMS Update," *Parade*, June 3, 2001, p. 7.

70 Daily mood diaries: E. A. Hardie, "Prevalence and Predictors of Cyclic and Noncyclic Affective Change," *Psychology of Women Quarterly* 21 (1997): 299–314; C. McFarland, M. Ross, and N. DeCourville, "Women's Theories of Menstruation and Biases in Recall of Menstrual Symptoms," *Journal of Personality and Social Psychology* 57 (1989): 522–531; J. Brooks-Gunn, "Adolescents as Daughters and as Mothers: A Developmental Perspective," in I. Sigel and G. Brody (eds.), *Methods of Family Research* (Hillsdale, N.J.: Erlbaum, 1990).

71 Daniel Kahneman with B. L. Fredrickson, C. A. Schreiber, and D. A. Redelmeier, "When More Pain Is Preferred to Less: Adding a Better End," *Psychological Science* 4 (1993): 401–405.

71 Taper down: Daniel Kahneman, "Assessments of Objective Happiness: A Bottom-Up Approach," in D. Kahneman, E. Diener, and N. Schwartz (eds.), *Understanding Well-Being: Scientific Perspectives on Enjoyment and Suffering* (New York: Russell Sage Foundation, 1999).

71 Democrats and students: J. Meyers, T. D. Wilson, and D. T. Gilbert, unpublished raw data reported by D. T. Gilbert, E. Driver-Linn, and T. D. Wilson, "The Trouble with Vronsky: Impact Bias in the Forecasting of Future Affective States," in P. Salovey and L. Feldman-Barrett (eds.), *The Wisdom of Feeling* (New York: Guilford, in press).

71 Other studies: T. R. Mitchell and L. Thompson, "A Theory of Temporal Adjustments of the Evaluation of Events: Rosy Prospection and Rosy Retrospection," in C. Stubbart, J. Porac, and J. Meindl (eds.), *Advances in Managerial Cognition and Organizational Information Processing*

(Greenwich, Conn.: JAI, 1994); T. R. Mitchell, L. Thompson, E. Peterson, and R. Cronk, "Temporal Adjustments in the Evaluation of Events: The 'Rosy View,'" *Journal of Experimental Social Psychology* 33 (1997): 421–448.

72 D. R. Wixon and James D. Laird, "Awareness and Attitude Change in the Forced-Compliance Paradigm: The Importance of When," *Journal of Personality and Social Psychology* 34 (1976): 376–384.

72 Michael Conway and Michael Ross, "Remembering One's Own Past: The Construction of Personal Histories," in R. Sorrentino and E. T. Higgins (eds.), *Handbook of Motivation and Cognition* (New York: Guilford, 1986). For more on the unreliability of personal recall, see Robert W. Pearson, Michael Ross, and Robyn M. Dawes, "Personal Recall and the Limits of Retrospective Questions in Surveys," in J. M. Tanur (ed.), *Questions About Questions: Inquiries into the Cognitive Bases of Surveys* (Thousand Oaks, Calif.: Sage, 1992).

72 Anne E. Wilson and Michael Ross, "From Chump to Champ: People's Appraisals of Their Earlier and Present Selves," *Journal of Personality and Social Psychology* 80 (2001): 572–584.

72 Robert Spitzer, "200 Subjects Who Claim to Have Changed Their Sexual Orientation from Homosexual to Heterosexual," paper presented to the American Psychiatric Association convention, 2001, and later remarks in a *Wall Street Journal* essay, May 23, 2001.

73 Moods and World Cup victory: J. P. Forgas, G. H. Bower, and S. E. Krantz, "The Influence of Mood on Perceptions of Social Interactions," *Journal of Experimental Social Psychology* 20 (1984): 497–513; N. Schwarz, F. Strack, D. Kommer, and D. Wagner, "Soccer, Rooms, and the Quality of Your Life: Mood Effects on Judgments of Satisfaction with Life in General and with Specific Domains," *European Journal of Social Psychology* 17 (1987): 69–79.

73 The setting and perceiving a face: M. Rothbart and P. Birrell, "Attitude and Perception of Faces," *Journal of Research Personality* 11 (1977): 209–215; H. G. Wallbott, "In and Out of Context: Influences of Facial Expression and Context Information on Emotion Attributions," *British Journal of Social Psychology* 27 (1988): 357–369.

73 Depressed people's recollections: P. M. Lewinsohn and M. Rosenbaum, "Recall of Parental Behavior by Acute Depressives, Remitted Depressives, and Nondepressives," *Journal of Personality and Social Psychology* 52 (1987): 611–619; M. Lewis, "Commentary," *Human Development* 35 (1992): 44–51.

73 Adolescent moods: R. F. Bornstein, D. J. Galley, D. R. Leone, and A. R.

Kale, "The Temporal Stability of Ratings of Parents: Test-Retest Reliability and Influence of Parental Contact," *Journal of Social Behavior and Personality* 6 (1991): 641–649.

73 Elizabeth F. Loftus, "Remembering What Never Happened," in E. Tulving (ed.), *Memory, Consciousness, and the Brain* (Philadelphia: Psychology Press/Taylor & Francis, 2000); E. F. Loftus and K. Ketcham, *The Myth of Repressed Memory* (New York: St. Martin's, 1994).

74 *Challenger* explosion recall: U. Neisser and N. Harsch, "Phantom Flashbulbs: False Recollections of Hearing the News About *Challenger*," in E. Winograd and U. Neisser (eds.), *Affect and Accuracy in Recall: Studies of "Flashbulb" Memories* (New York: Cambridge University Press, 1992).

74 Stephen J. Ceci and Maggie Bruck: S. J. Ceci, M. L. C. Huffman, E. Smith, and E. F. Loftus, "Repeatedly Thinking About a Non-Event: Source Misattributions Among Preschoolers," *Consciousness and Cognition* 3 (1994): 388–407; S. J. Ceci and M. Bruck, *Jeopardy in the Courtroom: A Scientific Analysis of Children's Testimony* (Washington, D.C.: American Psychological Association, 1995).

75 Richard Wiseman with C. Jeffreys, M. Smith, and A. Nyman, "The Psychology of the Seance," *Skeptical Inquirer* 23(2) (1999): 30–33.

75 Reagan source misattribution: Recounted by E. F. Loftus and K. Ketcham, *The Myth of Repressed Memory* (New York: St. Martin's, 1994).

75 Eyewitness confidence: I review this research in my *Social Psychology* (New York: McGraw-Hill, 2002).

75 Brian H. Bornstein and Douglas J. Zickafoose, " 'I Know I Know It, I Know I Saw It': The Stability of the Confidence-Accuracy Relationship Across Domains," *Journal of Experimental Psychology: Applied* 5 (1999): 76–88.

76 C. S. Lewis, *Mere Christianity* (New York: Macmillan, 1960), pp. 18–19.

76 Rainy day and suspension bridge: Norbert L. Schwarz and Gerald L. Clore, "Mood, Misattribution, and Judgments of Well-Being: Informative and Directive Functions of Affective States," *Journal of Personality and Social Psychology* 45 (1983): 513–523; Donald G. Dutton and Arthur P. Aron, "Some Evidence for Heightened Sexual Attraction Under Conditions of High Anxiety," *Journal of Personality and Social Psychology* 30 (1974): 510–517.

76 Richard E. Nisbett and Stanley Schachter, "Cognitive Manipulation of Pain," *Journal of Experimental Social Psychology* 2 (1966): 227–236.

76 Bibb Latané and John M. Darley, *The Unresponsive Bystander: Why Doesn't He Help?* (New York: Appleton-Century-Crofts, 1970).

77 Media influences: I review this research in *The American Paradox: Spir-*

itual Hunger in an Age of Plenty (New Haven: Yale University Press, 2000).

77 Third person effect: Julie M. Duck and Barbara-Ann Mullin, "The Perceived Impact of the Mass Media: Reconsidering the Third Person Effect," *European Journal of Social Psychology* 25 (1995): 77–93; J. M. Innes and H. Zeitz, "The Public's View of the Impact of the Mass Media: A Test of the 'Third Person' Effect," *European Journal of Social Psychology* 18 (1988): 457–463.

77 Pupil size: E. H. Hess, "Pupilometrics," in N. Greenfield and R. Sternbach (eds.), *Handbook of Psychophysiology* (New York: Holt, Rinehart, and Winston, 1972).

78 Blood pressure perception: Studies by Howard Leventhal and colleagues, as reported by Delia Cioffi, "Beyond Attentional Strategies: A Cognitive-Perceptual Model of Somatic Interpretation," *Psychological Bulletin* 109 (1990): 25–41.

78 Heaven and hell: Cited by Yueh-Ting Lee, quoted by B. Bower, "Fighting Stereotype Stigma," *Science News,* June 29, 1996 (www.sciencenews .org).

78 Mispredicted: D. T. Gilbert and J. E. J. Ebert, "Decisions and Revisions: The Affective Forecasting of Changeable Outcomes," *Journal of Personality and Social Psychology,* in press.

79–80 Examples: G. Loewenstein and D. Schkade, "Wouldn't It Be Nice? Predicting Future Feelings," in D. Kahneman, E. Diener, and N. Schwarz (eds.), *Well-Being: The Foundations of Hedonic Psychology* (New York: Russell Sage Foundation, 1998), pp. 85–105; D. T. Gilbert and T. D. Wilson, "Miswanting: Some Problems in the Forecasting of Future Affective States," in J. Forgas (ed.), *Feeling and Thinking: The Role of Affect in Social Cognition* (Cambridge: Cambridge University Press, 2000); T. D. Wilson, T. P. Wheatley, J. M. Meyers, D. T. Gilbert, and D. Axsom, "Focalism: A Source of Durability Bias in Affective Forecasting," *Journal of Personality and Social Psychology* 78 (2000): 821–836.

79 Women in labor: J. J. Christensen-Szalanski, "Discount Functions and the Measurement of Patient's Values: Women's Decisions During Child Birth," *Medical Decision Making* 4 (1984): 47–58.

79 George Macdonald, *What's Mine's Mine* (London: Kegan Paul, Trench, 1886).

80 Weekly snack preferences: J. Simonson, "The Effect of Purchase Quantity and Timing on Variety-Seeking Behavior," *Journal of Marketing Research* 27(2) (1990): 150–162.

80 Smokers: B. S. Lynch and R. J. Bonnie, "Toward a Youth-Centered Pre-

vention Policy," in B. S. Lynch and R. J. Bonnie (eds.), *Growing Up Tobacco Free: Preventing Nicotine Addiction in Children and Youths* (Washington, D.C.: National Academy Press, 1994).

Smokers quitting: Paul Slovic, "Cigarette Smokers: Rational Actors or Rational Fools?" in P. Slovic (ed.), *Smoking Risk, Perception, and Policy* (Thousand Oaks, Calif.: Sage, 2001).

81 Leo Tolstoy, *Anna Karenina* (D. Magarshack, trans.) (New York: Signet, 1877/1961), p. 468, quoted by D. T. Gilbert, E. Driver-Linn, and T. D. Wilson, "The Trouble with Vronsky: Impact Bias in the Forecasting of Future Affective States," in P. Salovey and L. Feldman-Barrett (eds.), *The Wisdom of Feeling* (New York: Guilford, in press).

81 HIV patients: E. M. Sieff, R. M. Dawes, and G. F. Loewenstein, "Anticipated Versus Actual Responses to HIV Test Results," *American Journal of Psychology* 112 (1999): 297–311.

81 Assistant professors: D. T. Gilbert, E. C. Pinel, T. D. Wilson, S. J. Blumberg, and T. P. Wheatley, "Immune Neglect: A Source of Durability Bias in Affective Forecasting," *Journal of Personality and Social Psychology* 75 (1998): 617–638.

82 Two things: Gilbert and Wilson, "Miswanting."

82 David A. Schkade and Daniel Kahneman, "Does Living in California Make People Happy? A Focusing Illusion in Judgments of Life Satisfaction," *Psychological Science* 9 (1990): 340–346.

82 Psalmist: Psalm 30:5.

82 Steven J. Sherman, "On the Self-Erasing Nature of Errors of Prediction," *Journal of Personality and Social Psychology* 39 (1980): 211–221.

83 Janet K. Swim and Lauri L. Hyers, "Excuse Me—What Did You Just Say?!: Women's Public and Private Reactions to Sexist Remarks," *Journal of Experimental Social Psychology* 35 (1999): 68–88.

83 Stanley Milgram, *Obedience to Authority* (New York: Harper and Row, 1974).

83 J. Sidney Shrauger, "The Accuracy of Self-Prediction: How Good Are We and Why?" paper presented at the Midwestern Psychological Association convention, Chicago, 1985; J. S. Shrauger, D. Ram, S. A. Greninger, and E. Mariano, "Accuracy of Self-Predictions Versus Judgments by Knowledgeable Others," *Personality and Social Psychology Bulletin* 22 (1996): 1229–1243; T. M. Osberg and J. S. Shrauger, "Self-Prediction: Exploring the Parameters of Accuracy," *Journal of Personality and Social Psychology* 51 (1986): 1044–1057; T. M. Osberg and J. S. Shrauger, "The Role of Self-Prediction in Psychological Assessment," in J. N. Butcher

and C. D. Spielberger (eds.), *Advances in Personality Assessment,* vol. 8 (Hillsdale, N.J.: Erlbaum, 1990).

83 Nicholas Epley and David Dunning, "Feeling 'Holier Than Thou': Are Self-Serving Assessments Produced by Errors in Self- or Other Prediction?" *Journal of Personality and Social Psychology* 79 (2000): 861–875.

84 Lao Tzu: W. Chan, *The Way of Lao Tzu* (Indianapolis: Bobbs-Merrill, 1963).

84 Between the idea: T. S. Eliot, *The Hollow Men* (1925).

84 H. Jackson Brown, Jr., *P.S. I Love You* (Nashville: Rutledge Hill, 1990), p. 79.

84 Optimism, health, and happiness: M. E. P. Seligman, *Learned Optimism* (New York: Pocket Books, 1998); S. E. Taylor and D. A. Armor, "Positive Illusions and Coping with Adversity," *Journal of Personality* 64 (1996): 873–898.

84 Neil D. Weinstein, "Unrealistic Optimism About Future Life Events," *Journal of Personality and Social Psychology* 39 (1980): 806–820; "Unrealistic Optimism About Susceptibility to Health Problems," *Journal of Behavioral Medicine* 5 (1982): 441–460.

84 Smokers: N. D. Weinstein, "Accuracy of Smokers' Risk Perceptions," *Annals of Behavioral Medicine* 20 (1998): 135–140.

84–85 HIV perceptions: D. Abrams, "AIDS: What Young People Believe and What They Do," paper presented at the British Association for the Advancement of Science conference, 1991; J. B. Pryor and G. D. Reeder, *The Social Psychology of HIV Infection* (Hillsdale, N.J.: Erlbaum, 1993).

85 Unwanted pregnancy: J. M. Burger and L. Burns, "The Illusion of Unique Invulnerability and the Use of Effective Contraception," *Personality and Social Psychology Bulletin* 14 (1988): 264–270.

85 San Francisco students: J. M. Burger and M. L. Palmer, "Changes In and Generalization of Unrealistic Optimism Following Experiences with Stressful Events: Reactions to the 1989 California Earthquake," *Personality and Social Psychology Bulletin* 18 (1991): 39–43.

85 Tara K. MacDonald and Michael Ross, "Assessing the Accuracy of Predictions About Dating Relationships: How and Why Do Lovers' Predictions Differ from Those Made by Observers?" *Personality and Social Psychology Bulletin* 25 (1999): 1417–1429.

85 Zero percent: L. A. Baker and R. E. Emery, "When Every Relationship Is Above Average: Perceptions and Expectations of Divorce at the Time of Marriage," *Law and Human Behavior* 17 (1993): 439–450.

85 Julie K. Norem, "Defensive Pessimism, Optimism, and Pessimism," in E.

C. Chang (ed.), *Optimism and Pessimism* (Washington, D.C.: APA Books, 2000).

85 Students' excess optimism: V. Prohaska, "'I Know I'll Get an A': Confident Overestimation of Final Course Grades," *Teaching of Psychology* 21 (1994): 141–143; J. A. Sparrell and J. S. Shrauger, "Self-Confidence and Optimism in Self-Prediction," paper presented at the American Psychological Association convention, 1984.

85 Optimism disappears: K. M. Taylor and J. A. Shepperd, "Bracing for the Worst: Severity, Testing, and Feedback Timing as Moderators of the Optimistic Bias," *Personality and Social Psychology Bulletin* 24 (1998): 915–926.

85 Higher grades: D. E. Goodhart, "The Effects of Positive and Negative Thinking on Performance in an Achievement Situation," *Journal of Personality and Social Psychology* 51 (1986): 117–124; J. K. Norem and N. Cantor, "Defensive Pessimism: Harnessing Anxiety as Motivation," *Journal of Personality and Social Psychology* 51 (1986): 1208–1217; C. Showers and C. Ruben, "Distinguishing Pessimism from Depression: Negative Expectations and Positive Coping Mechanisms," paper presented at the American Psychological Association convention, 1987.

**CHAPTER 5. INTUITIONS ABOUT
OUR COMPETENCE AND VIRTUE**

87 Self-reference effect: E. T. Higgins and J. A. Bargh, "Social Cognition and Social Perception," *Annual Review of Psychology* 38 (1987): 369–425; N. A. Kuiper and T. B. Rogers, "Encoding of Personal Information: Self-Other Differences," *Journal of Personality and Social Psychology* 37 (1979): 499–514; C. S. Symons and B. T. Johnson, "The Self-Reference Effect in Memory: A Meta-Analysis," *Psychological Bulletin* 121 (1997): 371–394.

87 Minor player: A. Fenigstein, "Self-Consciousness and the Overperception of Self as a Target," *Journal of Personality and Social Psychology* 47 (1984): 860–870.

87 Spotlight effect: T. Gilovich, V. H. Medvec, and K. Savitsky, "The Spotlight Effect in Social Judgment: An Egocentric Bias in Estimates of the Salience of One's Own Actions and Appearance," *Journal of Personality and Social Psychology* 78 (2000): 211–222.

88 Illusion of transparency: T. Gilovich, K. Savitsky, and V. H. Medvec, "The Illusion of Transparency: Biased Assessments of Others' Ability to Read One's Emotional States," *Journal of Personality and Social Psychology* 75 (1998): 332–346.

89 Cullen Murphy, "New Findings: Hold on to Your Hat," *Atlantic,* June 1990, pp. 22–23.

89 Paul Slovic and Baruch Fischhoff, "On the Psychology of Experimental Surprises," *Journal of Experimental Psychology: Human Perception and Performance* 3 (1977): 455–551.

90 Birds of a feather: I discuss similarity and attraction in my *Social Psychology,* 7th ed. (New York: McGraw-Hill, 2002).

90 Karl H. Teigen: "Old Truths or Fresh Insights? A Study of Students' Evaluations of Proverbs," *British Journal of Social Psychology* 25 (1986): 43–50.

92 Colleen M. Kelley and Larry L. Jacoby, "Adult Egocentrism: Subjective Experience Versus Analytic Bases for Judgment," *Journal of Memory and Language* 35 (1996): 157–175.

92 Physician hindsight: N. V. Dawson, H. R. Arkes, C. Siciliano, R. Blinkhorn, M. Lakshmanan, and M. Petrelli, "Hindsight Bias: An Impediment to Accurate Probability Estimation in Clinicopathologic Conferences," *Medical Decision Making* 8 (1988): 259–264.

92 Robyn Dawes, "Finding Guidelines for Tough Decisions," *Chronicle of Higher Education,* June 9, 1993.

93 Carl Rogers, "Reinhold Niebuhr's *The Self and the Dramas of History:* A Criticism," *Pastoral Psychology* 9 (1958): 15–17.

93 John Powell, *Happiness Is an Inside Job* (Valencia, Calif.: Tabor, 1989).

94 Groucho Marx, *Groucho and Me* (New York: Dell, 1960).

94 Success and failure experiments: W. K. Campbell and C. Sedikides, "Self-Threat Magnifies the Self-Serving Bias: A Meta-Analytic Integration," *Review of General Psychology* 3 (1999): 23–43.

94 Athletes: J. R. Grove, S. J. Hanrahan, and A. McInman, "Success/Failure Bias in Attributions Across Involvement Categories in Sport," *Personality and Social Psychology Bulletin* 17 (1991): 93–97; R. N. Lalonde, "The Dynamics of Group Differentiation in the Face of Defeat," *Personality and Social Psychology Bulletin* 18 (1992): 336–342; B. Mullen and C. A. Riordan, "Self-Serving Attributions for Performance in Naturalistic Settings: A Meta-Analytic Review," *Journal of Applied Social Psychology* 18 (1988): 3–22.

94 Michael Ross and Fiore Sicoly: "Egocentric Biases in Availability and Attribution," *Journal of Personality and Social Psychology* 37 (1979): 322–336.

94 More than 100 percent: J. Kruger and T. Gilovich, " 'Naive Cynicism' in Everyday Theories of Responsibility Assessment: On Biased Assump-

tions of Bias," *Journal of Personality and Social Psychology* 76 (1999): 743–753.

94 Divorced people: J. D. Gray and R. C. Silver, "Opposite Sides of the Same Coin: Former Spouses' Divergent Perspectives in Coping with Their Divorce," *Journal of Personality and Social Psychology* 59 (1990): 1180–1191.

94 Workers: Y. Imai, "Effects of Influencing Attempts on the Perceptions of Powerholders and the Powerless," *Journal of Social Behavior and Personality* 9 (1994): 455–468; B. Rice, "Performance Review: The Job Nobody Likes," *Psychology Today,* September 1985, pp. 30–36.

95 Pay raises: K. A. Diekmann, S. M. Samuels, L. Ross, and M. H. Bazerman, "Self-Interest and Fairness in Problems of Resource Allocation: Allocators Versus Recipients," *Journal of Personality and Social Psychology* 72 (1997): 1061–1074.

95 Students and bias: R. M. Arkin and G. M. Maruyama, "Attribution, Affect, and College Exam Performance," *Journal of Educational Psychology* 71 (1979): 85–93; M. H. Davis and W. G. Stephan, "Attributions for Exam Performance," *Journal of Applied Social Psychology* 10 (1980): 235–248; T. M. Gilmor and D. W. Reid, "Locus of Control and Causal Attribution for Positive and Negative Outcomes on University Examinations," *Journal of Research in Personality* 13 (1979): 154–160; B. Q. Griffin, A. L. Combs, M. L. Land, and N. N. Combs, "Attribution of Success and Failure in College Performance," *Journal of Psychology* 114 (1983): 259–266.

95 Teachers: R. M. Arkin, H. Cooper, and T. Kolditz, "A Statistical Review of the Literature Concerning the Self-Serving Attribution Bias in Interpersonal Influence Situations," *Journal of Personality* 48 (1980): 435–448; M. H. Davis, "The Case for Attributional Egotism," paper presented at the American Psychological Association convention.

95 Managers and Australians: R. Baumhart, *An Honest Profit* (New York: Holt, Rinehart & Winston, 1968); B. Headey and A. Wearing, "The Sense of Relative Superiority—Central to Well-Being," *Social Indicators Research* 20 (1987): 497–516.

95 Drivers: B. Guerin, "What Do People Think About the Risks of Driving? Implications for Traffic Safety Interventions," *Journal of Applied Social Psychology* 24 (1994): 994–1021; F. P. McKenna and L. B. Myers, "Illusory Self-Assessments—Can They Be Reduced?" *British Journal of Psychology* 88 (1997): 39–51; O. Svenson, "Are We All Less Risky and More Skillful Than Our Fellow Drivers?" *Acta Psychologica* 47 (1981): 143–148.

95 Dave Barry, *Dave Barry Turns 50* (New York: Crown, 1998).

95 Intelligence, looks, prejudice: "Vanity Fare," *Public Opinion,* August–

September 1984, p. 22; R. C. Wylie, *The Self-Concept,* vol. 2: *Theory and Research on Selected Topics* (Lincoln: University of Nebraska Press, 1979).

95 Ethics: S. N. Brenner and E. A. Molander, "Is the Ethics of Business Changing?" *Harvard Business Review,* January–February 1977, pp. 57–71; P. A. M. Van Lange, T. W. Taris, and R. Vonk, "Dilemmas of Academic Practice: Perceptions of Superiority Among Social Psychologists," *European Journal of Social Psychology* 27 (1997): 675–685.

95 Los Angeles residents: L. Larwood, "Swine Flu: A Field Study of Self-Serving Biases," *Journal of Applied Social Psychology* 18 (1978): 283–289; C. R. Snyder, "The 'Illusion' of Uniqueness," *Journal of Humanistic Psychology* 18 (1978): 33–41.

95 Baby boomers: Cited by K. C. Cole, *The Universe and the Teacup: The Mathematics of Truth and Beauty* (New York: Harcourt Brace, 1999), p. 35.

96 Old for their age: "Vanity Fare," p. 22.

96 *U.S. News:* "Oprah: A Heavenly Body? Survey Finds Talk-Show Host a Celestial Shoo-in," March 31, 1997, p. 18.

96 "Moral goodness": S. T. Allison, D. M. Messick, and G. R. Goethals, "On Better But Not Smarter Than Others: The Muhammad Ali Effect," *Social Cognition* 7 (1989): 275–296; P. A. M. Van Lange, "Being Better But Not Smarter Than Others: The Muhammad Ali Effect at Work in Interpersonal Situations," *Personality and Social Psychology Bulletin* 17 (1997): 689–693.

96 Caring versus doing: J. A. White and S. Plous, "Self-Enhancement and Social Responsibility: On Caring More, But Doing Less, Than Others," *Journal of Applied Social Psychology* 25 (1995): 1297–1318.

97 Perceived stereotypes: J. Kruger, "Personal Beliefs and Cultural Stereotypes About Racial Characteristics," *Journal of Personality and Social Psychology* 71 (1996): 536–548.

97 Liars: B. J. Sagarin, K. v. L. Rhoads, and R. B. Cialdini, "Deceiver's Distrust: Denigration as a Consequence of Undiscovered Deception," *Personality and Social Psychology Bulletin* 24 (1998): 1167–1176.

97 Bob Guccione: Quoted by P. Elmer-DeWitt, "Cyberporn," *Time,* July 3, 1995, pp. 38–45.

97 Cell phones: Richard H. Thaler reports that his colleague George Wu asked this question. "From Homo Economicus to Homo Sapiens," *Journal of Economic Perspectives* 14 (2000): 133–141.

97 Why false consensus occurs: R. M. Dawes, "The Potential Nonfalsity of the False Consensus Effect," in R. M. Hogarth (ed.), *Insights in Decision*

Making: A Tribute to Hillel J. Einhorn (Chicago: University of Chicago Press, 1990); J. Krueger and R. W. Clement, "Estimates of Social Consensus by Majorities and Minorities: The Case for Social Projection," *Personality and Social Psychology Review* 1 (1997): 299–313.

97 Pamela Anderson Lee quoted by B. Talbert, "Bob Talbert's Quote Bag," *Detroit Free Press*, p. 5E, citing *Allure* magazine, February 2, 1997.

97 False uniqueness: J. Suls, C. K. Wan, and G. S. Sanders, "False Consensus and False Uniqueness in Estimating the Prevalence of Health-Protective Behaviors," *Journal of Applied Social Psychology* 18 (1988): 66–79.

98 La Rochefoucauld, *Maxims* (1665).

98 Dacher Keltner and Robert J. Robinson, "Extremism, Power, and the Imagined Basis of Social Conflict," *Current Directions in Psychological Science* 5 (1996): 101–105.

98 Confidence in the future: M. Ross and I. R. Newby-Clark, "Construing the Past and Future," *Social Cognition* 16 (1998): 133–150.

98 More confident than correct: B. Fischhoff, P. Slovic, and S. Lichtenstein, "Knowing with Certainty: The Appropriateness of Extreme Confidence," *Journal of Experimental Psychology: Human Perception and Performance* 3 (1977): 552–564; L. A. Brenner, D. J. Koehler, V. Liberman, and A. Tversky, "Overconfidence in Probability and Frequency Judgments: A Critical Examination," *Organizational Behavior and Human Decision Processes* 65 (1996): 212–219.

98 Nuclear power plants: International Atomic Energy Agency (http://www.iaea.or.at/cgi-bin/db.page.pl/pris.oprconst.htm).

99 Warnings and admonitions: M. Alpert and H. Raiffa, "A Progress Report on the Training of Probability Assessors," in D. Kahneman, P. Slovic, and A. Tversky (eds.), *Judgment Under Uncertainty: Heuristics and Biases* (Cambridge: Cambridge University Press, 1982); S. Plous, "A Comparison of Strategies for Reducing Interval Overconfidence in Group Judgments," *Journal of Applied Psychology* 80 (1995): 443–454.

99 David Dunning with D. W. Griffin, J. D. Milojkovic, and L. Ross, "The Overconfidence Effect in Social Prediction," *Journal of Personality and Social Psychology* 58 (1990): 568–581.

99 Confidence in lie detection: B. M. DePaulo, K. Charlton, H. Cooper, J. J. Lindsay, and L. Muhlenbruck, "The Accuracy-Confidence Correlation in the Detection of Deception," *Personality and Social Psychology Review* 1 (1997): 346–357. See also M. L. Patterson, J. L. Foster, and C. D. Bellmer, "Another Look at Accuracy and Confidence in Social Judgments," *Journal of Nonverbal Behavior* 25 (2001): 207–219. They confirm that con-

fident people aren't more accurate in making social judgments, but that any individual tends to be more accurate when confident.

99 Robert Vallone with D. W. Griffin, S. Lin, and L. Ross, "Overconfident Prediction of Future Actions and Outcomes by Self and Others," *Journal of Personality and Social Psychology* 58 (1990): 582–592.

100 Overconfidence in self-change: Janet Polivy and C. Peter Herman, "The False-Hope Syndrome: Unfulfilled Expectations of Self-Change," *Current Directions in Psychological Science* 9 (2000): 128–131.

100 Roger Buehler with D. Griffin and M. Ross, "Exploring the 'Planning Fallacy': When People Underestimate Their Task Completion Times," *Journal of Personality and Social Psychology* 67 (1994): 366–381; R. Buehler, D. Griffin, and H. MacDonald, "The Role of Motivated Reasoning in Optimistic Time Predictions," *Personality and Social Psychology Bulletin* 23 (1997): 238–247; I. R. Newby-Clark, M. Ross, R. Buehler, D. J. Koehler, and D. Griffin, "People Focus on Optimistic Scenarios and Disregard Pessimistic Scenarios While Predicting Task Completion Times," *Journal of Experimental Psychology : Applied* 6 (2000): 171–182.

100 Hasegawa Nyozekan, *The Lost Japan* (1952).

102 Phillip E. Tetlock, "Close-Call Counterfactuals and Belief-System Defenses: I Was Not Almost Wrong But I Was Almost Right," *Journal of Personality and Social Psychology* 75 (1998): 639–652; "Theory-Driven Reasoning About Plausible Pasts and Probable Futures in World Politics: Are We Prisoners of Our Preconceptions?" *American Journal of Political Science* 43 (1999): 335–366.

102 Janet Metcalfe, "Cognitive Optimism: Self-Deception of Memory-Based Processing Heuristics?" *Personality and Social Psychology Review* 2 (1998): 100–110.

103 Live happily and make decisions: R. F. Baumeister, "The Optimal Margin of Illusion," *Journal of Social and Clinical Psychology* 8 (1989): 176–189; S. E. Taylor, *Positive Illusions* (New York: Basic Books, 1989).

103 William Hazlitt, "On Pedantry," *The Round Table* (1817).

103 Confucius, *Analects*.

CHAPTER 6. INTUITIONS ABOUT REALITY

106–107 Michael McCloskey, "Naive Theories of Motion," in D. Gentner and A. L. Stevens (eds.), *Mental Model* (Hillsdale, N.J.: Erlbaum, 1983).

108 Water-level task: H. Hecht and D. R. Proffitt, "The Price of Expertise: Effects of Experience on the Water-Level Task," *Psychological Science* 6 (1995): 90–95.

108 Physicians' misunderstandings: D. M. Eddy, "Variations in Physician

Practice: The Role of Uncertainty," in J. Dowie and A. S. Elstein (eds.), *Professional Judgment: A Reader in Clinical Decision Making* (New York: Cambridge University Press, 1988).

109 Coin tossing: For more on this, see Raymond S. Nickerson, "Ambiguities and Unstated Assumptions in Probabilistic Reasoning," *Psychological Bulletin* 120 (1996): 410–433.

109 The Monty Hall Dilemma: M. vos Savant, *The Power of Logical Thinking* (New York: St. Martin's, 1996); D. Granberg and T. Brown, "The Monty Hall Dilemma," *Personality and Social Psychology Bulletin* 21 (1995): 711–723.

109 Infants' head for numbers: K. Wynn, "Addition and Subtraction by Human Infants," *Nature* 358 (1992): 749–759, and "Psychological Foundations of Number: Numerical Competence in Human Infants," *Trends in Cognitive Science* 2 (1998): 296–303.

110 K. C. Cole, *The Universe and the Teacup: The Mathematics of Truth and Beauty* (New York: Harcourt Brace, 1999).

110 Robert Ornstein, *The Evolution of Consciousness* (New York: Prentice-Hall, 1991), *Time,* November 7, 1994, p. 6.

110 David A. Napolitan and George R. Goethals, "The Attribution of Friendliness," *Journal of Experimental Social Psychology* 15 (1979): 105–113.

111 Debaters: E. E. Jones and V. A. Harris, "The Attribution of Attitudes," *Journal of Experimental Social Psychology* 3 (1967): 2–24.

112 Quiz-game experiments: L. Ross, T. M. Amabile, and J. L. Steinmetz, "Social Roles, Social Control, and Biases in Social-Perception Processes," *Journal of Personality and Social Psychology* 35 (1977): 485–494.

112 Bush and Putin: R. Cohen, "Bush's Take on Putin a Bit Quick for Me," *Grand Rapids Press,* June 21, 2001, p. A14 (from the *Washington Post* Writers' Group); L. McQuillan, "Senator Criticizes Bush on Russia," *USA Today,* June, 20, 2001 (via usatoday.com); C. Matthews, "Look to Putin's Interests, Not His Eyes," *Grand Rapids Press,* June 25, 2001, p. A9 (from Newspaper Enterprise Association).

112 Verbs: K. Fiedler, G. R. Semin, and C. Koppetsch, "Language Use and Attributional Biases in Close Personal Relationships," *Personality and Social Psychology Bulletin* 17 (1991): 147–155; W. J. McGuire and C. V. McGuire, "Differences in Conceptualizing Self Versus Conceptualizing Other People as Manifested in Contrasting Verb Types Used in Natural Speech," *Journal of Personality and Social Psychology* 51 (1986): 1135–1143; P. A. White and D. P. Younger, "Differences in the Description of Transient Internal States to Self and Other," *Journal of Experimental Social Psychology* 24 (1988): 292–309.

113 Reversed perspectives: G. D. Lassiter and A. A. Irvine, "Videotaped Confessions: The Impact of Camera Point of View on Judgments of Coercion," *Journal of Applied Social Psychology* 16 (1986): 268–276; M. D. Storms, "Videotape and the Attribution Process: Reversing Actors' and Observers' Points of View," *Journal of Personality and Social Psychology* 27 (1973): 165–175.

113 Perspective changes with time: J. M. Burger, "Changes in Attributions Over Time: The Ephemeral Fundamental Attribution Error," *Social Cognition* 9 (1991): 182–193; J. M. Burger and J. L. Pavelich, "Attributions for Presidential Elections: The Situational Shift over Time," *Basic and Applied Social Psychology* 15 (1994): 359–371.

113 William C. Ward and Herbert M. Jenkins: "The Display of Information and the Judgment of Contingency," *Canadian Journal of Psychology* 19 (1965): 231–241.

113 Moon, adoptions, and fertility: These examples come from a wonderful book by T. Gilovich, *How We Know What Isn't So: The Fallibility of Human Reason in Everyday Life* (New York: Free Press, 1991).

115 Rupert Brown and Amanda Smith, "Perceptions of and by Minority Groups: The Case of Women in Academia," *European Journal of Social Psychology* 19 (1989): 61–75.

115 David L. Hamilton and Robert K. Gifford, "Illusory Correlation in Interpersonal Perception: A Cognitive Basis of Stereotypic Judgments," *Journal of Experimental Social Psychology* 12 (1976): 392–407.

115 Researchers debate: D. L. Hamilton and S. J. Sherman, "Stereotypes," in R. S. Wyer, Jr., and T. K. Srull (eds.), *Handbook of Social Cognition,* 2nd ed. (Hillsdale, N.J.: Erlbaum, 1994).

115–116 Capital punishment study: C. G. Lord, L. Ross, and M. Lepper, "Biased Assimilation and Attitude Polarization: The Effects of Prior Theories on Subsequently Considered Evidence," *Journal of Personality and Social Psychology* 37 (1979): 2098–2109.

116 10 to 1: Data from 1960, 1976, and 1980 presidential debated reported by D. R. Kinder and D. O. Sears, "Public Opinion and Political Action," in G. Lindzey and E. Aronson (eds.), *The Handbook of Social Psychology,* 3rd ed. (New York: Random House, 1985).

116 Predebate preference: G. D. Munro, P. H. Ditto, L. K. Lockhart, A. Fagerlin, M. Gready, and E. Peterson, "Biased Assimilation of Sociopolitical Arguments: Evaluating the 1996 U.S. Presidential Debate," *Basic and Applied Social Psychology,* in press.

116 Mark Snyder, Elizabeth D. Tanke, and Ellen Berscheid, "Social Perception and Interpersonal Behavior: On the Self-Fulfilling Nature of Social

Stereotypes," *Journal of Personality and Social Psychology* 35 (1977): 656–666.

116 Other experiments: For example, R. D. Ridge and J. S. Reber, "I Think She's Attracted to Me: The Effect of Men's Beliefs on Women's Behavior in a Job Interview Scenario," *Basic and Applied Social Psychology*, in press.

116 Peter Wason, "On the Failure to Eliminate Hypotheses in a Conceptual Task," *Quarterly Journal of Experimental Psychology* 12 (1960): 129–140.

117 Wason four-card problem: P. C. Wason, "Reasoning About a Rule," *Quarterly Journal of Experimental Psychology* 20 (1968): 273–281; P. C. Wason and P. N. Johnson-Laird, *The Psychology of Reasoning: Structure and Content* (Cambridge, Mass.: Harvard University Press, 1975); P. N. Johnson-Laird and P. C. Wason, "A Theoretical Analysis of Insight into a Reasoning Task," *Cognitive Psychology* 1 (1970): 134–138.

117 Reasoning and probabilities: N. Charter and M. Oaksford, "Human Rationality and the Psychology of Reasoning: Where Do We Go from Here?" *British Journal of Psychology* 92 (2001): 193–216.

118 Firefighters: C. A. Anderson, M. R. Lepper, and L. Ross, "Perseverance of Social Theories: The Role of Explanation in the Persistence of Discredited Information," *Journal of Personality and Social Psychology* 39 (1980): 1037–1049.

118 Sigmund Freud, *Civilization and Its Discontents* (New York: Cape & Smith, 1930).

119 Irving L. Janis, "Problems of International Crisis Management in the Nuclear Age," *Journal of Social Issues* 42(2) (1986): 201–220 (italics in original).

119 Robert Ornstein, *The Evolution of Consciousness* (New York: Prentice-Hall, 1991).

119 Gerd Gigerenzer, Peter M. Todd, and the ABC Research Group, *Simple Heuristics That Make Us Smart* (Oxford: Oxford University Press, 2119).

119 Heuristics-like perceptions: T. Gilovich, D. W. Griffin, and D. Kahneman, *The Psychology of Intuitive Judgment: Heuristics and Biases* (New York: Cambridge University Press, 2002).

120 Classics professor/truck driver: Adapted from R. E. Nisbett and L. Ross, *Human Inference: Strategies and Shortcomings of Social Judgment* (Englewood Cliffs, N.J.: Prentice-Hall, 1980).

121 Ruth Beyth-Maron and Shlomit Dekel, "A Curriculum to Improve Thinking Under Uncertainty," *Instructional Science* 12 (1983): 67–82.

122 Baruch Fischhoff and Maya Bar-Hillel, "Diagnosticity and the Base Rate Effect," *Memory and Cognition* 12 (1984): 402–410.

122 Amos Tversky and Daniel Kahneman, "Extensional Versus Intuitive Reasoning: The Conjunction Fallacy in Probability Judgment," *Psychological Review* 90 (1983): 293–315.

122 Seymour Epstein: with S. Donovan and V. Denes-Raj, "The Missing Link in the Paradox of the Linda Conjunction Problem: Beyond Knowing and Thinking of the Conjunction Rule, the Intrinsic Appeal of Heuristic Processing," *Personality and Social Psychology Bulletin* 24 (1999): 204–214.

123 Stuart J. McKelvie, "Bias in the Estimated Frequency of Names," *Perceptual and Motor Skills* 81 (1995): 1331–1338; "The Availability Heuristic: Effects of Fame and Gender on the Estimated Frequency of Male and Female Names," *Journal of Social Psychology* 137 (1997): 63–78; A. Tversky and D. Kahneman, "Availability: A Heuristic for Judging Frequency and Probability," *Cognitive Psychology* 5 (1973): 207–302.

123 Easy-to-imagine events: C. MacLeod and L. Campbell, "Memory Accessibility and Probability Judgments: An Experimental Evaluation of the Availability Heuristic," *Journal of Personality and Social Psychology* 63 (1992): 890–902; S. J. Sherman, R. B. Cialdini, D. F. Schwartzman, and D. K. Reynolds, "Imagining Can Heighten or Lower the Perceived Likelihood of Contracting a Disease: The Mediating Effect of Ease of Imagery," *Personality and Social Psychology Bulletin* 11 (1985): 118–127.

123 Ruth Hamill with T. D. Wilson and R. E. Nisbett, "Insensitivity to Sample Bias: Generalizing from Atypical Cases," *Journal of Personality and Social Psychology* 39 (1980): 578–589.

124 Fictional happenings: R. J. Gerrig and D. A. Prentice, "The Representation of Fictional Information," *Psychological Science* 2 (1991): 336–340; K. Oatley, "Why Fiction May Be Twice as True as Fact: Fiction as Cognitive and Emotional Simulation," *Review of General Psychology* 3 (1999): 101–117.

124 Canadians: A. N. Doob and J. Roberts, "Public Attitudes Toward Sentencing in Canada," in N. Walker and M. Hough (eds.), *Sentencing and the Public* (London: Gower, 1988).

124 Charlene Barshefsky, quoted by D. Broder, "Clinton Didn't Make the Case for Trade Bill," *Grand Rapids (Mich.) Press,* November 17, 1997 (*Washington Post* Writers Group).

125 100,000 child deaths: A. Gore, Jr., *Earth in the Balance: Ecology and the Human Spirit* (Boston: Houghton Mifflin, 1992).

125 Percentage who die or survive: T. M. Marteau, "Framing of Information: Its Influences upon Decisions of Doctors and Patients," *British Journal of Social Psychology* 28 (1989): 89–94; A. J. Rothman and P. Salovey,

"Shaping Perceptions to Motivate Healthy Behavior: The Role of Message Framing," *Psychological Bulletin* 121 (1997): 3–19.

125 Doctors: B. J. McNeil, S. G. Pauker, and A. Tversky, "On the Framing of Medical Decisions," in D. E. Bell, H. Raiffa, and A. Tversky, *Decision Making: Descriptive, Normative, and Prescriptive Interactions* (Cambridge, England: Cambridge University Press, 1988).

126 "Poor" vs. "welfare": Vox pop (poll by Yankelovich Partners, Inc.), p. 21.

126 "Foreign aid": P. Simon, "American Provincials," *Christian Century,* April 17, 1996, pp. 421–422.

126 "Forbid"/"not allow": J. A. Krosnick and H. Schuman, "Attitude Intensity, Importance, and Certainty and Susceptibility to Response Effects," *Journal of Personality and Social Psychology* 54 (1988): 940–952; H. Schuman and G. Kalton, "Survey Methods," in G. Lindzey and E. Aronson (eds.), *Handbook of Social Psychology,* vol. 1 (Hillsdale, N.J.: Erlbaum, 1985).

126 Lean/fat: I. P. Levin and G. J. Gaeth, "How Consumers Are Affected by the Framing of Attribute Information Before and After Consuming the Product," *Journal of Consumer Research* 15 (1988): 374–378.

126 "1 in 20": V. Denes-Raj, S. Epstein, and J. Cole, "The Generality of the Ratio-Bias Phenomenon," *Personality and Social Psychology Bulletin* 21 (1995): 1083–1092.

126 Success/failure rate: P. W. Linville, G. W. Fischer, and B. Fischhoff, "AIDS Risk Perceptions and Decision Biases," in J. B. Pryor and G. D. Reeder (eds.), *The Social Psychology of HIV Infection* (Hillsdale, N.J.: Erlbaum, 1992).

126 Regular/sale prices: J. E. Urbany, W. O. Bearden, and D. C. Weilbaker, "The Effect of Plausible and Exaggerated Reference Prices on Consumer Perceptions and Price Search," *Journal of Consumer Research* 15 (1988): 95–110.

126 Inflation and pay: D. Kahneman, J. L. Knetsch, and R. Thaler, "Fairness as a Constraint on Profit Seeking: Entitlements in the Market," *American Economic Review* 76 (1986): 728–741.

126 Monk: C. Crossen, *Tainted Truth: The Manipulation of Fact in America* (New York: Simon & Schuster, 1993).

129 Madeline L'Engle, *A Wind in the Door* (New York: Crosswicks, 1973).

CHAPTER 7. SPORTS INTUITION

133 Todd Obuchowski's hole-in-one: Reported by Chuck Shepherd, "News of the Weird," *Funny Times,* October 1998, p. 21.

133 David Howard and Melissa Geschwind, "South Dakota Man Has Lots of

Luck," *USA Today,* July 17, 2000 (reported in *Chance News,* August 10, 2000).

133 Scott Hatteberg: Associated Press, "Hat Trick: Triple Play to Grand Slam," *Seattle Times,* August 7, 2001, p. C4.

134 Thomas Gilovich, *How We Know What Isn't So: The Fallibility of Human Reason in Everyday Life* (New York: Free Press, 1991), p. 10.

134 Daniel Kahneman and Amos Tversky, "Subjective Probability: A Judgment of Representativeness," *Cognitive Psychology* 3 (1972): 430–454.

135 Bible code: "Bible Code Bunkum," *Science* 285 (1999): 2057.

135 Bulls in Tolstoy: D. E. Thomas, "Tolstoy Predicts Bulls' Sixth Championship (in Code of Course)," *Skeptical Inquirer,* November–December 1998, pp. 16–17.

136 Ruma Falk and Clifford Konold, "Making Sense of Randomness: Implicit Encoding as a Basis of Judgment," *Psychological Bulletin* 104 (1997): 301–318; R. Falk, "The Perception of Randomness," in *Proceedings of the Fifth International Conference for the Psychology of Mathematics Education* (Grenoble, France: Laboratoire I.M.A.G., 1981), pp. 222–229.

136 London bomb dispersion: R. D. Clarke, "An Application of the Poisson Distribution," *Journal of the Institute of Actuaries (London)* 72 (1946): 72, reported in W. Feller, *An Introduction to Probability Theory and Its Applications* (New York: Wiley, 1968), and more recently by Gilovich, *How We Know What Isn't So.*

136 Cancer cluster: Atul Gawande, "The Cancer-Cluster Myth," *New Yorker,* February 8, 1999, pp. 34–37.

137 Tubby Smith: Associated Press, "Utes, Wildcats Head to Title Game," *Holland Sentinel,* March 29, 1998, pp. B1–2.

137 Sylvia Hatchell: Associated Press, "North Carolina Women Have the Touch," *Valley News,* December 21, 1998, p. B8.

137 "Wanna get him the ball": C. Sprow, "Holland Runs and Guns to Win," *Holland Sentinel,* March 13, 1998, p. B1.

138 0-for-10: G. Brower, "Frustrated Dutchmen Left to Ponder Loss," *Holland Sentinel,* February 15, 2001, p. B1.

138 Thomas Gilovich, Robert Vallone, and Amos Tversky, "The Hot Hand in Basketball: On the Misperception of Random Sequences," *Cognitive Psychology* 17 (1985): 295–314.

138 76ers: Gilovich, *How We Know What Isn't So,* p. 12.

138 Alan Reifman, "Hot Hand Research," February 13, 1998, and "Results from NBA 3-Point Shot Contest—Hot Hand Still Rare," February 19, 2000, Society of Personality and Social Psychology listserv.

139 Dansville, N.Y.: B. Carlson, "A Run on Baby Girls at Noyes," *Livingston County News,* August 21, 1997, p. 1 (reported in *Chance News,* 6.10).
Joseph Lee Rodgers and Debby Doughty, "Does Having Boys or Girls Run in the Family?" *Chance,* Fall 2001, pp. 8–13.

140 Pi: C. Seife, "Randomly Distributed Slides of Pi," *Science* 293 (2001): 793.

140 Bruce Martin, "Coincidences: Remarkable or Random?" *Skeptical Inquirer,* September–October 1998, pp. 23–28.

141 Vinnie Johnson: A. Tversky and T. Gilovich, "The Cold Facts About the 'Hot Hand' in Basketball," *Chance: New Directions for Statistics and Computing* 2(1) (1989); "The 'Hot Hand': Statistical Reality or Cognitive Illusion," *Chance: New Directions for Statistics and Computing* 2(4) (1989): 31–34.

141 Red Auerbach quoted in T. Gilovich, *How We Know What Isn't So: The Fallibility of Human Reason in Everyday Life* (New York: Free Press, 1991), p. 17.

141 Billy Packer: January 10, 1995, letter to Mark Cook.

142 Gordon Wood: "Predicting Outcomes: Sports and Stocks," *Journal of Gambling Studies* 8 (1992): 201–222.

142 Santo on Sammy Sosa: WGN radio, May 19, 2001.

143 Santo on Todd Helton: WGN radio, August 29, 1998.

143 Santo on Blauser: WGN radio, May 30, 1998.

143 Batters do bat higher: J. Albert, "Exploring Baseball Hitting Data: What About Those Breakdown Statistics?" *Journal of the American Statistical Association* 89 (1994): 1066–1074.

143 Runner on first: H. Stern, "Statistics in Sports," Chance Lecture, Dartmouth College, December 13, 1997 (*Chance News* 8.01).

143 S. Christian Albright, "A Statistical Analysis of Hitting Streaks in Baseball," *Journal of the American Statistical Association* 88 (1993): 1175–1196.

144 Scott M. Berry, "Does 'the Zone' Exist for Home-Run Hitters?" *Chance* 12(1) (1999): 51–56.

144 Hal S. Stern, "A Statistician Reads the Sports Pages," *Chance* 10(2) (1997): 40–43.

146 Dale Miller and Saku Gunasegaram, "Temporal Order and the Perceived Mutability of Events: Implications for Blame Assignment," *Journal of Personality and Social Psychology* 59 (1990): 1111–1118.

146 Thomas Gilovich, personal communication, August 1, 2001.

146 Temporal contiguity, H. J. Einhorn and R. M. Hogarth, "Judging Probable Cause," *Psychological Bulletin* 99 (1986): 3–19.

146 *Sports Illustrated:* Alexander Wolff, "That Old Black Magic: The SI Jinx?" *Sports Illustrated,* January 21, 2001, pp. 50–61.

147 Rookies: Daniel Reisberg, "Advances in Cognitive Psychology," National Institute on the Teaching of Psychology meeting, St. Petersburg, Fla., 1996.

147 Cy Young Award winners: J. L. Spencer, "Superstition and the Regression Effect," *Skeptical Inquirer,* July–August 1999, p. 73.

147 Home runs: *Chance News,* 7.07, August 1998.

148 Paul E. Shaffner, "Specious Learning About Reward and Punishment," *Journal of Personality and Social Psychology* 48 (1985): 1377–1386.

148 Jeff Weaver: "Weaver Plays Sparkplug," AP report in *Holland (Mich.) Sentinel,* July 5, 2001, p. B1.

149 Coaching change: J. Kruger, K. Savitsky, and T. Gilovich, "Superstition and the Regression Effect," *Skeptical Inquirer,* March–April 1999, pp. 24–29.

149 Baseball: M. K. McBeath, D. M. Shaffer, and M. K. Kaiser, "How Baseball Outfielders Determine Where to Run to Catch Fly Balls," *Science* 268 (1995): 569–572.

150 Carl Sagan, "Basketball's Lessons for Science: There Is Theory Behind Those Magical Stars and Streaks," *New York Times,* November 7, 1993.

150 Gretzky: Malcolm Gladwell, "The Physical Genius: What Do Wayne Gretzky, Yo-Yo Ma, and a Brain Surgeon Have in Common?" *New Yorker,* August 2, 1999 (from www.gladwell.com).
Too much attention: Sian L. Beilock and Thomas H. Carr, "On the Fragility of Skilled Performance: What Governs Choking Under Pressure?" *Journal of Experimental Psychology: General* (2001).

150 Tiger Woods, *18 Holes with Tiger* (Dallas: Beckett, 1998).

CHAPTER 8. INVESTMENT INTUITION

152 Thaler on savings: R. Lowenstein, "Exuberance Is Rational," *New York Times Magazine,* February 17, 2001.

153 Cabdrivers: C. Camerer, L. Babcock, G. Loewenstein, and R. Thaler, "Labor Supply of New York City Cabdrivers: One Day at a Time," *Quarterly Journal of Economics* 112 (1997): 407–441.

153 Robert Shiller quoted by J. Cassidy, "All Together Now," *New Yorker,* March 27, 2000, pp. 122–126.

154 Terrance Odean, "Are Investors Reluctant to Realize Their Losses?" *Journal of Finance* 53 (1998): 1775–1798.

154 Daniel Kahneman and Amos Tversky, "Prospect Theory: An Analysis of Decision Under Risk," *Econometrica* 47 (1979): 263–291; D. Kahneman,

J. L. Knetsch, and R. H. Thaler, "Anomalies: The Endowment Effect, Loss Aversion, and Status Quo Bias," *Journal of Economic Perspectives* 5 (1991): 193–206; A. Tversky and D. Kahneman, "Loss Aversion and Riskless Choice: A Reference Dependent Model," *Quarterly Journal of Economics* 106 (1991): 1039–1061.

155 Two-point versus three-point shots: Richard Thaler's observations of coaches is reported by Lowenstein, "Exuberance Is Rational."

155 Richard H. Thaler, "Toward a Positive Theory of Consumer Choice," *Journal of Economic Behavior and Organization* 1 (1980): 39–60.

155 $2 versus lottery ticket: J. L. Knetsch and J. A. Sinden, "Willingness to Pay and Compensation Demanded: Experimental Evidence of an Unexpected Disparity in Measures of Value," *Quarterly Journal of Economics* 99 (1984): 507–521.

155 Cornell mugs: D. Kahneman, J. L. Knetsch, and R. Thaler, "Experimental Tests of the Endowment Effect and the Coase Theorem," *Journal of Political Economy* 98 (1990): 1325–1348; L. Van Boven, D. Dunning, and G. Loewenstein, "Egocentric Empathy Gaps Between Owners and Buyers: Misperceptions of the Endowment Effect," *Journal of Personality and Social Psychology* 79 (2000): 66–76.

155 Experiments on sunk cost: H. R. Arkes and P. Ayton, "The Sunk Cost and Concorde Effects: Are Humans Less Rational Than Lower Animals?" *Psychological Bulletin* 125 (1999): 591–600; C. M. Smith, R. S. Tindale, and L. Steiner, "Investment Decisions by Individuals and Groups in 'Sunk Cost' Situations: The Potential of Shared Representations," *Group Processes and Intergroup Relations* 1 (1998): 175–189.

156 Amos Tversky quoted in K. McKean, "Decisions, Decisions," *Discover,* June 1985, pp. 22–31.

156 Amos Tversky and Daniel Kahneman, "The Framing of Decisions and the Psychology of Choice," *Science* 211 (1981): 453–458. (Note: In the original experiment the play ticket was $10.)

156 Hal Arkes and Catherine Blumer, "The Psychology of Sunk Cost," *Organizational Behavior and Human Decision Processes* 35 (1985): 124–140.

156 Ford and Edsel: G. Whyte, "Decision Failures: Why They Occur and How to Prevent Them," *Academy of Management Executive* 5 (1991): 23–31.

157 Robert McNamara quoted by M. Howard, *The Causes of War* (Cambridge, Mass.: Harvard University Press, 1984), and cited by R. M. Dawes, *Rational Choice in an Uncertain World* (New York: Harcourt Brace, 1988).

157 Senator Jeremiah Denton quoted in Dawes, *Rational Choice in an Uncertain World.*

157 Gary Belsky and Thomas Gilovich, *Why Smart People Make Big Money Mistakes* (New York: Simon and Schuster, 1999).

157 Amos Tversky and Daniel Kahneman, "Judgment Under Uncertainty: Heuristics and Biases," *Science* 185 (1974): 1124–1130.

158 Gregory Northcraft and Margaret Neale, "Experts, Amateurs, and Real Estate: An Anchoring-and-Adjustment Perspective on Property Pricing Decisions," *Organizational Behavior and Human Decision Processes* 39 (1987): 84–97.

159 New business plans: A. Cooper, C. Woo, and W. Dunkelberg, "Entrepreneurs' Perceived Chances for Success," *Journal of Business Venturing* 3 (1988): 97–108.

159 Production estimates: J. B. Madsen, "Tests of Rationality versus an 'Over Optimist' Bias," *Journal of Economic Psychology* 15 (1994): 587–599.

159 S&P 500 predictions: T. Casby, *The Ten Biggest Investment Mistakes Canadians Make and How to Avoid Them* (Toronto: Stoddart, 2000).

159 Sell recommendations: G. Morgenson, "How Did So Many Get It So Wrong?" *New York Times,* December 31, 2000.

159 David Swensen, *Pioneering Portfolio Management* (New York: Free Press, 2000), p. 6.

159 Brad M. Barber and Terrance Odean, "Trading Is Hazardous to Your Wealth: The Common Stock Investment Performance of Individual Investors," *Journal of Finance* 55 (2000): 773–806.

159 Follow-up study: B. M. Barber and T. Odean, "Boys Will Be Boys: Gender, Overconfidence, and Common Stock Investment," *Quarterly Journal of Economics* 116 (2001): 261–292.

160 "Irrational exuberance": Greenspan's characterization of the market formed the title of Robert Shiller's *Irrational Exuberance* (Princeton, N.J.: Princeton University Press, 2000).

160 Burton G. Malkiel, "Nasdaq: What Goes Up . . . ," *Wall Street Journal,* April 14, 2000.

160 *New York Times:* A. Berenson and P. McGeehan, "Amid the Stock Market's Losses, a Sense the Game Has Changed," April 16, 2000.

161 Burton G. Malkiel, "Don't Sell Out," *Wall Street Journal,* September 26, 2001, p. A20.

161 Efficient market synopsis and joke: R. M. Stulz, "An Emotional High for Stocks?" *Science* 288 (2000): 2353.

162 Robert Frank, "Safety in Numbers," *New York Times Magazine,* November 28, 1999.

162 Five minutes: S. L. Aggarwal, "Stock Market Valuation: Fundamentals,

Randomness and Corrections," Chance Lectures at Dartmouth, December 13, 1997.

162 Burton G. Malkiel: *A Random Walk Down Wall Street* (4th ed.) (New York: Norton, 1989).

162 "Is the Stock Market Efficient?" *Science* 243 (1989): 1313–1318; "Returns from Investing in Equity Mutual Funds 1971 to 1991," *Journal of Finance,* June 1995, pp. 549–572.

162 Canadian funds: R. Chalmers, "Sizing Sizzle of Mutuals," *Edmonton Journal,* September 19, 1995, p. E1.

163 162 money managers: Data from Russell's growth, market-oriented, and value universes as reported by Todd E. Petzel, "Is It Luck or Is It Skill?" *Commonfund News,* December 1, 2001 (www.commonfund.org/cfnews /commentaries/petzel—2001–12.asp).

163 86 percent lagged: Jonathan Clements, "The Truth Investors Don't Want to Hear on Index Funds and Market Soothsayers," *Wall Street Journal,* May 12, 1998, p. C1.

163 200,000 professionals: Securities Industry Association report of 500,000 people licensed by the National Association of Securities Dealers, of whom 200,000 make their living at trading, as reported by W. A. Sherden, *The Fortune Sellers* (New York: Wiley, 1998).

163 Matthew Rabin, "Inference by Believers in the Law of Small Numbers," unpublished manuscript, January 27, 2000 (emlab.berkeley.edu/users/rabin/index.html).

164 John Allen Paulos, *Beyond Numeracy: The Ruminations of a Numbers Man* (New York: Knopf, 1991).

165 Malkiel on *Wall Street Journal* picks: G. Jasen, "Investment Dartboard: A Brief History of Our Contest," *Wall Street Journal,* October 7, 1998, p. C1.

165 Stock prices unpredictable: Malkiel, "What Goes Up."

165 Jane Bryant Quinn: Quoted by M. K. Anderson, "Columnist Upbeat on Economy," *Holland (Mich.) Sentinel,* May 22, 2001, p. A10.

165 John Templeton quoted in G. Moore, *Spiritual Investments: Wall Street Wisdom from the Career of Sir John Templeton* (Radnor, Pa.: Templeton Foundation Press, 1998).

165 The decade ahead: This is John Templeton's hunch. "The indexes usually contain mostly the larger corporations, which have proved to be very popular now for about 10 years. In my opinion, in the next 10 years, this temporary overvaluation of shares in larger companies will be corrected, so this would not be a good time to invest in index funds" (personal correspondence, July 25, 2001).

166 $1 invested in 1925: Ibbotson Associates, *Stocks, Bonds, Bills, and Inflation* (Chicago: Ibbotson Associates, 2000), cited by J. Lerner, "Yale University Investments Office: July 2000" (Cambridge, Mass.: Harvard Business School, 9–201–048, March 4, 2001).
Swenson, *Pioneering Portfolio Management,* p. 61.

166 The endowment funds: If there were no donations, and if each school were to draw 5 percent of their growth for operational spending, their net returns of 2 and 6 percent would accumulate, over fifty years, to $2.7 million and $18.7 million. Once again, a small difference in growth rates compounds to a huge difference in results. The huge effect of small return rate variations, when compounded over time, defies intuition, much as the rapidity of growth in exponential expressions defies high school students' intuitions. See E. Mullet and Y. Cherminat, "Estimation of Exponential Expressions by High School Students," *Contemporary Educational Psychology* 20 (1995): 451–456.

167 22-year-old: R. B. McKenzie and D. R. Lee, "Getting Rich in America," *Society,* November–December 1998, pp. 20–25.

167 1963 versus 1973: *Louis Rukeyser's Wall Street,* July 1999, p. 3.

167 Wellington Mara: Bill Pennington, "Longevity Has Its Rewards," *New York Times,* January 26, 2001.

167 John Templeton: Personal correspondence, July 25, 2001.

167 CommonFund: Benchmark study, March 6, 2001, with return results aggregated from Tables 36 and 37 of *2000 NACUBO Endowment Study* (from the National Association of College and University Business Officers).

168 Yale private equity: J. Lerner, "Yale University Investments Office: July 2000" (Cambridge, Mass.: Harvard Business School, 9–201–048, March 4, 2001).
Swenson, *Pioneering Portfolio Management,* p. 57 and table 5.2.

168 Donald Redelmeier and Amos Tversky, "On the Framing of Multiple Prospects," *Psychological Science* 3 (1992): 191–193.

169 Executive intuition: C. W. Allinson, E. Chell, and J. Haynes, "Intuition and Entrepreneurial Behaviour," *European Journal of Work and Organizational Psychology* 9 (2000): 31–43; N. Khatri and H. A. Ng, "The Role of Intuition in Strategic Decision Making," *Human Relations* 1 (2000): 57–86.

169 Bob Lutz and Ralph Larsen: A. M. Hayashi, "When to Trust Your Gut," *Harvard Business Review,* February 2001, pp. 59–65.

170 Herbert Simon: Ibid.

170 Rob Pittman: Ibid.

171 Chuck Ross, "Rejected," *New West,* February 12, 1979, pp. 39–43.

CHAPTER 9. CLINICAL INTUITION

172 Intuitive versus statistical prediction: The classic analysis that launched this field was Paul E. Meehl's *Clinical Versus Statistical Prediction: A Theoretical Analysis and a Review of Evidence* (Minneapolis: University of Minnesota Press, 1974). For published follow-up reviews see D. Faust and J. Ziskin, "The Expert Witness in Psychology and Psychiatry," *Science* 241 (1988): 31–35, and J. A. Swets, R. M. Dawes, and J. Monahan, "Psychological Science Can Improve Diagnostic Decisions," *Psychological Science in the Public Interest* 1 (2000): 1–26.

173 Paul E. Meehl, "Causes and Effects of My Disturbing Little Book," *Journal of Personality Assessment* 50 (1986): 370–375.

173 Canadian criminal offenders: J. Bonta, M. Law, and K. Hanson, "The Prediction of Criminal and Violent Recidivism Among Mentally Disordered Offenders: A Meta-Analysis," *Psychological Bulletin* 123 (1998): 123–142.

173 University of Minnesota research team: W. M. Grove, D. H. Zald, B. S. Lebow, B. E. Snitz, and C. Nelson, "Clinical Versus Mechanical Prediction: A Meta-Analysis," *Psychological Assessment* 12 (2000): 19–30.

174 Thomas Barefoot: Justice Blackmun's synopsis of psychiatric testimony quoted by Margaret A. Hagen, *Whores of the Court: The Fraud of Psychiatric Testimony and the Rape of American Justice* (New York: Regan/HarperCollins, 1997).

174–175 Judging children's testimonies: S. J. Ceci and M. L. C. Huffman, "How Suggestible Are Preschool Children? Cognitive and Social Factors," *Journal of the American Academy of Child and Adolescent Psychiatry* 36 (1997): 948–957.

175 Robyn M. Dawes on Meehl: "Resignation Letter to the American Psychological Association," *APS Observer,* January 1989, pp. 14–15.

175 Meehl, "Causes and Effects," and "Philosophy of Science: Help or Hindrance?" papers presented to the American Psychological Society convention, June 22, 1992.

176 David L. Rosenhan, "On Being Sane in Insane Places," *Science* 179 (1979): 250–258.

177 Lee Ross with M. R. Lepper, F. Strack, and J. Steinmetz, "Social Explanation and Social Expectation: Effects of Real and Hypothetical Explana-

tions on Subjective Likelihood," *Journal of Personality and Social Psychology* 35 (1977): 817–829.

178 Mark Snyder, "When Belief Creates Reality," in L. Berkowitz (ed.), *Advances in Experimental Social Psychology*, vol. 18 (New York: Academic Press, 1984).

178 Psychotherapists prefer questions: M. E. W. Dallas and R. S. Baron, "Do Psychotherapists Use a Confirmatory Strategy During Interviewing?" *Journal of Social and Clinical Psychology* 3 (1985): 106–122; J. Copeland and M. Snyder, "When Counselors Confirm: A Functional Analysis," *Personality and Social Psychology Bulletin* 21 (1995): 1210–1221; M. Snyder and C. J. Thomsen, "Interactions Between Therapists and Clients: Hypothesis Testing and Behavioral Confirmation," in D. C. Turk and P. Salovey (eds.), *Reasoning, Inference, and Judgment in Clinical Psychology* (New York: Free Press, 1988).

179 Make up own questions: P. G. Devine, E. R. Hirt, and E. M. Gehrke, "Diagnostic and Confirmation Strategies in Trait Hypothesis Testing," *Journal of Personality and Social Psychology* 58 (1990): 952–963; H. S. Hodgins and M. Zuckerman, "Beyond Selecting Information: Biases in Spontaneous Questions and Resultant Conclusions," *Journal of Experimental Social Psychology* 29 (1993): 387–407; W. B. Swann, Jr., and T. Giuliano, "Confirmatory Search Strategies in Social Interaction: How, When, Why, and with What Consequences," *Journal of Social and Clinical Psychology* 5 (1987): 511–524.

179 Confirmation bias persisted: M. Snyder, "Seek, and Ye Shall Find: Testing Hypotheses About Other People," in E. T. Higgins, C. P. Herman, and M. P. Zanna (eds.), *Social Cognition: The Ontario Symposium on Personality and Social Psychology* (Hillsdale, N.J.: Erlbaum, 1981); M. Snyder, B. Campbell, and E. Preston, "Testing Hypotheses About Human Nature: Assessing the Accuracy of Social Stereotypes," *Social Cognition* 1 (1982): 256–272.

179 Psychotherapy clients: R. M. Whitman, M. Kramer, and B. Baldridge, "Which Dream Does the Patient Tell?" *Archives of General Psychology* 8 (1963): 277–282.

Harold Renaud and Floyd Estess, "Life History Interviews with One Hundred Normal American Males: 'Pathogeneity' of Childhood," *American Journal of Orthopsychiatry* 31 (1961): 786–802.

180 The Violence Risk Appraisal Guide: J. A. Swets, R. M. Dawes, and J. Monahan, "Better Decisions Through Science," *Scientific American*, October 2000, pp. 82–87. A more technical version of this paper is avail-

able as "Psychological Science Can Improve Diagnostic Decisions," *Psychological Science in the Public Interest* 1(1) (2000): 1–26.

180 Caroline Myss: R. A. Baker, "Medical Intuitives: Do Your Chakras Need a Checkup?" *Skeptical Briefs,* December 1998, pp. 9–10.

180 School violence predictions: The Dallas Violence Risk Assessment is described by K. Ryan-Arredondo, K. Renquf, C. Egyed, M. Doxey, M. Dobbins, S. Sanchez, and B. Rakowitz, "Threats of Violence in Schools: The Dallas Independent School District's Response," *Psychology in the Schools* 38 (2001): 185–196.

180 Sexual reoffending: R. K. Hanson, "Will They Do It Again? Predicting Sex-Offense Recidivism," *Current Directions in Psychological Science* 9 (2000): 106–109; R. K. Hanson and D. Thornton, "Improving Risk Assessments for Sex Offenders: A Comparison of Three Actuarial Scales," *Law and Human Behavior* 24 (2000): 119–136.

180 Weather forecasters' self-assessments and accuracy: B. Fischhoff, "Debiasing," in D. Kahneman, P. Slovic, and A. Tversky (eds.), *Judgment Under Uncertainty: Heuristics and Biases* (New York: Cambridge University Press, 1982); Swets, Dawes, and Monahan, "Psychological Science Can Improve Diagnostic Decisions."

181 Paul Spengler with L. Anderson, "Experience, Expertness, and Effectiveness: Some Fine-Grained Analyses and Implications," paper presented at a symposium on "Clinical Judgment Is Finally Analyzed by Meta-Analysis," American Psychological Association, August 15, 1998. Other Ball State papers presented at the symposium included S. Aegisdottir and A. Maugherman, "Clinical Versus Statistical Prediction: Discussion of an Old Paradigm in a New Light," and M. J. White and G. Freels, "Some Effects of Experience on Clinical Judgments."

182 Dale E. McNiel with D. A. Sandberg and R. L. Binder, "The Relationship Between Confidence and Accuracy in Clinical Assessment of Psychiatric Patients' Potential for Violence," *Law and Human Behavior* 22 (1998): 655–669.

183 Mary Lee Smith with G. V. Glass and R. L. Miller, *The Benefits of Psychotherapy* (Baltimore: Johns Hopkins University Press, 1980), p. 183.

183 Better than nothing: S. M. Kopta, R. J. Lueger, S. M. Saunders, and K. I. Howard, "Individual Psychotherapy Outcome and Process Research: Challenges Leading to Greater Turmoil or a Positive Transition?" *Annual Review of Psychology* 30 (1999): 441–469.

183 NIMH therapy experiment: I. Elkin and eleven others, "National Institute of Mental Health Treatment of Depression Collaborative Research Program," *Archives of General Psychiatry* 46 (1989): 971–983.

183 Princess Diana: S. B. Smith, *Diana in Search of Herself: Portrait of a Troubled Princess* (New York: Times Books, 1999).

183 Therapeutic touch advocates: D. Krieger, *Accepting Your Power to Heal: The Personal Practice of Therapeutic Touch* (Santa Fe: Bear, 1993).

184 Therapeutic touch skeptics: B. Scheiber and C. Selby, "UAB Final Report of Therapeutic Touch—An Appraisal," *Skeptical Inquirer,* May–June 1997, pp. 53–54.

184 Experiments to date: L. Rosa, E. Rosa, L. Sarner, and S. Barrett, "A Close Look at Therapeutic Touch," *Journal of the American Medical Association* 279 (1998): 1005–1010; R. Long, P. Bernhardt, and W. Evans, "Perception of Conventional Sensory Cues as an Alternative to the Postulated 'Human Energy Field' of Therapeutic Touch," *Scientific Review of Alternative Medicine* 3(2) (1999): 53–59, 61.

184 22,000 trained: R. J. McNally, "EMDR and Mesmerism: A Comparative Historical Analysis," *Journal of Anxiety Disorders* 13 (1999): 225–236; G. M. Rosen, and J. Lohr, "Can Eye Movements Cure Mental Ailments?" *Skeptical Briefs,* March 1997, p. 12.

184 Without the eye movements: S. P. Cahill, M. H. Carrigan, and B. C. Frueh, "Does EMDR Work? And If So, Why? A Critical Review of Controlled Outcome and Dismantling Research," *Journal of Anxiety Disorders* 13 (1999): 5–33; J. M. Lohr, S. O. Lilienfeld, D. F. Tolin, and J. D. Herbert, "Eye Movement Desensitization and Reprocessing: An Analysis of Specific Versus Nonspecific Treatment Factors," *Journal of Anxiety Disorders* 13 (1999): 185–207; P. R. Davidson and K. C. Parker, "Eye Movement Desensitization and Reprocessing: A Meta-Analysis," *Journal of Consulting and Clinical Psychology* 69 (2001): 305–316.

184 Anthony G. Greenwald with E. R. Spangenberg, A. R. Pratkanis, and J. Eskenazi, "Double-Blind Tests of Subliminal Self-Help Audiotapes," *Psychological Science* 2 (1991): 119–122; A. G. Greenwald, "Subliminal Semantic Activation and Subliminal Snake Oil," paper presented to the American Psychological Association convention, Washington, D.C., 1991.

185 Light exposure experiments: C. I. Eastman, M. A. Young, L. F. Fogg, L. Liu, and P. M. Meaden, "Bright Light Treatment of Winter Depression: A Placebo-Controlled Trial," *Archives of General Psychiatry* 55 (1998): 883–889; A. J. Lewy and 7 others, "Morning vs. Evening Light Treatment of Patients with Winter Depression," *Archives of General Psychiatry* 55 (1998): 890–896; M. Terman, J. S. Terman, and D. C. Ross, "A Controlled Trial of Timed Bright Light and Negative Air Ionization for Treat-

ment of Winter Depression," *Archives of General Psychiatry* 55 (1998): 875–882.

185 ECT effectiveness: P. Bergsholm, J. L. Larsen, K. Rosendahl, and F. Holsten, "Electroconvulsive Therapy and Cerebral Computed Tomography," *Acta Psychiatrica Scandinavia* 80 (1989): 566–572; C. E. Coffey (ed.), *Clinical Science of Electroconvulsive Therapy* (Washington, D.C.: American Psychiatric Press, 1993).

185 NIH and APA: Consensus Conference, "Electroconvulsive Therapy," *Journal of the American Medical Association* 254 (1985): 2103–2108; American Psychiatric Association, *The Practice of ECT: Recommendations for Treatment, Training, and Privileging* (Washington, D.C.: American Psychiatric Press, 1990).

CHAPTER 10. INTERVIEWER INTUITION

187 Frank Bernieri quoted by Malcolm Gladwell, "The New-Boy Network: What Do Job Interviews Really Tell Us?" *New Yorker,* May 29, 2000, pp. 68–86.

188 Bella DePaulo with A. L. Blank, G. W. Swaim, and J. G. Hairfield, "Expressiveness and Expressive Control," *Personality and Social Psychology Bulletin* 18 (1992): 276–285.

188 Maurice Levesque and David Kenny, "Accuracy of Behavioral Predictions at Zero Acquaintance: A Social Relations Analysis," *Journal of Personality and Social Psychology* 65 (1993): 1178–1187.

188–189 Frank L. Schmidt and John E. Hunter, "The Validity and Utility of Selection Methods in Personnel Psychology: Practical and Theoretical Implications of 85 Years of Research Findings," *Psychological Bulletin* 124 (1998): 262–274.

189 Interview illusion: R. E. Nisbett, "Lay Personality Theory: Its Nature, Origin, and Utility," in N. E. Grunberg, R. E. Nisbett, et al., *A Distinctive Approach to Psychological Research: The Influence of Stanley Schachter* (Hillsdale, N.J.: Erlbaum, 1987).

189 Search consultant: "Reflections from the Lamp," Fall 1996 newsletter, Robert W. Dingman Co.

189 Robyn M. Dawes, *House of Cards: Psychology and Psychotherapy Built on Myth* (New York: Free Press, 1994).

190 Robyn M. Dawes, "Shallow Psychology," in J. S. Carroll and J. W. Payne (eds.), *Cognition and Social Behavior* (Hillsdale, N.J.: Erlbaum, 1976).

191 Intentions versus past behaviors: J. A. Ouellette and W. Wood, "Habit and Intention in Everyday Life: The Multiple Processes by Which Past

Behavior Predicts Future Behavior," *Psychological Bulletin* 124 (1998): 54–74.

192 Gladwell, "New-Boy Network."

192 Interviewer preconceptions: See, for example, T. H. Macan and R. L. Dipboye, "The Effects of the Application on Processing of Information from the Employment Interview," *Journal of Applied Social Psychology* 24 (1994): 1291–1314.

192 Prescreened applicants: D. M. Cable and T. Gilovich, "Looked Over or Overlooked? Prescreening Decisions and Postinterview Evaluations," *Journal of Personality and Social Psychology* 83 (1998): 501–508.

Carl Word, Mark Zanna, and Joel Cooper, "The Nonverbal Mediation of Self-Fulfilling Prophecies in Interracial Interaction," *Journal of Experimental Social Psychology* 10 (1974): 109–120.

193 Gladwell, "New-Boy Network."

194 Norval Glenn, "The Recent Trend in Marital Success in the United States," *Journal of Marriage and the Family* 53 (1991): 261–70. After studying the 1985 U.S. government population survey, Teresa Castro Martin and Larry L. Bumpass similarly estimate that two-thirds of recent marriages are destined for divorce or separation (see their "Recent Trends in Marital Disruption," *Demography* 26 [1989]: 37–51).

194 Gallup report: Diane Colasanto and James Shriver, "Mirror of America: Middle-Aged Face Marital Crisis," *Gallup Report*, no. 284, May 1989, pp. 34–38.

194 Cohabitation still intact: Brad Edmondson, "New Lifestage: Trial Marriage," *Forecast*, October 1997 (using National Center for Health Statistics data). Available at www.demographics.com/publications/fc/97 _fc/9710_fc/fco7106.htm.

194 Marriage and happiness: For more on the positive personal and social aftermath of marriage, see my *The American Paradox: Spiritual Hunger in an Age of Plenty* (New Haven: Yale University Press, 2000).

194 Zero percent: L. A. Baker and R. E. Emery, "When Every Relationship Is Above Average: Perceptions and Expectations of Divorce at the Time of Marriage," *Law and Human Behavior* 17 (1993): 439–450.

195 George Bernard Shaw: Preface to *Getting Married*.

195 Marriage stability predictors: T. R. Balakrishan et al., "A Hazard Model Analysis of the Covariates of Marriage Dissolution in Canada," *Demography* 24 (1987): 395–406; Colasanto and Shriver, "Mirror of America"; T. B. Heaton and E. L. Pratt, "The Effects of Religious Homogamy on Marital Satisfaction and Stability," *Journal of Family Issues* 11 (1990):

191–207; G. C. Kitson, K. B. Babri, and M. J. Roach, "Who Divorces and Why: A Review," *Journal of Family Issues* 6 (1985): 255–293; J. D. Teachman, K. A. Polonko, and J. Scanzoni, "Demography of the Family," in M. B. Sussman and S. K. Steinmetz (eds.), *Handbook of Marriage and the Family* (New York: Plenum, 1987); M. McGue and D. T. Lykken, "Genetic Influence on Risk of Divorce," *Psychological Science* 3 (1992): 368–373; J. R. Kahn and K. A. London, "Premarital Sex and the Risk of Divorce," *Journal of Marriage and the Family* 53 (1991): 845–855; D. M. Fergusson, L. J. Horwood, and F. T. Shannon, "A Proportional Hazards Model of Family Breakdown," *Journal of Marriage and the Family* 46 (1984): 539–549.

195 5 to 1 ratio: J. Gottman (with N. Silver), *Why Marriages Succeed or Fail* (New York: Simon & Schuster, 1994).

195 Usha Gupta and Pushpa Singh, "Exploratory Study of Love and Liking and Type of Marriages," *Indian Journal of Applied Psychology* 19 (1982): 92–97.

197 Michael A. Campion with D. K. Palmer and J. E. Campion, "Structuring Employment Interviews to Improve Reliability, Validity, and Users' Reactions," *Current Directions in Psychological Science* 7 (1998): 77–82.

197 Double the accuracy: W. H. Wiesner and S. P. Cronshaw, "A Meta-Analytic Investigation of the Impact of Interview Format and Degree of Structure on the Validity of the Employment Interview," *Journal of Occupational Psychology* 61 (1988): 275–290. A more recent synopsis of research confirms that structured interviews substantially surpass the usefulness of unstructured interviews: Schmidt and Hunter, "Validity and Utility of Selection Methods."

197 Gladwell, "New-Boy Network."

CHAPTER II. RISK INTUITION

198 Terrorism: L. C. Johnson, "The Declining Terrorist Threat," *New York Times,* July 10, 2001.

198–199 Accident data: *Statistical Abstract of the United States;* rail crossing data from Federal Railroad Administration reported in Associated Press, "Rush Is on to Improve Safety of Train Crossings," *Holland (Mich.) Sentinel,* June 3, 2001, p. A11.

199 Studies of intuited versus actual risk: P. Slovic, "Perception of Risk," *Science* 236 (1987): 280–285, and *The Perception of Risk* (London: Earthscan, 2000).

199 Thirty-seven times safer: Personal communication from Kevin T. Fearn, Research and Statistics Department, National Safety Council, October

8, 2001. During the 1980s, U.S. travelers were twenty-six times safer per mile on planes than cars, according to National Safety Council, *Accident Facts* (Chicago: National Safety Council, 1991).

199 22 heads: The odds of heads on a first coin flip are 1 in 2. The odds of two consecutive heads are 1 in 4. The odds of 22 consecutive heads are 1 in 4,194,304.

200 Defenders of objectivity: For example, F. B. Cross, "The Risk of Reliance on Perceived Risk," www.fplc.edu/RISK/vol3/winter/cross.htm.

200 John Stossel, "The Real Cost of Regulation," *Imprimis,* May 2001, pp. 1–5.

200 Gallup: "Commercial Aviation," *Gallup Report,* March–April 1989, pp. 32–33.

200 Barry Sonnenfeld quoted by J. Winokur, "Curmudgeon," *Funny Times,* August 2001, p. 4. Ironically, Sonnenfeld survived and escaped injury when, on February 16, 1999, the executive jet in which he was riding ran off the runway at the Van Nuys, Calif., airport, crashed into several nearby aircraft, and caught fire (http://airsafe.com/events/celebs /mib.htm).

200 27 months, 16 million flights: M. Tolchin, "Major Airlines Go Two Years Without a Fatality," *New York Times* report in *Grand Rapids (Mich.) Press,* April 17, 1994, p. A10.

1,118 fatalities: *Time,* January 14, 2002, p. 16.

200 140,000 years: Or 21,000 years with a daily flight, reports Arnold Barnett, quoted by Adam Bryan, "Fly Me; Why No Airline Brags: 'We're the Safest,'" *New York Times,* June 9, 1996, sec. 4, p. 1.

200 Fifty more planes: The Air Transport Association reports that 483 passengers were killed in plane crashes from 1995–99 (97 per year). During these years, the National Safety Council's Research and Statistics Department tells me, Americans were thirty-seven times safer per passenger mile in planes than in motor vehicles. Multiplying 37 by 97 we can estimate that nearly 3,600 people would have to die in plane crashes during an average year for flying to be as dangerous as cars, trucks, and motorcycles. In the 1990s there was an average of 79 airline passenger deaths per year. Dividing 3,600 minus 79 by 60 passengers yields 58 planes like those on September 11 that would need to crash for flying to equal the dangers of driving.

201 Basketball: 631,186 injuries in 1998, according to "NEISS Data Highlights—1998," Consumer Product Safety Review, Fall 1999.

201 John Allen Paulos quoted by K. C. Cole, *The Universe and the Teacup* (New York: Harcourt Brace, 1998), p. 33.

201 Passenger/driver intuitions: D. G. MacGregor and P. Slovic, "Perceived

Risk and Driving Behavior: Lessons for Improving Traffic Safety in Emerging Market Countries," in H. von Holst, A. Nygren, and A. E. Anderson (eds.), *Transportation, Traffic Safety, and Health–Human Behavior* (Heidelberg, Germany: Springer-Verlag Berlin, 2000).

202 Richard Wilson quoted by M. Specter, "10 Years Later, Through Fear, Chernobyl Still Kills in Belarus," *New York Times,* March 31, 1996, p. 1. Although Wilson's statement referred to the people of Chernobyl, many nuclear engineers think it applicable to the wider world.

202 Learn and extinguish: G. C. L. Davey, "Classical Conditioning and the Acquisition of Human Fears and Phobias: A Review and Synthesis of the Literature," *Advances in Behavior Research and Therapy* 14 (1992): 29–66, "Preparedness and Phobias: Specific Evolved Associations or a Generalized Expectancy Bias?" *Behavioral and Brain Sciences* 18 (1995): 289–297; A. Ohman, "Face the Beast and Fear the Face: Animal and Social Fears as Prototypes for Evolutionary Analyses of Emotion," *Psychophysiology* 23 (1986): 123–145.

202 Spiders than flowers: E. W. Cook III, R. L. Hodes, and P. J. Lang, "Preparedness and Phobia: Effects of Stimulus Content on Human Visceral Conditioning," *Journal of Abnormal Psychology* 95 (1986): 195–207.

203 Bombing fears: S. Mineka and R. Zinbarg, "Conditioning and Ethological Models of Anxiety Disorders: Stress-in-Dynamic-Context Anxiety Models," in D. Hope (ed.), *Perspectives on Anxiety, Panic, and Fear: Nebraska Symposium on Motivation* (Lincoln: University of Nebraska Press, 1996).

203 National Safety Council: Thirty-five deaths from venomous snakes, lizards, and spiders from 1994 through 1996, as reported in "Injury Facts" (www.nsc.org/lrs/statinfo/99016.htm).

203 6,900 times: A. Barnett, "Air Safety: End of the Golden Age?" *Chance* 1(2) (1990): pp. 8–12. Arnold Barnett also found that, over a two-year period, there were 0.02 front-page cancer-death stories per 1,000 annual deaths, and 138 front-page stories about deaths from some other cause per 1,000 annual deaths. Reported by J. A. Paulos, *A Mathematician Reads the Newspaper* (New York: Basic Books, 1995).

203 Baruch Fischhoff, "Heuristics and Biases in Application," in T. Gilovich, D. W. Griffin, and D. Kahneman (eds.), *The Psychology of Intuitive Judgment: Heuristics and Biases* (New York: Cambridge University Press, 2002).

203 67 fatalities: According to the International Shark Attack File at the Florida Museum of Natural History, as reported by T. McCarthy, "Why Can't We Be Friends?" *Time,* July 30, 2001, pp. 34–41.

206 Skiing versus preservatives: Slovic, "Perception of Risk."

206 Chauncey Starr, "Social Benefit versus Technological Risk," *Science* 165 (1969): 1232–1238.

206 Gender and risk: J. P. Byrnes, D. C. Miller, and W. D. Schafer, "Gender Differences in Risk Taking: A Meta-Analysis," *Psychological Bulletin* 125 (1999): 367–383.

206 One evolutionary psychologist: Margo Wilson, quoted by R. Bennett, "Risky Business," *Science News,* September 16, 2000, p. 190.

206 George Loewenstein with E. U. Weber, C. K. Hsee, and N. Welch, "Risk as Feelings," *Psychological Bulletin* 127 (2001): 267–286.

207 President Clinton quoted by R. Monastersky, "A Shelter in the Storm," *Science News,* May 22, 1999, p. 335.

207 1 in 4.4 million: NOAA reports 4,460 tornado deaths from 1950 through 1999, or 89 per year. The population averaged about 220 million over those fifty years. So the odds of any person being killed by a tornado during any year was 1 in about 2.5 million. Over the past twenty-five years (perhaps a more adequate indicator given modern housing and alarm systems) there have been fifty-five tornado deaths per year while the population has averaged close to 240 million, yielding 1 in 4.4 million. An MIT web site offers a 1 in 8.7 million estimate, without giving its basis.

207 Airplane safety seats: M. Kinsley, "Less Cost, More Risk," *Time,* July 15, 1996, p. 46.

208 15 to 5 in 10,000: People will pay considerably more to reduce the risk of insect spray poisoning from 5 to 0 in 10,000 than from 15 to 5 in 10,000, report W. K. Viscusi and W. A. Magat, *Learning About Risk: Consumer and Worker Responses to Hazard Information* (Cambridge, Mass.: Harvard University Press, 1987).

208 $50: Cole, *Universe and the Teacup,* p. 31, and Time/CNN poll, *Time,* September 24, 2001, p. 88.

208 David Beckmann: Personal communication, July 25, 2001, and August 31, 2001.

209 3 million/20 jumbo jets: R. Peto, *Mortality from Smoking in Developed Countries, 1950–2000: Indirect Estimates from National Vital Statistics* (New York: Oxford University Press, 1994).

209 Half a billion: A. D. Lopez, "Measuring the Health Hazards of Tobacco: Commentary," *Bulletin of the World Health Organization* 77(1) (1999): 82–83.

209 Philip Morris: B. Herbert, "Economics 101 at Big Tobacco U.," *New York Times,* July 23, 2001.

209 Twelve minutes: "A Fistful of Risks," *Discover,* May 1996, pp. 82–83.

Dave Barry: *The Dave Barry 2002 Calendar* (Kansas City: Andrews McMeel, 2002).

210 96/58 percent: D. G. Altman, D. W. Levine, G. Howard, and H. Hamilton, "Tobacco Farming and Public Health: Attitudes of the General Public and Farmers," *Journal of Social Issues* 53 (1997): 113–128.

210 Canada: Statistics Canada. *Statistical Report on the Health of Canadians.* Prepared by the Federal, Provincial and Territorial Advisory Committee on Population Health for the Meeting of Ministers of Health, Charlottetown, PEI, September 16–17, 1999.

210 Next single cigarette: P. Slovic, "What Does It Mean to Know a Cumulative Risk? Adolescents' Perceptions of Short-Term and Long-Term Consequences of Smoking," *Journal of Behavioral Decision Making* 13 (2000): 259–266.

210 Canadian picture warnings: "A Picture Is Worth a Thousand Words," American Psychological Association *Monitor,* June 2001, p. 14.

210 David Dreman, *Contrarian Investment Strategy: The Psychology Stock Market Success* (New York: Random House, 1979).

210 Kimihiko Yamagishi, "When a 12.86% Mortality Is More Dangerous Than 24.14%: Implications for Risk Communication," *Applied Cognitive Psychology* 11 (1997): 495–506.

211 20 out of 100: P. Slovic, J. Monahan, and D. M. MacGregor, "Violence Risk Assessment and Risk Communication: The Effects of Using Actual Cases, Providing Instructions, and Employing Probability vs. Frequency Formats," *Law and Human Behavior* 24 (2000): 271–296.

211 .000001: N. Kraus, T. Malmfors, and P. Slovic, "Intuitive Toxicology: Expert and Lay Judgments of Chemical Risks," *Risk Analysis* 12 (1992): 215–232.

211 7 out of 100: V. Denes-Raj and S. Epstein, "Conflict Between Intuitive and Rational Processing: When People Behave Against Their Better Judgment," *Journal of Personality and Social Psychology* 66 (1994): 819–829.

211 Slovic with Monahan and MacGregor, "Violence Risk Assessment and Risk Communication."

211 Lifetime accident statistics: MacGregor and Slovic, "Perceived Risk and Driving Behavior."

211 Put the tears back on: M. L. Finucane, E. Peters, and P. Slovic, "Judgment and Decision Making: The Dance of Affect and Reason," in S. L. Schneider and J. Santeau (eds.), *Emerging Perspectives on Decision Research* (New York: Cambridge University Press, in press).

211 Sociopaths and emotional response: D. T. Lykken, "A Study of Anxiety in the Sociopathic Personality," *Journal of Abnormal and Social Psychology* 55 (1957): 6–10.

212 Liking and perceived risks and benefits: P. Slovic, M. Finucane, E. Peters, and D. G. MacGregor, "The Affect Heuristic," in T. Gilovich, D. W. Griffin, and D. Kahneman (eds.), *The Psychology of Intuitive Judgment: Heuristics and Biases* (New York: Cambridge University Press, 2002).

212 George Loewenstein et al., "Risk as Feelings."

CHAPTER 12. GAMBLERS' INTUITION

213 $17 billion in 1974: "Gambling on the Increase," *Science* 279 (1998): 485; B. Lemley, "The New Math of Gambling," *Discover,* May 2000, pp. 60–65. Although I have seen estimates of monies gambled as high as $800 billion, $500 billion and $450 billion are my conservative estimates based on the General Accounting Office's 2000 estimate of $54 billion lost and based on many forms of betting returning about 90 percent of the wager (though only 50 percent by lotteries). The National Gambling Impact Study Commission estimated $43 billion in revenues from all forms of casinos and race tracks (implying some $400 million bet), $17 billion from lottery revenues (implying $34 billion bet), and $80 to $380 billion from sports betting—which also leads to an estimate of more than $500 billion bet.

213 Baseball and casinos: National League attendance for 2000 was 39,683,109, and American League attendance was 31,675,798 (www.baseball-reference.com/leagues). Casino data from American Gaming Association (www.americangaming.org/survey2000/summary/summary.html).

213 $54 billion: B. L. Ungar, "Impact of Gambling: Economic Effects More Measurable Than Social Effects," General Accounting Office Report to the Honorable Frank R. Wolf, House of Representatives, April 2000.

213 $6 billion: Actually, $6.1 billion in 2000, reports the Las Vegas Convention and Visitors Authority (www.lasvegas24hours.com/gen_resfaq.html).

213 Forty-eight states: Forty-seven states, reports R. C. Leone, "The False Promise of Casinos," *New York Times,* June 25, 2001. Gambling is illegal in Hawaii and Utah. Although horse-track betting is legal in Tennessee, the state had no operating race tracks as of December 1999, reports Ungar, "Impact of Gambling."

213 Montana: D. Crary, "Gambling Takes Toll on Small Towns," Associated Press, *Holland (Mich.) Sentinel,* February 20, 2000, p. A9.

214 Saving for rainy day: M. Brady, "Foolish Gambling," *Motley Fool,* April 3, 1997.

214 John J. Egan, "State-Sanctioned Gambling Is a Bad Bet," *U.S. Catholic,* November 1997, pp. 24–57.

214 Massachusetts: M. J. Sandel, "The Hard Questions: Bad Bets," *New Republic,* March 10, 1997, p. 27.

214 Connecticut: J. Lender, "State Lottery Officials Apologize for Racy Ad," *Hartford Courant,* January 25, 1996, p. A3.

214 William Safire, "Cutting My Losses," *New York Times,* March 29, 1999.

214 64 percent: During 1997–98, according to Common Cause, as reported in "Is Gambling an Issue in Presidential Politics?" *Christianity Today,* May 24, 1999, p. 46.

214 Poker machines: V. Novak, "They Call It Video Crack," *Time,* June 1, 1998, pp. 58–59.

214 David Beasley: E. Walsh, "Gambling's Election Win," *Washington Post,* November 6, 1998, p. A1.

214 Britain's National Lottery: "The National Lottery Fact Pack," cited by E. Hill and J. Williamson, "Choose Six Numbers, Any Numbers," *Psychologist,* January 1998, pp. 17–21.

215 60 percent: A. Hardie and G. Chamberlain, "Scots Forsake the Land of Their Fathers," *Scotsman,* August 27, 2001, p. 5. The "National Lottery Fact Pack" estimated that 65 percent of Brits regularly played the National Lottery.

215 90 to 93 cents: *Casino Player* magazine, cited by G. Wells, "You Win Some, You Lose More," *Grand Rapids (Mich.) Press,* April 25, 1999, F1, F7.

216 Brett Pulley, "Living Off the Daily Dream of Winning a Lottery Prize," *New York Times,* May 22, 1999.

216 15.4 million: H. J. Shaffer, M. N. Hall, J. Vander Bilt, "Estimating the Prevalence of Disordered Gambling Behavior in the United States and Canada: A Meta-Analysis," Harvard Medical School Division on Addictions, December 15, 1997, p. 43. (Presented to the National Gambling Impact Study Commission.)

216 Gamblers Anonymous: As reported by Gamblers Anonymous International Service Office and cited in "Family News from Dr. James Dobson," July 1999. (Dobson was a Republican appointee to the National Gambling Impact Study Commission.) The 2001 data were provided by Gamblers Anonymous International Secretary, Karen H., by personal correspondence on August 15, 2001.

216 Twenty-eight-year-old: M. Allen, "For $250 Million, Convenience Stores Beat Day at Beach," *New York Times,* July 27, 1998.

216 10 percent: C. T. Clotfelter and P. J. Cook, *Selling Hope: State Lotteries in America* (Cambridge, Mass.: Harvard University Press, 1989), p. 92.

216 Economist: E. L. Grinols and J. D. Omorov, "Development or Dreamfield Delusions? Assessing Casino Gambling's Costs and Benefits," *Journal of Law and Commerce,* University of Pittsburgh School of Law, Fall 1996, pp. 58–60, cited by the National Coalition Against Legalized Gambling (www.ncalg.org/facts_about.htm).

216 Dollar and a nightmare: Quoted by E. Nieves, "Lottery Casualties: When the $1 Dream Becomes a Nightmare," *New York Times,* May 29, 1997.

216 Scott Harshbarger: Pulley, "Living off the Daily Dream of Winning a Lottery Prize."

216–217 Chelsea/Wellesley: Cited by Sandel, "Bad Bets," *New Republic,* p. 27.

217 "Gambling creates wealth": Quoted by L. Lots, "Getting Sick of Gambling Fever," *Church Herald,* May 1995, p. 58.

217 William Temple, "Gambling and Ethics," issued by Churches' Committee on Gambling, 215 Abbey House, London (undated).

217 William Safire, "Lotteries Are Losers," *New York Times,* June 21, 1999.

218 Urination problems: "Operators of the Casino Niagara in Niagara Falls, Ontario, told the *Ottawa Citizen* that customers' urinating around slot machines has become a 'severe problem,' " reported C. Shepherd, "News of the Weird," *Funny Times,* September 1997, p. 21.

218 Roger Jones quoted by P. Belluck, " 'I'll Throw in 5 Bucks,' and Record Lottery Prize Is Claimed," *New York Times,* May 22, 1998.

218 Long odds and "subjective overestimation": D. M. Sanbonmatsu, S. S. Posavac, and R. Stasney, "The Subjective Beliefs Underlying Probability Overestimation," *Journal of Experimental Social Psychology* 33 (1997): 276–295.

218 Hal S. Stern, "A Statistician Reads the Sports Pages," *Chance* 11(4) (1998): 17–21.

218 Frank Capaci: Belluck, " 'I'll Throw in 5 Bucks.' "

218 Thirteen Ohio workers: P. Belluck, "You Gotta Believe! 13's the Lucky Number," *New York Times,* July 31, 1998.

219 Billion plus tickets: Including 328 million losing tickets sold in the Big Game lotteries leading up to Maria Grasso's win and 562 million losing tickets sold in the Powerball lottery won by the Lucky 13.

219 Joe: Quoted by Nieves, "Lottery Casualties."

219 Publishers Clearinghouse: Reported by PCH marketing executive Todd Sloan in a *Fortune* interview, reported by C. Shepherd, "News of the Weird," *Funny Times,* September 1997, p. 21.

219 1 in 100 million: As reported in personal e-mail correspondence from Publishers Clearinghouse Customer Service, August 20, 2001.

219 NATO bombs: M. Orkin, *What Are the Odds? Chance in Everyday Life* (New York: Freeman, 2000).

220 Carmen Castellano: J. Rodriguez, "S.J. Retiree Claims Lottery Bonanza," *Mercury News,* June 29, 2001.

220 Laurie Snell, "A Lottery Mystery," *Chance News* 6.03 (Dartmouth University). Figure from "Using Lotteries in Teaching a Chance Course," written by the Chance Team for the Chance Teachers Guide, August 1, 1998.

220 Thomas Holtgraves and James Skeel, "Cognitive Biases in Playing the Lottery: Estimating the Odds and Choosing the Numbers," *Journal of Applied Social Psychology* 22 (1992): 934–952.

221 Maryland's Pick 3: C. Clotfelter and P. Cook, "The Gambler's Fallacy in Lottery Play," *Management Science* 39: 1521–1525.

221 New Jersey's Pick 3: D. Terrell, "A Test of the Gambler's Fallacy: Evidence from Para-Mutuel Games," *Journal of Risk and Uncertainty* 8 (1994): 309–317. This and the Maryland study were cited by M. Rabin, "Inference by Believers in the Law of Small Numbers," unpublished manuscript, Department of Economics, University of California, Berkeley, 2001.

222 Thomas Gilovich, "Superstition and the Regression Effect," *Skeptical Inquirer,* March–April 1999, pp. 24–29.

222 Ruma Falk, "Do Men Have More Sisters Than Women?" *Teaching Statistics* 4 (1982): 60–62.

222 Ellen J. Langer, "The Psychology of Chance," *Journal for the Theory of Social Behavior* 7 (1977): 185–208.

223 More than fifty experiments: P. K. Presson and V. A. Benassi, "Illusion of Control: A Meta-Analytic Review," *Journal of Social Behavior and Personality* 11 (1996): 493–510; S. C. Thompson, W. Armstrong, and C. Thomas, "Illusions of Control, Underestimations, and Accuracy: A Control Heuristic Explanation," *Psychological Bulletin* 123 (1998): 143–161.

223 Throw hard: M. Henslin, "Craps and Magic," *American Journal of Sociology* 73 (1967): 316–330.

223 To improve luck: Gilovich, "Superstition and the Regression Effect."

223 Sports near misses: T. Gilovich and C. Douglas, "Biased Evaluations of Randomly Determined Gambling Outcomes," *Journal of Experimental Social Psychology* 22 (1986): 228–241.

223 National Opinion Research Center, "Gambling Impact and Behavior Study," report to the National Gambling Impact Study Commission, April 1, 1999.

223 Ann Landers, syndicated column, July 5, 1998 (in *Holland [Mich.] Sentinel* and other newspapers).

224 1.6 million years: Arnold Barnett lecture on "Odds in Everyday Life," reported in *Chance News,* 7.07.
    Drive ten miles: Michael Orkin's calculation, as reported by S. Mirsky, "Dumb, Dumb, Duh Dumb," *Scientific American,* November 2001, p. 95.

224 Britain's National Lottery: R. Uhlig, "Hawking Fires a Brief Tirade Against the Lottery," *Daily Telegraph* (London), February 4, 1996.

224 To die: "National Lottery and Death Rates," *Chance News,* July 15, 1999. Reported from *Daily Express* (London), August 13, 1998. In the U.K., twenty-two people die every twenty minutes. Thirteen percent of the population watches the draw, from which one can estimate that three viewers die for every winner.

225 $1.51 million: My thanks to my accounting professor friend, Scott Vandervelde, for computing forty years of weekly compounded deposits and interest for me.

CHAPTER 13. PSYCHIC INTUITION

227 James Van Praagh quoted by J. Mendelsohn, "He Sees Dead People," *USA Weekend,* May 5–7, 2000, p. 16.

227 Gallup Poll: F. Newport and M. Strausberg, "Poll Analyses: Americans' Belief in Psychic and Paranormal Phenomena Is Up Over Last Decade," Gallup News Service, June 8, 2001 (*Gallup Poll Monthly,* June 2001, pp. 14–17).

227 $1 billion: M. Nisbett, "Psychic Telephone Networks Profit on Yearning, Gullibility," *Skeptical Inquirer,* May–June 1998, pp. 5–6.

227 Guy Claxton, *Hare Brain, Tortoise Mind* (London: Fourth Estate, 1998).

228 96 percent: R. A. McConnell, "National Academy of Sciences' Opinion on Parapsychology," *Journal of the American Society for Psychical Research* 85 (1991): 333–365.

228 Thomas Jefferson: This 1807 quote appears in F. Hitching, *The World Atlas of Mysteries* (London: Pan Books, 1978), p. 182. A slightly different version was quoted by P. Diaconis, "Statistical Problems in ESP Research," *Science* 201 (1978): 131–136. Diaconis drew the quote from H. H. Nininger, *Our Stone-Pelted Earth* (Boston: Houghton Mifflin, 1933). I have been unable to identify the original Jefferson source.

228 486 predictions: H. Strentz, "Become a Psychic and Amaze Your Friends!" *Atlanta Journal,* January 1, 1986, p. 15A.

228 Psychic intuitions for police: M. Reiser, *Police Psychology* (Los Angeles: LEHI, 1982).

229 Jane Ayers Sweat and Mark Durm, "Psychics: Do Police Departments Really Use Them?" *Skeptical Inquirer* 17 (1993): 148–158.
Terrance Gainer quoted in B. Radford, "'Psychic Flies' Feed on Levy Disappearance," *Skeptical Inquirer,* November–December 2001, p. 12.

229 Robert Baker, "Black Noses and Blue Nonsense," *Skeptical Inquirer,* Fall 1991, pp. 67–71.

230 The Randi $1 million challenge: J. Randi, 2000 Club mailing list e-mail letter, which (as one who has joined others in pledging $1,000 to this fund) I received on February 4, 1999. The actual $1 million has reportedly been provided by an anonymous U.S. donor, and it "generates $50,000 to $60,00 in interest annually for Randi's paranormal education foundation" (G. Barrett, "Can the Living Talk to the Dead?" *USA Today,* June 20, 2001, pp. 1D, 2D).

230 James Hydrick: Al Seckel, "Mere Puffery: The Confessions of a Leading Psychic," *Santa Monica News,* 1998. (www.illusionworks.com/confession.htm).

230 All-in-one priest: C. Ballard, "John Edward Is the Oprah of the Other Side," *New York Times,* July 29, 2001 (www.nytimes.com).

231 Ray Hyman, "Cold Reading: How to Convince Strangers That You Know All About Them," in K. Frazier (ed.), *Paranormal Borderlands of Science* (Buffalo, N.Y.: Prometheus, 1981).

232 Kelly Bulkeley quoted by W. Bauman, "Dreams at the Intersection of Science and Religion," *Research News,* April 2001, p. 6.

232 Half of students: W. S. Messer and R. A. Griggs, "Student Belief and Involvement in the Paranormal and Performance in Introductory Psychology," *Teaching of Psychology* 16 (1989): 187–191.

233 Henry A. Murray and D. R. Wheeler, "A Note on the Possible Clairvoyance of Dreams," *Journal of Psychology* 3 (1937): 309–313.

233 Ray Hyman, "Where's the Science in Psi?" *Psychology Today,* July–August 2000, p. 50.

233 National Research Council, D. Druckman and J. A. Swets (eds.), *Enhancing Human Performance: Issues, Theories, and Techniques* (Washington, D.C.: National Academy Press, 1988).

233 CIA: R. Hyman, "Evaluation of the Military's Twenty-Year Program on Psychic Spying," *Skeptical Inquirer,* March–April 1996, pp. 21–23, 27; D. Waller, "The Vision Thing," *Time,* December 11, 1995, p. 48.

234 Daryl J. Bem quoted in *Skeptical Inquirer* 8 (1984): 194.

234 John Beloff, "Why Parapsychology Is Still on Trial," *Human Nature,* December 1978, pp. 68–74.

234 Richard Wiseman: Personal communication, 2000.

235 Daryl J. Bem and Charles Honorton, "Does Psi Exist? Replicable Evidence for an Anomalous Process of Information Transfer," *Psychological Bulletin* 115 (1994): 4–18.

235 Ray Hyman, "Anomaly or Artifact? Comments on Bem and Honorton," *Psychological Bulletin* 115 (1994): 19–24; "The Evidence for Psychic Functioning: Claims vs. Reality," *Skeptical Inquirer,* March–April 1994, pp. 24–26.

235 Julie Milton and Richard Wiseman, "Does Psi Exist? Lack of Replication of an Anomalous Process of Information Transfer," *Psychological Bulletin* 125 (1999): 387–391.

235 Hold the phone: J. Milton, "Should Ganzfeld Research Continue to be Crucial in the Search for a Replicable Psi Effect? Part I. Discussion Paper and Introduction to an Electronic-Mail Discussion," *Journal of Parapsychology* 63 (1999): 309–334.

236 Michael Shermer, "If That's True, What Else Would Be True?" *Skeptic* 7 (4) (1999): 102–103.

237 Susan Blackmore, "The Lure of the Paranormal," *New Scientist,* September 22, 1990, pp. 62–65.

237 K. C. Cole, *The Universe and the Teacup: The Mathematics of Truth and Beauty* (New York: Harcourt Brace, 1999), p. 133.

238 Dubrovnic: D. Cronkite, "The Dubrovnic Coincidence," *Perspectives,* December 1999, p. 3.

238 Time and chance: Ecclesiastes 9:11 NRSV.

238 Anatol Rapoport, "Ideological Commitments in Evolutionary Theories," *Journal of Social Issues* 47 (1991): 83–99.

238 James Redfield, *The Celestine Prophecy* (Hingham, Mass.: Wheeler, 1993).

238 John Allen Paulos, *Beyond Numeracy* (New York: Knopf, 1991).

239 Persi Diaconis and Frederick Mosteller, "Methods for Studying Coincidences," *Journal of the American Statistical Association* 84 (1989): 853–861.

239 Patricia Ann Campbell: From an Associated Press report, May 2, 1983.

239 Twins collide: C. Shepherd, "News of the Weird," *Funny Times,* April 1997, p. 15.
Philip Dodgson and Philip Dodgson: "Through the Looking Glass," *Psychologist,* January 1997, p. 48.

239 Ernie and Lynne Carey: "Daughters Give Birth on Same Day," *Los Angeles Times,* March 14, 1998, p. A15.

239 Charles Schulz: Schulz died of a heart attack Saturday evening, February 12, 2000. The Sunday papers in which his last strip appeared were available in some locales on Saturday, the day of his death.

239 Kristin Nalvik Loendahl: Reported by Chuck Shepherd, "News of the Weird," *Funny Times,* October 1998, p. 21.

240 Oregon Pick 4: L. Brancaccio, "We Print Winning Numbers in Advance!" *Columbian,* July 3, 2000 (reported in *Chance News,* August 10, 2000).

240 Stephen Samuels and George McCabe quoted by Diaconis and Mosteller, "Methods for Studying Coincidences."

241 Lost faith and parapsychology: J. E. Alcock, "Parapsychology: The 'Spiritual' Science," *Free Inquiry,* Spring 1985, pp. 25–35; J. Beloff, "Science, Religion and the Paranormal," *Free Inquiry,* Spring 1985, pp. 36–41.

241 Extrasensorial healers: S. Kapitzka, "Antiscience Trends in the U.S.S.R," *Scientific American,* August 1991, pp. 32–38.

241 Thirty-two Russian scientists: "Science Needs to Combat Pseudoscience: A Statement by Thirty-Two Russian Scientists and Philosophers," *Skeptical Inquirer,* January–February 1999, pp. 37–38. Reprinted from *Izvestiya,* July 17, 1998.

242 Job: 42:3, NRSV.

242 Leo Tolstoy, *My Confessions* (Boston: Dana Estes, 1904).

242 J. B. S. Haldane, *Possible Worlds and Other Papers* (Freeport, N.Y.: Books for Libraries Press, 1928; reprinted 1971).

242 Isaiah: 55:8–9, NRSV.

243 Anselm: *Proslogian, prooeem.* PL 153 225A. "Faith seeks understanding" now forms part of the Catechism of the Catholic Church (#158).

243 Owen Gingerich, "Is There a Role for Natural Theology Today?" *Real Issue,* February 6, 1999 (www.origins.org/real/n9501/natural.html). Einstein: I say "reportedly" because I could locate this quotation on 9,090 websites but was unable to verify an original source.

244 Peter Berger on Adam Seligman, "Protestantism and the Quest for Certainty," *Christian Century,* August 26–September 2, 1998, pp. 782–784.

244 Critically analyze: I have critiqued New Age claims related to reincarnation, near-death experiences, and astrology in *Psychology,* 6th ed. (New York: Worth, 2001). I have critiqued prayer experiments in "Is Prayer Clinically Effective? *Reformed Review* 53 (2) (2000): 95–102, also available at davidmyers.org/religion/prayer.html.

244 Robert A. Emmons, "Spiritual Intelligence: Toward a Theory of Person-

ality and Spirituality," in *The Psychology of Ultimate Concerns* (New York: Guilford, 1999).

245 Growing evidence: I have reported on such evidence in *The Pursuit of Happiness* (New York: Avon, 1993) and in *The American Paradox: Spiritual Hunger in an Age of Plenty* (New Haven: Yale University Press, 2000).

EPILOGUE

247 Norman Cousins: "The Taxpayers Revolt: Act Two," *Saturday Review,* September 16, 1978, p. 56.

247 College students think smarter: G. T. Fong, D. H. Frantz, and R. E. Nisbett, "The Effects of Statistical Training on Thinking About Everyday Poblems," *Cognitive Psychology* 18 (1986): 253–292; D. R. Lehman, R. O. Lempert, and R. E. Nisbett, "The Effects of Graduate Training on Reasoning: Formal Discipline and Thinking About Everyday-Life Events," *American Psychologist* 43 (1988): 431–442; S. W. VanderStoep and J. J. Shaughnessy, "Taking a Course in Research Methods Improves Reasoning About Real-Life Events," *Teaching of Psychology* 24 (1997): 122–124.

247 Project on Redefining the Meaning and Purpose of Baccalaureate Degrees, *Integrity in the College Curriculum* (Washington, D.C.: Association of American Colleges, 1995).

248 George Soros, *The Crisis of Global Capitalism* (New York: Public Affairs, 1998), p. 85.

248 Brain waves jump: B. Libet, "Unconscious Cerebral Initiative and the Role of Conscious Will in Voluntary Action," *Behavioral and Brain Sciences* 12 (1985): 181–187.

249 Psalmist: Psalm 4, 6, 14, *Jerusalem Bible.*

Index

Bell, Alexander Graham, 101
Belsky, Gary, 157, 158, 164
Bem, Daryl, 234, 235
Bennett, John, 45–46
Berger, Peter, 244
Bernall, Cassie, 125
Bernieri, Frank, 187
Berra, Yogi, 89
Berscheid, Ellen, 116
Beyth-Marom, Ruth, 121–22
Bible/biblical verses, 238, 242,
    249
"Bible code" craze, 135
Biederman, Irving, 28
biological predisposition, 202–3
Bird, Larry, 138, 141
Birnie, Matthew, 39
Blackmore, Susan, 237
Blauser, Jeff, 143
blindsight, 4–5, 127
Blumer, Catherine, 156
body, 21, 37–39, 42, 114, 127
Bohr, Niels, 4
Bonhoeffer, Dietrich, 246
Bono, Christopher, 31–32, 46
Boone, Pat, 45
Boorstin, Daniel, 104
Bornstein, Brian, 75
brain, 9, 67, 237; blindsight and, 4;
    brain-damaged patients, 36–37,
    45, 127; emotional pathways of,
    37–39; information processing of,
    241–42; intuitive expertise and,
    51; neural networks of, 18, 248–
    49. See also consciousness; left
    brain; right brain
breast cancer, 202, 205
Brown, Michael, 61
Brown, Rupert, 115
Browne, Sylvia, 230

Browning, Robert, 179
Bruck, Maggie, 74, 75
Bryant, Kobe, 146, 150
Buehler, Roger, 100
Buffet, Warren, 163–64, 236
Bulkeley, Kelly, 232
Bumpass, Larry L., 293n
Bush, George W., 112, 252n
business management, 57, 94–95
Buss, David, 68
bystander inaction, 76–77

Campion, Michael, 197
Camus, Albert, 245
Cantor, Nancy, 35
Capaci, Frank, 218, 223
Carey, Ernie and Lynn, 239
Carlston, Donal, 40
Carter, Jimmy, 92, 114
Castellano, Carmen, 220
Ceci, Stephen, 74, 75
Celestine Prophecy (Redfield), 135,
    238
chance. See randomness
Chapman, Loren and Jean, 176
Chapman, Mark, 115
Charles, Prince of Wales, 2
Chartrand, Tanya, 15, 42
Chase, William, 54
checkers, 54
chess, 5, 16, 52, 176; learned
    expertise and, 54–55, 56; reading
    patterns in, 150
chicken sexing, 55, 56, 176
children, 3, 9, 10, 35; crime statistics
    and, 124–25; emotional memories
    of, 39; false memories and, 74–75;
    hyperactivity and, 114; insight
    and, 62; intuitive learning of, 17–
    18, 127; mass media and, 77;

nonverbal expressions of, 48;
  safety regulations and, 207–8
Christie, Agatha, 15
Chronicles of Narnia (Lewis), 247
clairvoyance, 227, 241
Claxton, Guy, 227
clinicians, 172–73, 176, 181
Clinton, Bill, 71, 96, 114, 207, 213
Clinton, Hillary, 114
clusters, randomness and, 136–37
co-evolution, 48
Coats, Erick, 47
Cobain, Kurt, 176
cognitive errors, 68
cognitive science, 17, 23, 24, 247
Cohen, Richard, 112
coincidence, 237–40
cold reading, psychics and, 231–32
Cole, K. C., 110, 198, 209, 237
Columbine High School massacre,
  124–25
common sense, 89, 93
communication, nonverbal, 4
communism, 102, 112
computers, 5, 44, 181
confirmation bias, 116–17, 128, 179
conformity, 77
Confucius, 103
consciousness, 3, 15, 24, 243;
  automatic processes and, 29;
  heightened state of, 244–45;
  neurology and, 248–49; tacit
  knowledge and, 57. *See also* brain
consensus, false, 97
contagious moods, 42
control, illusion of, 222–23
control, lack of, 206
controlled experiments, 72
Conway, Michael, 72
Cooper, Joel, 193

Copernicus, 60
cortex, of brain, 37–38
cost-benefit analysis, 207
Cousins, Norman, 247
Craioveanu, Mihai and Deborah, 58
creativity, 4, 59–63, 127
credit card companies, 181
criminal offenders, 172, 173, 174, 180
Cromwell, Oliver, 119
"curse of knowledge," 91–92
Czyzewska, Maria, 52

Damasio, Antonio, 36, 37
Darley, John, 40, 76
Dawes, Robyn, 24, 92–93, 175, 189
de Klerk, F. W., 102
decision making, 6, 15
decline effect, 234
Deep Blue (chess computer), 56
defensive pessimism, 85
Defying the Crowd (Sternberg &
  Lubart), 60
Dekel, Shlomit, 121–22
democracy, 248
Denton, Jeremiah, 157
DePaulo, Bella, 188
Diaconis, Persi, 239
Diana, Princess of Wales, 10, 96,
  183, 228
DiBiasi, Patricia, 239
dichotic listening/viewing, 25
DiMaggio, Joe, 144, 145
Dixon, Jeanne, 229
Dodgson, Philip, 239
Domjan, Michael, 38
Doughty, Debby, 139
Doyle, Arthur Conan, 28
Drapeau, Jean, 100
dreams, 23, 226, 232–33
Dreman, David, 210

Dreyfus, Hubert and Stuart, 54, 57
dual attitude system, 33–35, 127
dual processing, 4
Dunning, David, 83, 99
durability bias, 79, 81
Durm, Mark, 229

economics: intuitive entrepreneurs,
169–71; randomness and, 152,
161–65; risk and reward, 166–69
Edison, Thomas, 60
education, 247–48
Edward, John, 227, 230–31
Egan, John, 214
Einstein, Albert, 1, 61, 243
Ekman, Paul, 44
electroconvulsive therapy (ECT),
185–86
Eliot, T. S., 2, 68, 191
emergency situations, behavior in,
76–77
Emmons, Robert, 244, 245
Emotional Intelligence (Goleman),
36
emotions, 4, 26, 30; durability of, 81;
economics and, 152; emotional
intelligence, 36, 127, 211; gender
and, 46–47; health and, 114;
positive memories and, 71; self-
awareness and, 88; social
intelligence and, 35–37; wisdom
of body and, 37–39
empathic accuracy, 43–44
empathy, 46, 49
endowment effect, 155–56
environment, creative, 60
Epley, Nicholas, 83
Epstein, Seymour, 30, 35, 49, 122
Estess, Floyd, 179
ethics, 95

everyday experience, 244
evolution, 40
evolutionary psychologists, 48
experiential knowing, 30
experiments: belief perseverance,
115–18; conformity, 77;
construction of memory, 73–74;
controlled, 72; economic
irrationality, 158; face recognition,
68; false memory, 174–75;
familiarity/fondness, 39–40; lie
detection, 44; life history recall,
69; praise and punishment, 148;
prediction of behavior, 82–83;
quiz-game, 112; unconscious
learning, 52. *See also*
psychology/psychologists
expertise, 59–60
explicit memory, 22
expressiveness, 188–89
extrasensory perception (ESP), 147,
226, 227, 228, 233–34, 235
extraversion, 112, 178–79, 187, 188
eye movement desensitization and
reprocessing (EMDR), 184
eyewitnesses, 75

face recognition, 5
facial expressions, 27, 33, 42, 45, 46
facial features, 53
faith, 243
Falk, Ruma, 136, 222
false consensus, 97–98
false-hope syndrome, 100
false memories, 74, 174–75
familiarity-fondness link, 39–40
fears, primal, 202
feelings, misprediction of, 78–82,
128
feelings, risks as, 211–12

physics, 58, 104–5, 109, 110; extrasensory perception (ESP) and, 228; laws of, 18; sports and, 29

pi (o), digits of, 140, 144

Piaget, Jean, 108

Picasso, Pablo, 61

Pipher, Mary, 49

Pirsig, Robert, 172

Pittman, Rob, 170

placebo effect, 182, 185

PMS (premenstrual syndrome), 70

poets, 52, 62

Poincaré, Henri, 63

Polanyi, Michael, 57

police psychics, 228–29

Polivy, Janet, 100

pornography, 77

positive reinforcement, 149

postmodernists/postmodernity, 8, 199, 232

Potter, Beatrix, 170

Powell, John, 93–94

Presley, Elvis, 189

Prickett, Tricia, 187

prime time power, 145–46

priming, 26–29, 127

probabilities, 106, 142, 144, 207, 218–22

procedural memory. *See* implicit memory

prosopagnosia, 5, 127

prototypes, 120

proverbs, 90–91, 113, 229

psychics, 226–36

psychoanalysis, 24

psychology/psychologists, 3, 15, 89; critical inquiry and, 235; maxims of, 100; popular psychology, 9. *See also* experiments

psychotherapy, 182–86, 239

Pulley, Brett, 216

punishments and rewards, 148–49

Putin, Vladimir, 112

puzzle games, 8

Quinn, Jane Bryant, 165

Rabin, Matthew, 163

Rabin, Yitzhak, 135

race/racial prejudice, 95, 193

Randi, James, 230, 304n

randomness, 134–37, 137–45, 152, 161–65, 220–22

Rapoport, Anatol, 238

rational analysis, 8, 18, 129; defeat of, 211; gender differences and, 46, 49; moral judgments and, 40; social intuition and, 33

rational knowing, 30

Rawls, John, 40

Reagan, Ronald, 75, 115, 158

reality, 1, 2, 93; construction of, 73; controlled experiments and, 72; mass media and, 77; prediction of behavior and, 84, 86; well-being and, 81

Reason, James, 16

Redelmeier, Donald, 114, 168

Redfield, James, 135, 238

Reifman, Alan, 138

reincarnation, 243

Rejection (White), 170

religion, 50, 243–46, 245

Renaud, Harold, 179

representativeness heuristic, 120–23, 128

repression (psychological), 10

responsibility, 94